Understanding Project Management

Understanding Project Management

A Practical Guide

Third Edition

Dave C. Barrett

CS BUSINESS PRESS

CANADIAN SCHOLARS

Toronto | Vancouver

Understanding Project Management: A Practical Guide, Third Edition
Dave C. Barrett

First published in 2024 by
CS Business Press / Canadian Scholars, imprints of CSP Books Inc.
180 Bloor Street West, Suite 1401
Toronto, Ontario
M5S 2V6

www.canadianscholars.ca

Library and Archives Canada Cataloguing in Publication

Title: Understanding project management : a practical guide / Dave C. Barrett.
Names: Barrett, Dave C., 1959- author.
Description: Third edition. | Includes bibliographical references and index.
Identifiers: Canadiana (print) 2024040758X | Canadiana (ebook) 20240407598 | ISBN 9781773384214 (softcover) | ISBN 9781773384221 (PDF) | ISBN 9781773384238 (EPUB)
Subjects: LCSH: Project management. | LCSH: Work breakdown structure.
Classification: LCC HD69.P75 B367 2024 | DDC 658.4/04—dc23

Material from the following publication has been reproduced with the permission of Project Management Institute Inc. *A Guide to the Project Management Body of Knowledge, PMBOK® Guide*, 7th ed. Copyright and all rights reserved.

Cover design by Krista Mitchell
Page layout by S4Carlisle Publishing Services

24 25 26 27 28   5 4 3 2 1

Printed and bound in Ontario, Canada

Canada

To Paula, my wife, best friend, and collaborator in all things.
Your steadfast belief in me made this book possible.

CONTENTS

LIST OF SAMPLE DOCUMENTS AND TEMPLATES

Cost Estimates

Detailed Budget

Project HR Requirements

Project Roles and Responsibilities

RACI Chart

Quality Management Plan

Risk Register

Communication Management Plan

Project Documentation Guidelines

Meeting Agenda

PREFACE

Hello and welcome to *Understanding Project Management: A Practical Guide*, Third Edition. This book was written for those new to the field of project management or those looking for a practical, common-sense approach to managing projects.

Over the years, I've found that textbooks written for introductory project management courses are often a difficult read. They are typically written at a highly detailed level and are most appropriate for very experienced Project Managers managing large, complex projects. For most people, though, this tends to present project management as an overwhelming set of processes and documentation that is not suited for their projects. It also suggests that project management needs to be bureaucratic, be time-consuming, and involve a great volume of tedious documentation. Not a great first impression to make.

This text takes a different approach. Its basis is simplicity. Project management is broken down into a series of simple common-sense processes to help manage any project. It is structured around a case study that follows a moderately sized project from initiation to completion. Throughout the case study project, the relevant project management concepts, processes, and documents are specifically demonstrated. The reader can see how project management is employed from start to finish.

The processes and templates outlined in this text should not be viewed as an inflexible set of instructions to be performed during every project. The variability of projects in terms of size, complexity, content, and many other characteristics would make this approach ineffective. Instead, the processes and templates provided should become part of your tool kit, which may then be applied as appropriate given the conditions present in the current project.

My project management philosophy is that every process performed and document produced must have a practical purpose that benefits the goals of the project. Ultimately, project management is about getting things done, on time and within budget, resulting in a satisfied customer. Any processes that do not serve this purpose should not be performed.

We can apply project management not only to our jobs but also to our lives. It is my sincere hope that the principles and processes contained in this text will bring you greater productivity, efficiency, and simplicity at work and at home.

NEW TO THE THIRD EDITION

Building on the content of previous editions, *Understanding Project Management: A Practical Guide*, Third Edition includes the following:

- A short history of project management has been added to chapter 1: "Understanding the Project Environment."
- An overview of agile, waterfall, and hybrid approaches has been added to chapter 1: "Understanding the Project Environment."
- An overview of key concepts from the *PMBOK Guide*, Seventh Edition has been added to chapter 1: "Understanding the Project Environment."
- A discussion of remote project teams (including international project teams) has been added to chapter 7: "Project Team Planning."
- A reference to Earned Value Management has been added to chapter 11: "Executing, Monitoring, and Controlling the Plan." A new appendix has been added to demonstrate the use of Earned Value Management during the case study project.
- The agile-related content in Part III has been expanded to include an overview of agile project management, a new Scrum-related case study, and a discussion of hybrid project management.

ACKNOWLEDGEMENTS

This book represents the culmination of my 20-plus years as a project management practitioner and more than 20 years of teaching the subject to post-secondary students. Not long after starting my teaching career, I realized that I had a story to tell based on this experience and I needed to write a text that would explain the benefits of project management in a simple, practical way.

Once again during this edition, I'm grateful for the support of the many people I've had the opportunity to work with at Canadian Scholars. Thanks to Emma Melnyk, who helped shape the content and focus of this edition. As a Project Manager myself, I appreciated the effective and timely management of the production process by Lizzie Di Giacomo. Thanks as well to the copy editor, Cindy Angelini, whose thoughtful edits and questions improved the quality of the final product.

I'd like to thank Simone Craig, Rich Crowley, Madelyn Lecsek, Catherine Maharaj, and Dushyant Puri for feedback and advice related to the expanded agile section of this edition. I'd also like to thank Fatehjit Kochar, Lisa Pollard, and Fernando Santiago for their detailed review of and suggested updates to the new Earned Value Management appendix. Thanks as well to Ian Adare, Rachit Chaudhary, Ferdinand Del Mundo, Laurel Giasson, Fadi Habib, Jose Hernandez, Dave Knight, Sladjan Mocevic, Barb Rice, Jeffrey Thomson, and German Turno for their input and to Melissa Smith of Lakehouse Creative for her continued work on the illustrations of the textbook.

And finally, I'd like to thank Paula Barrett. As an author, I'm fortunate to be married to a professional writer and Professor of Public Relations. She has been my sounding board, providing inspiration, feedback, creative ideas, and editing. A significant amount of the case study project can be credited to Paula. Her impact on the final quality of this work cannot be fully measured.

PART I

INTRODUCTION TO PROJECT MANAGEMENT

Prior to studying the various processes required to manage projects, a discussion of introductory project management concepts and terminology is essential. These concepts and terms provide a solid foundation for the processes and documents presented throughout the remainder of the text.

1 Understanding the Project Environment

HOW TO USE THIS TEXT

Textbook Case Study

This text is structured around a case study that follows a moderately sized project from initiation to completion. At each step, the relevant **project management** concepts, tools, and documents are presented and then demonstrated within the case study. To get the most from this text, read each case study instalment and consider how and why the project management tools are being used. The concepts and tools of project management are less relevant in the abstract but come alive during actual projects.

Document Templates

Document templates are employed throughout the text as a way of demonstrating how the concepts of project management may be implemented. This should not be interpreted as a suggestion that projects must use all the project templates exactly as written. Project management does not equate to the completion of document templates. Instead, each template should be viewed as an indication of the type of thinking that should take place during the project. While you are welcome to use these templates within a project, the actual format and level of detail depend on the needs of the project. For example, when creating a project schedule, the actual format may be activities listed on a whiteboard, in a spreadsheet, or in project management software. The thinking and actions that take place are more important than the format of the documents.

Legend: Textbook Navigation

To help identify key sections of the text, the symbols shown in figure 1.1 will be used.

An example where we apply a concept or theory

The next instalment of the ongoing case study

Important summary concepts and ideas

The key terminology of project management

Questions for further discussion and exploration

Figure 1.1: Symbols Used in the Text

WHAT IS A PROJECT?

When setting out to study the field of project management, a key question is "What is it that makes something a project?" While projects tend to share many characteristics, there are two conditions that are fundamental and therefore must be present:

- The project is temporary—there is a beginning and an end.
- The outcome of the project is unique—that is, different in some way from anything else produced.

The **Project Management Institute** (2021, p. 4) provides the following definition of a **project**: "a temporary endeavour undertaken to create a unique product, service, or result."

Within organizations, projects are initiated in order to create something new or to implement change in order to deliver value to the organization. This could be an updated product design, a marketing campaign, or a revamp of the company's website. When projects are completed, the finished product, service, or results are transferred to the operations of the company.

As every project is unique, projects vary in their scope, duration, and complexity. The requirements of the project can be well-known and stable or unknown and volatile.

Projects may also vary significantly in size. Consider, for example, an insurance company call centre department:

- A small project could involve a review of recently completed calls in order to recommend changes to the phone scripts used by the Customer Service Representatives.
- A medium-sized project could involve an upgrade of computer software to improve the call centre's automatic call routing.
- A large project could involve a relocation of the call centre to another city.

A project is defined as a temporary endeavour undertaken to create a unique product, service, or result.

WHAT IS OPERATIONS?

Non-project work is known as **operations**. Operations involve the ongoing creation of the goods or services of an organization.

Examples of operations include the following:

- The production facility of a car company
- The call centre of an insurance company
- The storefront of a coffee company

Following the completion of a project, the product, service, or result created by the project is normally transitioned from the project to operations. This transition is covered in detail in chapter 15: "Closing the Project."

Operations is the area responsible for the ongoing creation of the goods or services of an organization.

WHAT IS PROJECT MANAGEMENT?

Given the definition of projects as temporary and unique activities, the next question is how best to manage them. The use of project management promotes an orderly progression from the start to the end of the project. It involves the use of various **processes** and documents to effectively plan and execute the project. The Project Management Institute (2021, p. 4) defines *project management* as "the application of knowledge, skills, tools, and techniques to project activities to meet the project requirements." However, it is important to realize that projects do not only produce outputs, but by doing so, they provide value to the organization.

Project management may refer to a profession (i.e., the project management profession), a job title (i.e., a Project Manager), or an activity (e.g., the Marketing Manager performs a number of project management activities). Some organizations may perform project management with strict adherence to formal processes, while other organizations may use informal processes. As projects may vary in terms of their scope, duration, and complexity, determining the appropriate number of project management processes to use can be challenging. For example, if an insufficient amount of project management is used, the project may underperform due to a lack of planning and control. However, if too much project management is used, the project may be burdened with an unnecessary amount of process. Understanding the characteristics of the project and then determining the appropriate amount of project management required is an important decision for the Project Manager to make.

Professional project management organizations publish ethical standards for those working within the profession. For example, the Project Management Institute, within its *PMI Code of Ethics and Professional Conduct* document, identifies honesty, responsibility, respect, and fairness as important values for project managers to uphold.

A SHORT HISTORY OF PROJECT MANAGEMENT

Project management can trace its origins back to ancient civilizations such as the Egyptians and Romans. Some level of project management would have been used to plan and execute complex projects such as the pyramids and aqueducts.

Industrialization and mass production in the early 20th century brought about the need for more systematic project management techniques. During this time period, Henry L. Gantt introduced the **Gantt Chart**, which provides a visual representation of the project schedule.

The processes of project management were further advanced during World War II, as projects such as the Manhattan Project required a greater level of coordination. In the postwar period, the private sector began to embrace project management in industries such as construction and aerospace.

The field of project management continued to progress, with the establishment of professional organizations such as the Project Management Institute (PMI) in 1969 and the publication of the first edition of the *Project Management Body of Knowledge* (*PMBOK Guide*) in 1996. During this time period, alternative approaches, primarily developed for systems development projects, emerged and became known as agile or adaptive project management.

Project management continues today as a well-established discipline and profession. It is applied across industries including construction, engineering, information technology, finance, and others.

Project management is defined as the application of knowledge, skills, tools, and techniques to project activities to meet project requirements.

PROJECT MANAGEMENT APPROACHES

Project management does not consist of a single set of processes. Instead, various approaches have been developed. These approaches, which I will describe, may be broadly grouped into the following three categories: waterfall, agile, and hybrid.

Waterfall Project Management

Waterfall project management[1] is an approach where the project plan is developed in detail and then subsequently followed for the remainder of the project (see figure 1.2). For many projects, the process of developing a plan

---

1   The introduction of the term *waterfall* is generally attributed to Winston W. Royce, based on a paper written by Royce in 1970, though he did not actually use this term in the paper. On the contrary, he warned of some of the risks inherent in following a strictly sequential software development method.

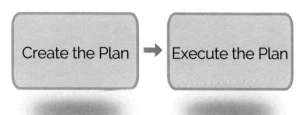

Figure 1.2: Waterfall Project Management

and then executing the plan is an effective project management approach. This is especially true for projects in which the requirements are well understood and not likely to change significantly, the technology used is relatively stable, or the duration of the project is relatively short. Additionally, projects involving construction, events, or procurement are well-suited to this approach, as are any projects that require the coordination of high-cost equipment or materials.

Waterfall project management is also referred to as traditional project management or predictive project management. The term *waterfall* evokes an image of the work of the project flowing from one stage to the next, much like a waterfall flows downward from one level to the next. However, this term sometimes carries a negative connotation, with the implication that waterfall projects are absolutely rigid and each stage of the project must be 100% complete before the next can begin and that changes cannot be made once planning is complete. On the contrary, projects using this approach often incorporate significant levels of flexibility, including the facilitation of changes throughout the project.

This textbook subscribes to this flexible implementation of the waterfall project management approach throughout part II.

Agile Project Management

While the waterfall approach is useful for many projects, there are situations where this approach may not be effective. In many cases, particularly those related to software development, the output of the project is difficult to completely define prior to execution, due to changing consumer tastes, market conditions, or advances in technology. In these instances, problems often occur when the customer is expected to finalize their requirements in advance and then wait an extended period of time in order to receive the results.

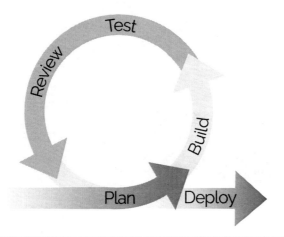

Figure 1.3: Agile Project Management

Agile project management is an approach in which the output of the project is developed in iterations and delivered to customers in frequent increments (see figure 1.3). The use of agile project management has greater potential in an environment of uncertainty and continual change because instead of attempting to minimize or manage change, change is expected and embraced. Agile project management is also referred to as adaptive project management.

Agile project management will be described in detail in part III.

Hybrid Project Management

Many organizations do not use a purely waterfall or agile approach but instead employ a hybrid approach tailored to the project and organization. **Hybrid project management** is a combination of waterfall and agile project management (see figure 1.4).

For example, some organizations may use a waterfall approach for some projects (e.g., technology infrastructure) and agile for other projects (e.g., software development). Organizations may also integrate agile elements into their waterfall projects (e.g., employing the use of daily stand-up meetings for project teams) or waterfall elements into their agile projects (e.g., determining the anticipated availability of project output to a customer).

Hybrid project management will be described in detail in part III.

Use of Waterfall, Agile, and Hybrid

As mentioned previously, many projects will naturally gravitate to a particular project management approach based on the characteristics of the organization's

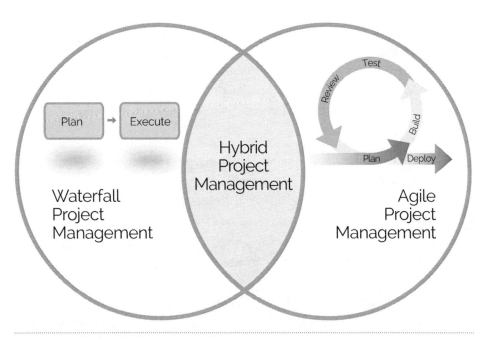

Figure 1.4: Hybrid Project Management

projects. As well, many organizations are interested in the benefits of agile project management and are investigating the use of both agile and hybrid project management. Figure 1.5 displays a summary of a survey on the worldwide use of waterfall, agile, and hybrid project management. The figure demonstrates that, as of the time of the survey, waterfall project management was used in over 44%

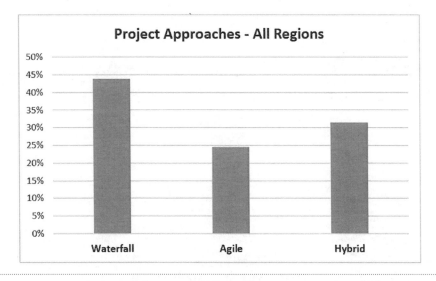

Figure 1.5: Project Approaches Across All Regions (Source: Pulse of the Profession, PMI, 2024)

of projects, while agile and hybrid project management accounted for approximately 56% of projects.

The use of the approaches varies by industry. For example, in the construction industry, waterfall is dominant. On the other hand, in the IT industry, usage is more evenly distributed between waterfall, agile, and hybrid.

Here is an example of the use of different project management approaches.

The creation of a new movie demonstrates the use of waterfall. When making the movie, a number of sequential phases will be followed, such as concept development, scriptwriting, storyboarding, filming, editing, and theatrical release.

Alternatively, the creation of the movie could use a hybrid approach. For example, often the development of the script goes through multiple iterations before moving to the next phase of the movie.

Many stand-up comedians use an agile approach when developing a new routine. After writing the initial set of jokes, they test them in small comedy clubs with live audiences. Based on the audience response to each performance, they determine which jokes work and how to adjust their delivery. Through a number of iterations, they continually improve their performance. Once it meets their desired standard, they are ready to perform it in larger venues or record it for release on a streaming service.

Different project management approaches have been developed: waterfall, agile, and hybrid. Each is appropriate for certain types of projects.

THE PROJECT LIFE CYCLE

As indicated earlier in this chapter, projects produce a product, service, or result. The question then becomes how best to organize the activities needed to complete the project. What follows is a basic process for creating something new:

1. Determine the overall parameters of the project, such as why this project should be performed, when it needs to be completed, and what funds are available to complete the project.
2. Plan the details of the work to be performed, including what will be produced, when it will be completed, and the resulting cost.
3. Produce the product, service, or result based on the planning.
4. End the project, comparing the results achieved to the original parameters of the project.

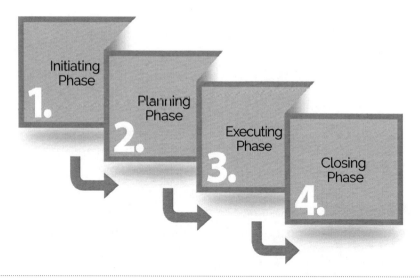

Figure 1.6: Project Life Cycle

Each of the above steps is represented by a project **phase**. The collection of phases representing the entire project is known as the **project life cycle** (PLC). The PLC used in this text is shown in figure 1.6.

Each phase represents a time period of the project when similar activities take place. Project phases are advantageous as they provide clarity to the project team regarding the type of activities required during each time period. The end of a phase is often used as a review point to assess whether the project should continue. These review points are known as **phase gates**. For example, at the end of the Initiating Phase, a decision may be made regarding whether the project should proceed to the Planning Phase.

Different organizations and projects may use other names for each phase or contain a different number of phases. For example, for systems development projects, planning is often replaced by analysis and design. On other projects, executing may be known as implementation, development, or construction.

The width of the phases in figure 1.6 is not representative of the duration or the amount of work required. Instead, the Initiating and Closing phases are normally very brief and require a minimum of resources. Increased time and resources are required during the Planning and Executing phases.

The project life cycle (PLC) consists of the following four phases: Initiating, Planning, Executing, and Closing.

Types of Project Life Cycles

There are four types of project life cycles that may be defined for a project, each tailored to suit specific project requirements and organizational needs. They are as follows.

Predictive Life Cycle

A **predictive life cycle** follows a sequential approach in which planning is completed prior to the creation of the project's output. This life cycle is useful when project requirements may be clearly defined, with minimal changes expected, and when the project's output is delivered at the end of the project. This life cycle is used during waterfall projects and is described in detail throughout part II.

Iterative Life Cycle

An **iterative life cycle** consists of repeating cycles of planning followed by the creation of output. Each cycle or iteration allows for refinement and improvement of the project's output, with each iteration building upon on the previous one(s). This life cycle is useful when project requirements are not fully known up front or may change significantly during the project and when the output is delivered at the end of the project (though early delivery of partial functionality may be possible). The iterative life cycle will be described in more detail in chapter 18: "Hybrid Project Management."

Incremental Life Cycle

An **incremental life cycle** involves breaking a project into small, manageable parts, called increments, that are provided in successive deliveries. Each increment represents a portion of the overall project. This life cycle is useful when the requirements of each increment may be clearly defined and when early delivery of each increment is desired. The incremental life cycle will be described in more detail in chapter 18: "Hybrid Project Management."

Agile Life Cycle

An **agile life cycle** is both iterative and incremental. It is well-suited for projects with evolving requirements and when delivery of each increment is desired. The agile life cycle will be described in more detail in chapter 16: "An Overview of Agile" and chapter 17: "The Scrum Framework."

There are four types of project life cycles that may be defined for a project, each tailored to suit specific project requirements and organizational needs.

Introduction to the Case Study

DECO PRODUCTIONS

Deco Productions is a medium-sized software company located in the Midwest that employs more than 300 people. Casey Serrador founded the company in 2012. As an avid photographer, Casey guides the company in the development of software related to photography and video production.

The company name was inspired by Casey's interest in the Art Deco period. She was drawn to the streamlined forms and smooth lines inherent in the period and looks to instill this modern elegance into the culture and products of her company. Additionally, the Art Deco period's focus on technological and social progress is a priority shared by Deco Productions.

The company's goal is simple: to provide industry-leading, quality products and services to its customers. This best-in-class strategy requires a culture of constant innovation with frequent product updates in order to stay ahead of the competition.

Deco Productions promotes an open and collaborative environment. Work hours are flexible, and many employees spend time both in the office and working from home. The office has an open-concept design with a few private rooms reserved for customer meetings and private conversations.

Casey's philosophy is that people make better decisions when they have a stake in the outcomes of the organization. This is accomplished through an employee profit-sharing program. She also believes that the people closest to the work are best able to understand how the work should be performed. Employees and teams are empowered to modify their own processes in order to improve the company's performance.

Virtual town hall meetings—where Casey and her management team describe the company's recent progress and upcoming challenges—are held on a monthly basis. Employees have the opportunity to ask questions and provide ideas. There are numerous instances of ideas raised during the meeting that were subsequently implemented, to the benefit of the company.

Deco Productions develops camera and video software for the following markets:

- Consumers (mobile device camera applications)
- Camera manufacturers
- Video camera manufacturers

(continued)

One of Deco Productions' software products is DecoCam. DecoCam is an industry-leading software application for the mobile device market. Consumers are able to purchase and download the product to their mobile devices. The product employs state-of-the-art technology to produce digital pictures with superior colour and clarity.

A new version of DecoCam (Version 4) has been proposed. This version would introduce a new feature known as the Photo Assistant. This feature would perform as follows:

- Before taking a picture, the user has the option of selecting the Photo Assistant.
- The user is prompted to take a short video, of up to 10 seconds, of the immediate surroundings.
- The Photo Assistant analyzes the video and recommends an optimal setting in terms of the direction, angle, and content of the picture.

While the initial cost estimate to create this feature is high, it is expected that the Photo Assistant will be popular with consumers and help ensure DecoCam maintains its position as a market leader. Though this initiative has not yet been approved, many in the organization are hopeful that the project will commence shortly.

PROJECT STAKEHOLDERS

Projects are not performed in isolation but instead involve or impact individuals, groups, and organizations known as **project stakeholders**. Project stakeholders may be internal or external to the project's company.

It is important to identify and manage the relationship with the project stakeholders, as they may positively or negatively impact the project's outcomes.

Project stakeholders typically involved in or impacted by projects are shown in figure 1.7.

Two key project stakeholders that are required for every project are the **Project Sponsor** and **Project Manager**. The Project Sponsor provides the funding for the project. While a Project Sponsor does not actively manage the project, they provide overall guidance and approve major decisions during the project. The Project Manager's function is to actively manage the project, ideally using sound project management principles.

Project stakeholders are individuals, groups, and organizations that are involved in or impacted by a project.

Figure 1.7: Project Stakeholders

PROJECT CONSTRAINTS

While customers would ideally prefer that a project produces as much as possible, there are limitations to what can be achieved. These limitations are known as **project constraints**.

The three fundamental project constraints are often referred to as the triple constraint:

- Scope: the required features and characteristics of the product, service, or result
- Time: the amount of time available to complete the project
- Cost: the budget available to complete the project

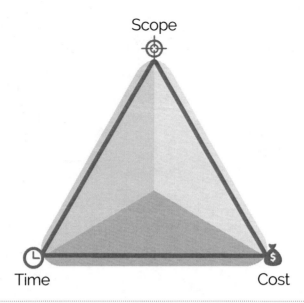

Figure 1.8: The Triple Constraint

The triangle diagram in figure 1.8 clearly displays the relationship between the constraints. Each constraint is connected to the other two constraints. The challenge for the Project Manager is to deliver the results of the project while satisfying each of the project constraints. In other words, they must deliver the required scope by the due date and stay within the budget. Difficulty occurs when one or more of the constraints is exceeded. For example, if additional features are required, this may also affect the time constraint (it may take longer) and the cost constraint (the budget may be exceeded).

Over time, additional constraints have been recognized and added to the original three constraints:

- Quality: the desired level of performance required for the project
- Resources: the availability of people, material, and equipment to complete the project
- Risk: the amount of risk that may be tolerated for the project

The diagram in figure 1.9 displays the more complex relationship between the six project constraints. As shown, each of the constraints may impact the other five.

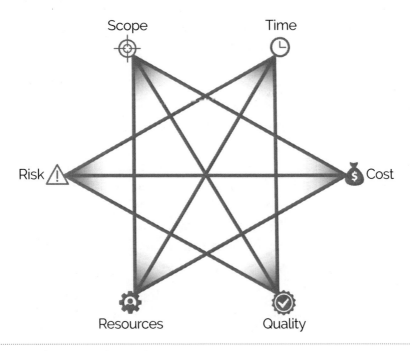

Figure 1.9: Six Project Constraints

For example, let's say that a project is already underway when it becomes apparent that the project's target date may not be met. Rather than delaying the project, the Project Manager looks at the following options:

- Overtime could be scheduled, or additional workers could be added to the project. However, this tends to increase the costs of the project (that is, it affects the cost constraint), and additional workers may not be available (resource constraint).
- The workers could attempt to work faster and get more work done in the remaining time. However, this tends to cause problems (quality constraint) and may damage the reputation of the organization (risk constraint).
- A discussion could be held with the Project Sponsors in order to reduce the results of the project (scope constraint).

This example demonstrates an important characteristic of constraints: when one constraint changes, it often impacts many, if not all, of the other constraints. One would hope that changes to constraints are a rare event on a project. Unfortunately, they are relatively common. During projects, budgets often change, schedules change, resources are unavailable or delayed, changes to the scope of the project are proposed, and so on. Managing the interaction among project constraints becomes an ongoing task.

The challenge for the Project Manager is to determine the best course of action to take if issues occur that cause changes to the project's constraints. The Project Manager must balance the satisfaction of the customer with the performance of the project. Excellent communication and diplomacy skills are required in order to arrive at an acceptable solution. A Project Manager's skill in these areas often means the difference between the success and failure of the project.

The six project constraints are scope, time, cost, quality, resources, and risk.

PROGRAMS AND PORTFOLIOS

This text focuses primarily on the management of projects. However, there are two additional project-related structures that are often present within organizations—programs and portfolios—and along with them come the corresponding disciplines of program management and portfolio management.

When a number of projects in an organization share a common business objective, grouping them together in order to coordinate their activities is often useful. This collection of projects is known as a **program** and is managed by a Program Manager (see figure 1.10).

The Project Manager of each project within the program works under the direction of the Program Manager. A key benefit of program management is the increased effectiveness of coordination between projects in areas such as the following:

- Coordinating decisions across projects
- Coordinating schedules of projects
- Coordinating resources across projects

Programs are groups of projects that share a common business objective.

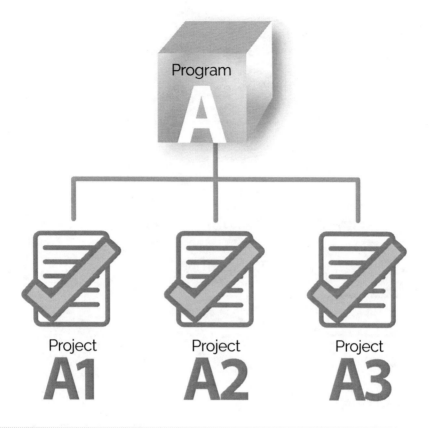

Figure 1.10: Program

There are usually a significant number of possible projects and programs that an organization may undertake. However, due to financial and resource constraints, organizations must choose a subset of these initiatives to perform at any one time in order to achieve the strategic objectives of the organization. This subset of projects and programs is known as the organization's project **portfolio** (see figure 1.11).

The process of managing the content of the portfolio, including adding, prioritizing, and removing its projects and programs, is called portfolio management. A Portfolio Manager is a senior role within an organization due to the strategic nature of the work involved.

Portfolios are the project initiatives an organization has selected to perform in order to achieve the strategic objectives of the organization.

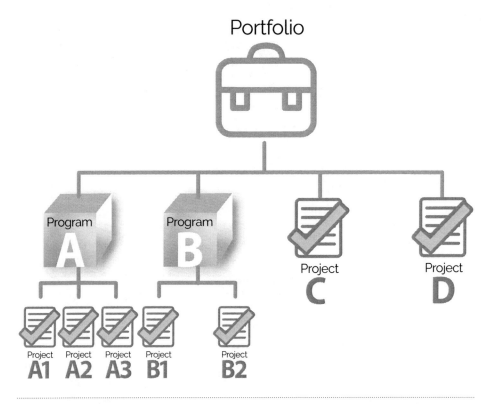

Figure 1.11: Portfolio

Case Study Update: Programs and Portfolios

Casey Serrador signs in to the video meeting. It is 8:55 a.m. and almost time for the monthly senior management strategy meeting to begin. Casey's senior management team, the heads of each division within Deco Productions, attend the meeting.

After a review of the company strategy and a discussion of Casey's recent interview on a cable business news special, the agenda turns to the selection of the next major company initiative. There are three possibilities:

1. An update to Deco Productions' suite of video camera software that has been recently requested by one of Deco Productions' key customers (a major video camera manufacturer)
2. The creation of a completely new service that would allow DecoCam customers to upload pictures to a system that would automatically create physical books, such as yearbooks or vacation albums
3. An update to the DecoCam application that would introduce the Photo Assistant feature

Each initiative is presented by a different executive, who outlines both the strategic benefits and the likely costs to be incurred.

Jackson Woodhouse, Vice-President, Customer Support, presents the first option. Most of the discussion revolves around the strategic importance of the customer and the likelihood that they could be lost to one of Deco Productions' competitors if the project is not completed.

Catherine Bianchi, Vice-President, Product Development, presents the second option. Concerns are raised that other companies already provide the proposed functionality and that it doesn't differentiate Deco Productions in any significant way.

Arun Singh, Vice-President, Mobile Products Distribution, presents the third option. The possible development of the Photo Assistant feature generates a great deal of discussion. While the feature is bold and unique, the costs are also projected to be high. If the project fails, it would cause a significant hit to the company's bottom line.

After a period of discussion, the decision becomes clear. Casey summarizes the discussion by confirming that the DecoCam Version 4 project containing the Photo Assistant application will be starting soon. As part of the discussion, a goal for DecoCam V4 is defined: a 5% increase in the mobile camera software market share.

The executive team then shifts its focus to how best to organize this initiative. After a further period of discussion, the DecoCam V4 Program is created, consisting of the following projects:

- DecoCam V4 Development
- DecoCam V4 Installation
- DecoCam V4 Technical Writing
- DecoCam V4 Product Launch

Each member of the management team considers how this new program impacts their area of responsibility. Arun Singh looks at the list of projects. The DecoCam V4 Product Launch project will be performed within his department. He makes a mental note to get a Project Manager assigned to this project as soon as possible.

THE PROJECT MANAGEMENT INSTITUTE AND *PMBOK GUIDE*

The structure of this textbook is consistent with the *PMBOK Guide*, Sixth Edition, published by the Project Management Institute. The sixth edition of the *PMBOK Guide* provides a detailed step-by-step guide for managing projects, which tends to be an effective framework within which those new to project management can learn and appreciate the discipline.

PMBOK Guide, Seventh Edition

The newest edition, the *PMBOK Guide*, Seventh Edition, presents a holistic approach to project management by providing a set of guiding values and beliefs. This broader perspective can help experienced project managers make better decisions and adapt more effectively to changing conditions. The seventh edition represents a shift from a process-based focus of the sixth edition to a principle-based one with an increased emphasis on value creation.

Project Management Principles

In the *PMBOK Guide*, Seventh Edition, the Project Management Institute (2021, p. 5) outlines 12 Project Management Principles that provide guidance for those within the project management profession:

1. Be a diligent, respectful, and caring steward
2. Create a collaborative project team environment
3. Effectively engage with stakeholders
4. Focus on value
5. Recognize, evaluate, and respond to system interactions
6. Demonstrate leadership behaviours
7. Tailor based on context
8. Build quality into processes and deliverables
9. Navigate complexity
10. Optimize risk responses
11. Embrace adaptability and resiliency
12. Enable change to achieve the envisioned future state

These principles are consistent with the content of this textbook. Some principles apply generally throughout the textbook (e.g., "4. Focus on value"), and others apply directly to one or more chapters (e.g., "8. Build quality into processes and deliverables" applies primarily to chapter 4: "Scope Planning" and chapter 8: "Quality Planning").

Performance Domains

In the *PMBOK Guide*, Seventh Edition, the Project Management Institute (2021, p. 7) also defines eight groups of related project activities called *Project Performance Domains*. Guided by the 12 Project Management Principles, these domains are crucial for the effective completion of projects and delivery of value to project stakeholders.

The eight Project Performance Domains are listed in table 1.1. The relevant textbook chapter or chapters are indicated for each Project Performance Domain.

Table 1.1: Project Performance Domains

Name	Description	Textbook Chapters
Stakeholder	The Stakeholder Performance Domain addresses activities and functions associated with stakeholders.	Chapter 3: "Stakeholder Planning" Chapter 11: "Executing, Monitoring, and Controlling the Plan" Chapter 17: "The Scrum Framework"
Team	The Team Performance Domain addresses activities and functions associated with the people who are responsible for producing project deliverables that realize business outcomes.	Chapter 7: "Project Team Planning" Chapter 13: "Managing the Human Resources Aspects of the Project" Chapter 17: "The Scrum Framework"
Development Approach and Life Cycle	The Development Approach and Life Cycle Performance Domain addresses activities and functions associated with the development of approach, cadence, and life cycle phases of the project.	Chapter 1: "Understanding the Project Environment" Chapters 16 to 18 (part III: Agile and Hybrid Project Management)
Planning	The Planning Performance Domain addresses activities and functions associated with the initial, ongoing, and evolving organization and coordination necessary for delivering project deliverables and outcomes.	Chapters 3 to 10 (part II: Waterfall Project Management) Chapter 17: "The Scrum Framework"
Project Work	The Project Work Performance Domain addresses activities and functions associated with establishing project processes, managing physical resources, and fostering a learning environment.	Chapter 11: "Executing, Monitoring, and Controlling the Plan" Chapter 12: "Managing Disruptions to the Plan—Issues and Change" Chapter 13: "Managing the Human Resources Aspects of the Project" Chapter 14: "Project Procurement" Chapter 17: "The Scrum Framework"
Delivery	The Delivery Performance Domain addresses activities and functions associated with delivering the scope and quality that the project was undertaken to achieve.	Chapter 4: "Scope Planning" Chapter 8: "Quality Planning" Chapter 17: "The Scrum Framework"
Measurement	The Measurement Performance Domain addresses activities and functions associated with assessing project performance and taking appropriate actions to maintain acceptable performance.	Chapter 11: "Executing, Monitoring, and Controlling the Plan" Chapter 15: "Closing the Project" Chapter 17: "The Scrum Framework"
Uncertainty	The Uncertainty Performance Domain addresses activities and functions associated with risk and uncertainty.	Chapter 9: "Risk Planning"

Project Management Certifications

The Project Management Institute administers a number of project management–related certifications. Two popular choices are the Project Management Professional (PMP) and the Certified Associate in Project Management (CAPM). The PMP is designed for the experienced project management practitioner, as several years of direct project management experience are required before the certification may be attained. The CAPM, in contrast, does not require previous project management experience, so it is an ideal choice for those entering the project management field. More information about these certifications and others may be found on the Project Management Institute's website (www.pmi.org).

KEY TERMINOLOGY

Agile Life Cycle: An approach that includes the refinement of output inherent in an iterative life cycle and the frequent deliveries of output inherent in an incremental life cycle

Agile Project Management: An approach in which the output of the project is developed in iterations and delivered to customers in frequent increments

Gantt Chart: A chart illustrating the dependencies between activities in a project schedule, with activities listed in rows and activity durations depicted as horizontal bars

Hybrid Project Management: A combination of waterfall and agile project management

Incremental Life Cycle: An approach that consists of breaking a project into smaller, manageable parts called *increments* that are provided in successive deliveries; each increment represents a portion of the overall project

Iterative Life Cycle: An approach that consists of repeating cycles of planning followed by the creation of output; each cycle or iteration allows for refinement and improvement of the project's output, with each iteration building upon on the previous one

Operations: The area responsible for the ongoing creation of the goods or services of an organization

Phase: A time period of the project when similar activities take place

Phase Gate: A review that takes place at the end of a phase in order to determine whether to proceed to the next phase

Portfolio: The collection of projects and programs that the organization actively manages in order to achieve its strategic objectives

Predictive Life Cycle: A sequential approach in which planning is completed prior to the creation of the project's output

Process: A series of actions taken to achieve a result

Program: A number of projects that are related in some way, such as a common business objective

Project: A temporary endeavour undertaken to create a unique product, service, or result

Project Constraints: Limits to what a project is able to achieve; the six project constraints are scope, time, cost, quality, resources, and risk

Project Life Cycle: A collection of project phases that represents the entire project

Project Management: The application of knowledge, skills, tools, and techniques to project activities to meet the project requirements

Project Management Institute: A global professional organization that defines standards and guidelines for the project management field

Project Manager: The individual who is assigned to manage the project and ensure that the objectives are completed

Project Sponsor: The individual who provides the financial resources, support, and approval for the project

Project Stakeholders: Individuals or groups who have some involvement or are affected in some way by the project

Waterfall Project Management: An approach in which the project plan is developed in detail and subsequently followed for the remainder of the project

KEY CONCEPTS

1. A project is defined as a temporary endeavour undertaken to create a unique product, service, or result.
2. Operations involve the ongoing creation of the goods or services of an organization.
3. Project management is defined as the application of knowledge, skills, tools, and techniques to project activities to meet the project requirements.
4. Different project management methodologies have been developed: waterfall, agile, and hybrid. Each is appropriate for certain types of projects.
5. The project life cycle (PLC) consists of the following four phases: Initiating, Planning, Executing, and Closing.
6. There are four types of project life cycles that may be defined for a project, each tailored to suit specific project requirements and organizational needs.
7. Project stakeholders are individuals, groups, and organizations that are involved in or impacted by a project.
8. The six project constraints are scope, time, cost, quality, resources, and risk.
9. Programs are groups of projects that share a common business objective.
10. Portfolios are the project initiatives an organization has selected to perform in order to achieve the strategic objectives of the organization.

DISCUSSION QUESTIONS

1. Create a list of projects from your personal experience. Do they all meet the criteria of being temporary and unique? What other attributes do they share?

2. What personal traits would be helpful for someone managing a project? What personal traits would be helpful for someone managing the operations of an organization? What are the similarities and differences between the two roles?

3. Perform an online search to research the history of project management. Based on your findings, what factors led to the development of project management?

4. What are the key differences between the Initiating Phase and the Planning Phase?

5. Perform an online search to identify a current project that would be best suited to each of the following: waterfall project management, agile project management, and hybrid project management.

6. Think of an example from your personal, work, or school activities where a change in one constraint caused an impact to one or more other constraints. Describe the example.

7. Create a list of the possible personal projects that you could potentially undertake over the next two years. How will you determine which of the projects you will perform?

PART II

WATERFALL PROJECT MANAGEMENT

In this part, project management based on the predictive life cycle—also known as waterfall project management—will be discussed, and the ongoing case study introduced in chapter 1 will be followed from its initiation to its completion.

2 Starting the Project

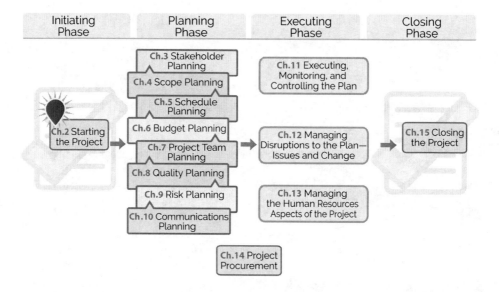

Initiating Phase	Planning Phase	Executing Phase	Closing Phase

Ch.2 Starting the Project

Ch.3 Stakeholder Planning
Ch.4 Scope Planning
Ch.5 Schedule Planning
Ch.6 Budget Planning
Ch.7 Project Team Planning
Ch.8 Quality Planning
Ch.9 Risk Planning
Ch.10 Communications Planning

Ch.11 Executing, Monitoring, and Controlling the Plan
Ch.12 Managing Disruptions to the Plan— Issues and Change
Ch.13 Managing the Human Resources Aspects of the Project

Ch.15 Closing the Project

Ch.14 Project Procurement

INTRODUCTION TO STARTING THE PROJECT

In the previous chapter, the DecoCam V4 Program was defined as consisting of four projects. The remainder of this case study will focus on one of the projects: the DecoCam V4 Product Launch.

This chapter describes the activities that take place during the first phase of the PLC: the Initiating Phase. While it is a relatively short phase, it is very important that it is completed effectively. The Initiating Phase provides the foundation for the remainder of the project.

There are two main steps when starting the project, as shown in figure 2.1.

The first step involves determining the overall options for the project and results in the creation of the **Business Case**. Assuming the project moves forward, the next step is to set the overall goals and objectives of the project,

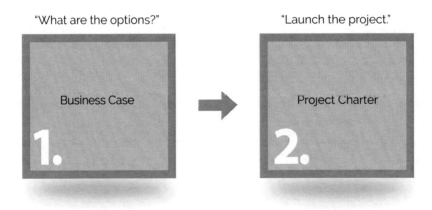

"What are the options?"

"Launch the project."

Business Case

Project Charter

1.

2.

Figure 2.1: Starting the Project

through the creation of the **Project Charter**. The project should then be officially launched through a **Project Kickoff Meeting** with key project stakeholders.

WHAT ARE THE OPTIONS?

When starting a project, there are often a number of broad options to consider for how the project may be implemented or even whether the project should be performed at all. Determining the options and selecting the best course of action is known as creating the Business Case (see figure 2.2). The advantage of this process is that it provides a clear direction and focus for the project.

When creating the Business Case, the likely costs are compared to the potential benefits. Estimated costs may be tangible (e.g., labour costs) or

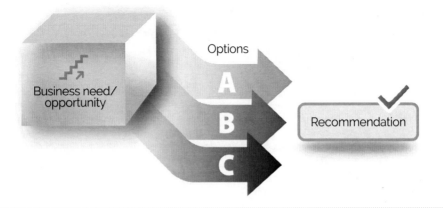

Options

Business need/ opportunity

A

B

C

Recommendation

Figure 2.2: Creating the Business Case

intangible (e.g., increased risk of missing a deadline). Benefits may be tangible (e.g., increased sales) or intangible (e.g., increased brand recognition).

The completion of a Business Case provides the management of the organization with the information necessary to determine the best course of action when initiating the project. The senior management of the organization is typically responsible for the final approval of the recommended option, as it may result in significant resources being spent and it could impact other initiatives within the organization.

Here is an example that uses the Business Case process. It is spring break, and you are considering a vacation. After thinking about your options, you make the following list:

- Flying to a resort destination for a week. The benefit is that this will likely be the most memorable and relaxing option. However, financially it will be the costliest of the three options.
- Driving to a nearby lodge for a few days. While this would still be memorable, it would almost certainly be less so than the first option. However, the financial cost will be much lower.
- Staying home (not travelling). Since you are not travelling, the benefit is that you will not be incurring the expenses of the first two options and will be able to catch up on some school assignments. However, you will lose out on the potential relaxation and memorable times of the other options.

Based on this cost-benefit analysis, a decision may be made.

The following is the Business Case report template:[1]

BUSINESS CASE	
Proposed Project	[At this point, the project is not yet approved, so it may not have its final name, or the name may change. The current name or identifier should be included here.]
Date Produced	[The date the Business Case is produced]
Background	[This section should include information that will help the reader understand the context and background history regarding the potential project. This section should not be written assuming that the background is common knowledge but instead should be specific in order to create a common understanding of the context.]

---

1   The format of this project document, and the subsequent project documents in the text, is provided as a typical example of the document. However, this is not to imply that there is one standard format; organizations will customize the format of the project documents according to their needs.

Business Need/ Opportunity	[This section should demonstrate the business need or opportunity that the proposed project will address.]
Options	[This section documents the potential approaches to complete the project. There are always a minimum of two options: perform the project or do nothing.]

Cost-Benefit Analysis
[This section contains the detailed costs and benefits of each option listed in the previous section. The costs may include considerations such as financial expenditures, the amount of time required, possible risks, and the potential for reduced quality. The benefits may include the potential of increased sales, market share, and brand recognition, and the reduction of errors and ongoing costs. Each option should be clearly identified and listed separately.]

Recommendation
[This section contains the recommended option from the previous section.]

Case Study Update: Creating the Business Case

Working late on a Friday afternoon, Sophie Featherstone is updating the final project documents for a recently completed project. Sophie has been with Deco Productions for just over two years, working as a Senior Project Manager in the Product Distribution department.

As she packs up to leave, her phone rings. Checking the call display, she sees that it is Arun Singh, Vice-President, Mobile Products Distribution.

"Hello, Sophie. Glad you're still here," says Arun. "I need you to manage the product launch for the new version of DecoCam. This is the biggest update to DecoCam that we've had. Its goal is a 5% increase in market share, so there is a lot riding on this one. Given all the good work you've done over the last couple of years, I know you're up to it."

Sophie replies, "Sounds great, Arun. It will be great to work with you again."

Hanging up the phone, Sophie pulls out her notebook and starts a to-do list. She has a lot of work to do to get this project up and running quickly.

There are usually many different options for completing a project. On a notepad, she jots down three main options:

A.   Soft product launch: consisting of minimal promotional activities that would rely primarily upon word of mouth from the existing DecoCam users.

B.   Moderate product launch: consisting of option A plus promotions through the company's existing communication channels.

C.   Full product launch: consisting of option B plus the development of a promotional video and creation of trade show materials.

(continued)

Over the next few days, Sophie consults with a number of people within the company. This helps her define the high-level content and develop a reasonable estimate for each option.

As she completes her work, one of the options emerges as the best choice, and it becomes clear what her recommendation will be. She books a meeting with the Project Sponsor, Arun, who will select the final option.

The following is the resulting Business Case developed during the case study project:

DECO PRODUCTIONS	**BUSINESS CASE**
Proposed Project	DecoCam V4 Product Launch
Date Produced	March 2, 2026
Background	Deco Productions is updating its DecoCam product to include a new feature known as the Photo Assistant. The subject of this Business Case is the work involved to launch this new product.
Business Need/ Opportunity	DecoCam is currently the leading camera-related application in the mobile market, and it is important that this leadership position is maintained. An effective launch of the new version of DecoCam will positively impact the sales of the new product, leading to increased revenues and market share of this product. An important objective of this project is that it must be ready to launch once the development of the new product is complete.

Options	The following are the high-level options:
	A. Soft product launch
	  • Product information would be updated on the company website and printed materials, but otherwise no additional promotional activities would take place.
	B. Moderate product launch
	  • This would include option A along with promotional activities using the company's existing communication channels.
	C. Full product launch
	  • This would include option B along with a promotional video and the creation of trade show materials.

Cost-Benefit Analysis
Option A—Soft product launch
Costs
• Budget: $10,000
• Possibility of delaying the product launch date: 1%
Benefits
• Market share: estimated that DecoCam will maintain its current market share
Option B—Moderate product launch
Costs
• Budget: $25,000
• Possibility of delaying the product launch date: 5%
Benefits
• Market share: estimated that DecoCam will increase its current market share by 3% within one year of the product launch
• Brand recognition: moderate increase in the recognition of Deco Productions as a provider of high-quality photography- and video-related products
Option C—Full product launch
Costs
• Budget: $60,000
• Possibility of delaying the product launch date: 10%
Benefits:
• Market share: estimated that DecoCam will increase its current market share by 6% within one year of the product launch
• Brand recognition: significant increase in the recognition of Deco Productions as a provider of high-quality photography- and video-related products
Recommendation
Given the potential for increased market share and brand recognition, option C (full product launch) is recommended.

The options for the project are documented in the Business Case.

LAUNCH THE PROJECT

With the work and decisions that have been completed to this point, the next step is to officially launch the project by creating the Project Charter. Creation of the Project Charter signals that the project has started and authorizes the Project Manager to proceed with the project. The creation of a Project Charter also ensures that there is agreement between the Project Sponsor, Project Manager, and other key stakeholders. The Project Charter will typically contain information such as the following:

- Project goals: these define what the project will achieve and how it supports the goals of the organization.

- Project objectives: these define the specific and measurable outcomes that are required to achieve the project goals.
- Project budget: the budget represents the funds that are available for the project. The amount may be based on initial estimates performed during the Initiating Phase or may represent the amount that was originally allocated for the project.
- Project Sponsor and Project Manager: these are two important roles required in order to proceed with the project.
- Additional key project stakeholders: during the Initiating Phase, project stakeholders are identified. Those stakeholders who will be actively involved in the project and play a significant role are listed in the Project Charter.
- Overall project **milestones**: significant points in the project, known as milestones, are listed in the Project Charter. Examples of overall milestones are the start of the project and the target date for the completion of the project.
- Overall project risks: any risks (i.e., unexpected events that could affect the outcome of the project) known at this point in the project should be listed in the Project Charter.

The following is the Project Charter template:

PROJECT CHARTER	
Project Name	[This section contains the project name that should appear consistently on all project documents. Organizations often have project naming conventions.]
Date Produced	[The date the Project Charter is produced]
Project Goals	[This section defines what the project will achieve and how it supports the goals of the organization.]
Project Objectives	[This section defines the specific and measurable outcomes that are required to achieve the project goals.]
Project Budget	[This section contains the funds available for the project.]
Project Sponsor	[Name of Project Sponsor and job title]
Project Manager	[Name of Project Manager and job title]
Additional Key Project Stakeholders	
[The names of key stakeholders who are known at this point in the project, including their job title or project role]	

Overall Project Milestones	**Dates**
[A list of the key milestones that are known at this point in the project]	[Milestone dates]
Overall Project Risks	
[A list of the overall risks that are known at this point in the project]	

Case Study Update: Creating the Project Charter

Sophie has accomplished a great deal over the last couple of weeks. The Business Case that she created was very useful for selecting the best option for the product launch. Her boss appreciated how well the options were presented and accepted her recommendation to proceed with the full product launch option.

Over the last few days, Sophie has been in various discussions with a number of stakeholders within Deco Productions, including Casey and Arun. Through these discussions, she has clarified her understanding of the project's goals and objectives, key milestones, and possible risks. The only problem is that she suspects that she is the only one who understands the big picture of the project. Additionally, Sophie is concerned that there are many people within the organization who are not aware of this project, let alone that she is the Project Manager.

She decides that it's time to summarize this information in a written report—the Project Charter. Given the number of stakeholders who will be affected by her project, she checks her calendar in order to book a Project Kickoff Meeting.

The following is the Project Charter for the case study project:

DECO PRODUCTIONS	**PROJECT CHARTER**
Project Name	DCV4Launch—DecoCam V4 Product Launch
Date Produced	March 25, 2026
Project Goals	The goal of the project is to successfully launch DecoCam V4 in order to support the company's goal of a 5% increase in DecoCam's market share.
Project Objectives	The objectives of the project are, by May 8, 2026: • Update the product information on the company website and printed materials. • Promote DecoCam V4 through existing communication channels. • Create a promotional video that achieves at least 10,000 views within three months. • Create the trade show materials. • Complete the project within the $60,000 budget.
Project Budget	$60,000
Project Sponsor	Arun Singh, Vice-President, Mobile Products Distribution

(continued)

Project Manager	Sophie Featherstone, Senior Project Manager	
Additional Key Project Stakeholders		
Casey Serrador, CEO, Deco Productions		
Jackson Woodhouse, Vice-President, Customer Support		
Catherine Bianchi, Vice-President, Product Development		
Overall Project Milestones	**Dates**	
Project starts	March 23, 2026	
Initiating Phase complete	March 25, 2026	
Planning Phase complete	April 3, 2026	
Executing Phase complete	May 8, 2026	
Project complete	May 13, 2026	
Overall Project Risks		
Errors are present in the product launch materials.		
Delays during the project cause the product launch to be late.		

 Creation of the Project Charter signals that the project has started and authorizes the Project Manager to proceed with the project.

The Project Kickoff Meeting

It is usually advisable for the Project Manager to schedule a Project Kickoff Meeting once the Project Charter is published. Key project stakeholders, including the Project Sponsor, other senior managers, and project team members, should be invited to attend. The agenda for this meeting should include the following:

- Introduction of the project stakeholders (if they have not previously met)
- Review of the organization's strategy and goals
- Discussion of the project goals, objectives, and budget
- Overview of key milestones throughout the project
- Discussion of any known risks or current issues

The desired result of this meeting is that the key stakeholders understand and support the project. The meeting should allow for any issues or concerns to be raised, as it will be more effective to address these early on rather than later in the project.

This demonstrates the first phase gate in the project. That is, a review takes place at the end of the Initiating Phase to determine whether to proceed to the Planning Phase. If the Project Sponsor agrees with the information in the Project Charter, approval should be provided. While this may be given verbally at the Project Kickoff Meeting, the approval should be communicated in writing by the Project Sponsor to the Project Manager.

With the approval of the Project Charter and completion of the Project Kickoff Meeting, the project leaves the Initiating Phase and is ready to enter the Planning Phase of the PLC.

> The project officially begins when the Project Sponsor approves the Project Charter.

KEY TERMINOLOGY

Business Case: A documented study to determine the costs and benefits of a proposed initiative that will be used as a basis for future project work

Milestone: An important event that occurs during a project

Project Charter: A document that signals that the project has started and authorizes the Project Manager to proceed with the project

Project Kickoff Meeting: A meeting held with key project stakeholders at the end of the Initiating Phase to officially launch the project

KEY CONCEPTS

1. The options for the project are documented in the Business Case.
2. Creation of the Project Charter signals that the project has started and authorizes the Project Manager to proceed with the project.
3. The project officially begins when the Project Sponsor approves the Project Charter.

DISCUSSION QUESTIONS

1. Should a Business Case be created for every project? If yes, why should one always be created? If no, when would a Business Case not be required?
2. Think of a home renovation project that you have either been involved in or observed. Create a list of all of the stakeholders for this project.
3. How do project goals differ from project objectives? Do you need to define both in the Project Charter?

4. What are some of the negative outcomes that could occur if a Project Charter is not produced?

5. Is a Project Kickoff Meeting necessary? Describe the benefits of holding this meeting.

6. Perform an online search to research the challenges associated with the Initiating Phase of a project. Based on your findings, what are some problems that may occur during this phase?

3   Stakeholder Planning

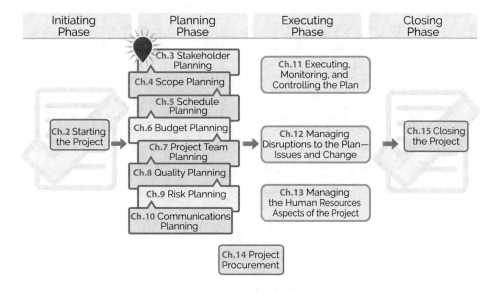

INTRODUCTION TO THE PLANNING PHASE

With the completion of the Initiating Phase, the goals and objectives have been established and the project has officially started. The Initiating Phase should have answered the question of why the project is being performed.

The project now moves into the Planning Phase. During this period, the details of the project are determined and the following questions are answered:

- Who will be involved or affected by the project? Who will deliver the project?
- What will the project create? What are the risks? What will it cost?
- Where will the work be performed?

- When will the work be completed?
- How will the work be performed?

The chapters related to the Planning Phase (chapters 3 to 10) are presented in a logical order that demonstrates how the overall project plan is created in the case study. It is important to understand that this progression of planning is not a completely linear process. Decisions made in one area of planning may impact previously developed plans. For example, after defining the content of the project (scope), detailed cost planning may then require the project scope to be revisited and updated. Planning documents should therefore not be considered final during the project but should instead be viewed as living documents. Throughout the Planning Phase, they are often updated as plans evolve. As well, during the Executing Phase, changes are often necessary due to changing conditions, and these changes should be reflected in the project plans.

Each chapter's planning processes should be thought of as providing an additional component to the overall project plan. Each component can impact any or all of the previously developed plans. None of the components are complete until *all* components are complete.

The creation of the project plan is important because it contains the characteristics of the project to be completed, enables decisions to be made, and is used to guide the execution of the project.

Once the project begins to be executed, real-world activities and problems begin to occur. Project Managers often find themselves confronted with issues that they didn't predict during planning. The duration and cost of the actual work are often very different from what was estimated. In short, plans are often proven to be incorrect during the execution of the project.

Some may see this as a reason to eliminate the planning process. Instead, this is why planning is important. The planning process immerses the Project Manager and the project team in the details of the project, as they are required to look at the project from many angles and become intimately familiar with the details. This prepares the Project Manager and project team to handle the unpredictable events that naturally occur during the execution of the project.

Dwight D. Eisenhower, the 34th President of the United States, once said that plans are worthless, but planning is everything. He went on to explain, "That is the reason it is so important to plan, to keep yourself steeped in the character of the problem that you may one day be called upon to solve or to help solve" (Eishenhower, 1957).

A mistake sometimes made by those new to project management is to employ a "one-size-fits-all" approach to project planning and, therefore, to plan every project with the same level of detail and rigour. Instead, the challenge for the Project Manager is to determine the appropriate amount of planning that should be performed for a given project. This will depend on a number of factors, including the size, complexity, cost, and risk level of the project.

INTRODUCTION TO STAKEHOLDER PLANNING

Before delving into the details of the project's requirements, it is useful to consider the project stakeholders who will be involved in or affected by the project.

Project stakeholders are important throughout the project. The project itself is based on project stakeholder requirements. The scope, schedule, and budget will require the appropriate stakeholder approval, and the acquisition of the project personnel often requires stakeholder negotiation and agreement. The perceived quality of the project will be based on the perception of the stakeholders.

The purpose of stakeholder planning is not only to identify all of the project's stakeholders but also to build effective and appropriate relationships with each stakeholder.

There are two main steps when planning for project stakeholders (see figure 3.1).

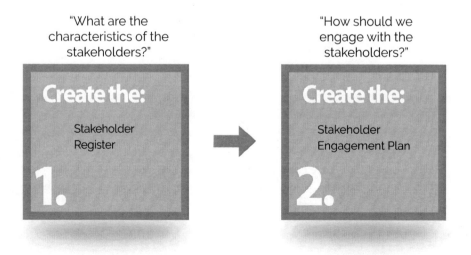

Figure 3.1: Stakeholder Planning

WHAT ARE THE CHARACTERISTICS OF THE STAKEHOLDERS?

The key stakeholders of the project were previously identified during the Initiating Phase and were documented in the Project Charter. During planning, this list is expanded as additional stakeholders are identified. Each stakeholder is reviewed to assess their level of power, interest, and support.

Power

Power is the capacity to influence others to change their attitude and behaviour.[1] For stakeholders, during projects, power relates to the stakeholders' ability to positively or negatively affect the project. This power may come from a number of sources, such as their formal job position, their role in the project, or their perceived expertise.

The following are examples of stakeholders who may have higher levels of power:

- The CEO of the company (job position)
- The person managing resources for the organization (role)
- An industry expert in a field relevant to the project (perceived expertise)

These stakeholders may have lower levels of power:

- Project team members
- Other managers in the organization
- The general public

The assessment of power can be difficult, as it may not be readily apparent. For example, while project team members may generally possess a lower level of power, a project team member with a unique skill set would likely possess a higher level of power. Power levels may also shift over the course of a project. For example, the general public may possess a low level of power at the start of a project, but if an individual or group attracts the attention of the media, their power level may increase.

---

1   For more information about power and the related topic of influence, please refer to the section Understanding Power and Influence in chapter 13.

The assessment of power often requires an understanding of the internal politics that almost always exist within organizations.

Interest

A stakeholder's **interest** is the level of concern or engagement that they have with the project. A stakeholder with a high level of interest is aware of and feels invested in the project, while a stakeholder with a lower level of interest is less aware of and less invested in the project.

Examples of stakeholders who may have higher levels of interest include the following:

- The Project Sponsors
- Project team members
- A customer who will receive the end product

Examples of stakeholders who may have lower levels of interest include the following:

- A bank manager providing a loan to finance the project
- A manager from a department not directly involved in the project
- An inspector who verifies the project is following municipal building codes

As with the level of power, the level of interest may be difficult to assess. Using the example above, the Project Sponsor would need to be observed in order to determine their level of interest.

Support

The third category for assessing stakeholders is their level of **support**. A stakeholder's level of support indicates their willingness to provide assistance to the project or, conversely, the likelihood that they will disrupt the project.

The Project Sponsor is normally a supportive stakeholder, given that they benefit from the results of the project. For example, they may provide assistance in resolving a key issue. Government regulatory agencies are normally neutral stakeholders, as they would likely neither help nor hinder a project, other than to enforce the required regulations. An activist group may be unsupportive. For example, they may actively oppose the outcome of the project through protests.

While not all stakeholders can or need to be supportive, moving stakeholders from unsupportive to supportive is usually positive for the project.

The following is the template for the **Stakeholder Register**:

STAKEHOLDER REGISTER					
Project Name	[This section contains the project name that should appear consistently on all project documents. Organizations often have project naming conventions.]				
Name	**Project Role**	**Level of Power**	**Level of Interest**	**Level of Support**	
[Name of the person or group]	[Project role/title or the reason that they are a stakeholder]	[High/ Low]	[High/ Low]	[Supportive/ Neutral/ Unsupportive]	

Case Study Update: Creating the Stakeholder Register

After completing the Project Kickoff Meeting, Sophie starts to think about the planning work ahead. There are so many things to start working on. Her first priority is to create a list of all the stakeholders that she is aware of at this point in the project.

The company's CEO, Casey Serrador, is the first name on the list. By nature of her role, Casey has an extremely high level of power. Sophie knows from past experience that Casey's interest level is also high. Casey is a hands-on CEO who is fully engaged in the products of her company and is highly supportive of her employees.

Next, Sophie adds Arun Singh to the list. As the Project Sponsor, Arun has a high level of power. Arun will want this project to be successful and, given the high visibility of this project, he will likely be very interested. Sophie can count on a high level of support from him.

There will be three additional project teams working on the other DecoCam V4 Program projects—Development, Installation, and Technical Writing. Sophie has assessed that each of the Project Managers will possess a fairly high level of power, as their actions and decisions could positively or negatively affect her project. However, she knows that their primary interest will be in their own projects and that therefore they will have a lower level of interest in hers. In terms of support, Sophie expects that they will be neutral.

In conversation with Arun, Sophie becomes aware of a potential issue. Jackson Woodhouse, Vice-President of Customer Support, is very upset that his project idea (upgraded camera software for a key customer) was bypassed in favour of the Photo Assistant option. Jackson is an important stakeholder, and Sophie will need the cooperation of a number of people in his department. While Sophie feels his power and interest are high, she is worried about whether he will be supportive of her project. She will do her best to gain his support for the project, but at this point in time she will assume that he will be unsupportive.

Catherine Bianchi is well-known. Through working with her on a number of projects, Catherine has become a mentor for Sophie, providing feedback and career advice to her. Sophie knows that her power, interest, and support will be high.

At this point, there are no team members assigned to Sophie's project, but she knows that this will be changing soon. Part of the planning process is to identify and acquire the necessary team members to complete the project. For now, she adds *project team* to her list, knowing that she will be able to fill in the names later. Her project team will have a lower level of power compared to other stakeholders. Their interest should be high, and they should also be supportive. It will become an issue later if there are any uninterested or unsupportive team members assigned to the project.

Finally, there will be a number of other employees at Deco Productions who will be involved with or affected by the project. For example, they may provide services for or receive certain outputs of the project. In general, they will have a low level of power and interest, and their level of support will likely be neutral.

From past experience, Sophie knows that additional stakeholders will become apparent throughout the project and, as they do, she will add them to her list. For now, this is a good start.

The following is the Stakeholder Register for the project:

DECO PRODUCTIONS	STAKEHOLDER REGISTER			
Project Name	DCV4Launch—DecoCam V4 Product Launch			
Name	**Project Role**	**Level of Power**	**Level of Interest**	**Level of Support**
Casey Serrador	Founder and CEO	High	High	Supportive
Arun Singh	Project Sponsor	High	High	Supportive
Other V4 Project Managers	Project Managers of the other V4 projects	High	Low	Neutral
Jackson Woodhouse	Vice-President, Customer Support	High	High	Unsupportive

(continued)

Name	Project Role	Level of Power	Level of Interest	Level of Support
Catherine Bianchi	Vice-President, Product Development	High	High	Supportive
Project team	Project team	Low	High	Supportive
Deco Productions employees	Employees of Deco Productions with some level of contact with the project	Low	Low	Neutral

> Project stakeholders should be identified and analyzed to assess their level of power, interest, and support.

HOW SHOULD WE ENGAGE WITH THE STAKEHOLDERS?

The next step is to plan how to build or maintain effective relationships with each of the stakeholders that focus on their individual characteristics and needs. The Project Manager should proactively cultivate these relationships throughout the project.

Building effective relationships with stakeholders is very important, as it will help the Project Manager in virtually all aspects of managing the project, including communicating with stakeholders, resolving issues, and making changes to the project.

While each stakeholder relationship is unique, some general approaches the Project Manager can take are outlined in figure 3.2.

The assessment of each stakeholder's level of power and interest should be periodically reviewed during the project, as they may vary over time. Table 3.1 presents a description of each general approach.

Another aspect to consider when developing the Stakeholder Engagement Plan is the level of support for each stakeholder. The Project Manager should strive

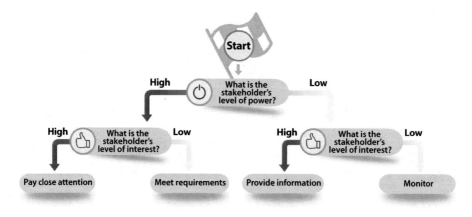

Figure 3.2: Stakeholder Engagement—General Approaches

Table 3.1: Stakeholder General Approach Descriptions

		Low	High
Stakeholder Power	**High**	**Meet Requirements** *(power—high, interest—low)* Given their high degree of power, these stakeholders are important. Their lower level of interest necessitates that the Project Manager's main priority is to understand the requirements of this stakeholder and ensure they are met.	**Pay Close Attention** *(power—high, interest—high)* While all stakeholders are significant to some degree, this type of stakeholder is a key player in the project. The Project Manager should pay close attention to this stakeholder and attempt to build as strong a relationship as possible.
	Low	**Monitor** *(power—low, interest—low)* No action required other than to periodically monitor the stakeholder in order to detect any change in power or interest.	**Provide Information** *(power—low, interest—high)* Focus on providing this stakeholder with information that keeps them well-informed.

Stakeholder Interest

to increase the level of stakeholder support where appropriate. The ability to do so is greatly enhanced when effective stakeholder relationships have been developed.

The template for the **Stakeholder Engagement Plan** is as follows:

STAKEHOLDER ENGAGEMENT PLAN		
Project Name	[This section contains the project name that should appear consistently on all project documents. Organizations often have project naming conventions.]	
Name	**About the Stakeholder**	**How to Engage the Stakeholder**
[Name of the person or group]	[Background and characteristics of the stakeholder]	[Include one of the following: **Pay close attention**: **Meet requirements**: **Provide information**: **Monitor**: In addition, provide details of the approach to be taken to effectively engage with the stakeholder.]

Case Study Update: Creating the Stakeholder Engagement Plan

Sophie considers each of the stakeholders on her list. She asks herself the question "What can I do to effectively engage with them?"

One of the approaches that has helped her when developing her Stakeholder Engagement Plan is to use empathy to see things from their point of view. Once she does, she can more clearly evaluate their needs and decide how best to approach them.

(continued)

From her past interactions, she knows that Casey is passionate about the quality of her company's products and, above all, values open and clear communication. Sophie stops and thinks about what it would be like to be the CEO of a company, one that she started. With this insight, she jots down a few ideas, including dropping by Casey's office periodically and being ready for the types of questions she tends to ask.

Another stakeholder to consider is Jackson. He may be a challenge for Sophie, since his project idea was bypassed in favour of DecoCam V4, and she is concerned he may be unsupportive of her project. She thinks about how Jackson would likely feel. He has been with the company for many years and likely feels some level of frustration as well as feeling underappreciated by the company. Based on this, Sophie decides that she will seek out his advice during the project and regularly provide positive feedback to his department. She hopes this will increase his level of support for the project.

She continues this process with each of the remaining stakeholders.

The following is the Stakeholder Engagement Plan that was produced:

DECO PRODUCTIONS	**STAKEHOLDER ENGAGEMENT PLAN**	
Project Name	DCV4Launch—DecoCam V4 Product Launch	
Name	**About the Stakeholder**	**How to Engage the Stakeholder**
Casey Serrador	As CEO of the company, Casey is an extremely important stakeholder. Casey is very outgoing and supportive, but she can be very demanding when it comes to the quality of her company's products and services. She does not tolerate people who are vague or evasive, and she requires open and clear communication. She also promotes an open-door policy that encourages employees to drop by her desk if they would like to talk to her.	**Pay close attention:** • As part of this project, reports will not be provided directly to Casey, as Arun (Project Sponsor) will perform this task. • However, Casey is likely to make efforts to interact with the project team at various intervals. • Drop by her office periodically to demonstrate key aspects of the project (at least twice during the project). • Provide high-level overviews, but be prepared to provide details if she requests more information. • Be open and direct with her regarding any requests for information. • Let the project team know that she may be dropping by for demos periodically.

Arun Singh	Arun is relatively new to the organization and seems concerned about creating a good first impression with this project. He is very supportive and friendly but somewhat more reserved in nature compared to Casey's style of management. He has shown a great deal of interest in the financial aspects of the project and has expressed concern regarding the budget.	**Pay close attention:** • Book informational meetings with Arun to provide him with updates and ensure that he is comfortable with the progress of the project. These can be held at increased or decreased intervals depending on his feedback. • Invite Arun to the biweekly team demonstration of completed deliverables. • Keep him updated regarding the budget information and alert him immediately if there is any indication that the budget will be exceeded.
Other V4 Project Managers	Many projects are interdependent, so it is important to foster positive relationships between the project teams.	**Meet requirements:** • Schedule an initial meeting with each Project Manager to review their timeline and any dependencies between projects. • Respond to any requests for assistance and provide assistance when appropriate. • Send a summary of key dates to each Project Manager once the schedule is completed. Send updates to them if the key dates change during the project.
Jackson Woodhouse	Jackson has been with the organization for many years and is very loyal to the company. He has very strong convictions and is focused on providing support for Deco Productions' largest clients. In the past, he has been critical of the mobile device camera applications. He values direct discussion and likes to "tell it like it is."	**Pay close attention:** • Early in the project, drop by Jackson's office to acknowledge and listen to his concerns about his preferred project option (upgraded camera software for a key customer). • Encourage his input and feedback. • During status updates and reports, acknowledge the value of his department's support.
Catherine Bianchi	As the head of the Product Development area, Catherine has a keen interest in all of Deco Productions' products. She is very friendly and supportive and has given Sophie valuable career advice on a number of occasions.	**Meet requirements:** • Continue to meet with Catherine to gain her advice and mentoring. • Prior to publishing major project documents, pass them by her for comments.
Project team	As the project team has not yet been assigned, this section cannot be completed. It is anticipated that experienced DecoCam employees will be assigned shortly.	**Provide information:** • Keep all teams well-informed by ensuring that all project documents are accessible. • Foster a positive team environment by periodically suggesting team lunches or gatherings at the end of the workday. • Check in with each team member regularly to see how their work is going and receive any feedback or concerns.

(continued)

Name	About the Stakeholder	How to Engage the Stakeholder
Deco Productions employees	The employees of the company are often interested in new products that are developed.	**Monitor:** • No specific actions are planned at this time. • Answer any requests for information or updates when appropriate.

Develop a plan to engage with each stakeholder.

DISTRIBUTION OF STAKEHOLDER DOCUMENTS

While most of the project management documents described in this text are shared within the organization, the stakeholder documents contained in this chapter are generally not shared.

Since these stakeholder documents contain assessments of each stakeholder, they could be misinterpreted if read by a stakeholder, potentially harming the relationship. Therefore, care should be taken to keep these documents confidential. For example, the stakeholder documents could be shared with only the project team for a given project and would not be shared with other stakeholders.

Keep the Stakeholder Register and Stakeholder Engagement Plan confidential.

KEY TERMINOLOGY

Interest: The stakeholder's level of concern or engagement that they have with a project

Power: The capacity to influence others to change their attitude and behaviour

Stakeholder Engagement Plan: A planning document containing the Project Manager's planned actions to effectively engage with each identified stakeholder

Stakeholder Register: A planning document listing the stakeholders of the project and including their perceived power, interest, and level of support

Support: The attitude the stakeholder displays toward the project, ranging from supportive to neutral to unsupportive

KEY CONCEPTS

1. Project stakeholders should be identified and analyzed to assess their level of power, interest, and support.

2.   Develop a plan to engage with each stakeholder.

3.   Keep the Stakeholder Register and Stakeholder Engagement Plan confidential.

DISCUSSION QUESTIONS

1.   Think of a project from your personal, work, or school activities. Identify the stakeholders for this endeavour.

2.   Think of an example of a project stakeholder for each of the four combinations of power and interest:

     •   High power, high interest

     •   High power, low interest

     •   Low power, high interest

     •   Low power, low interest

3.   What could cause a project stakeholder to change from being unsupportive to being supportive?

4.   What skills are most important in order to effectively engage with project stakeholders?

5.   Perform an online search researching the benefits of stakeholder management. Based on your findings, describe any additional benefits of stakeholder management not mentioned in this chapter.

4   Scope Planning

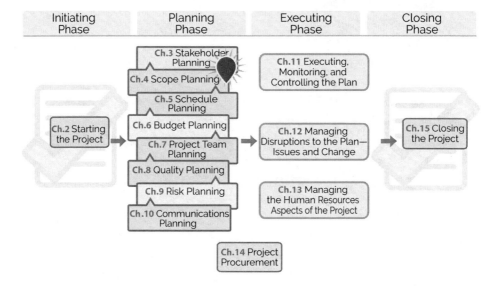

| Initiating Phase | Planning Phase | Executing Phase | Closing Phase |

Ch.3 Stakeholder Planning

Ch.4 Scope Planning

Ch.5 Schedule Planning

Ch.6 Budget Planning

Ch.7 Project Team Planning

Ch.8 Quality Planning

Ch.9 Risk Planning

Ch.10 Communications Planning

Ch.2 Starting the Project

Ch.11 Executing, Monitoring, and Controlling the Plan

Ch.12 Managing Disruptions to the Plan— Issues and Change

Ch.13 Managing the Human Resources Aspects of the Project

Ch.14 Project Procurement

Ch.15 Closing the Project

INTRODUCTION TO SCOPE PLANNING

While the Project Charter defines the project's goals and objectives, it does not provide detailed information about what will be produced during the project. Therefore, additional planning should be performed in order to provide a clear definition of the requirements and details of the project's scope.

There are two main steps when planning the project scope, as shown in figure 4.1.

The first step is to determine the list of items needed for the project. These items are documented in the **Project Requirements Document**. The next step is to determine what the project will produce. The output of this step consists

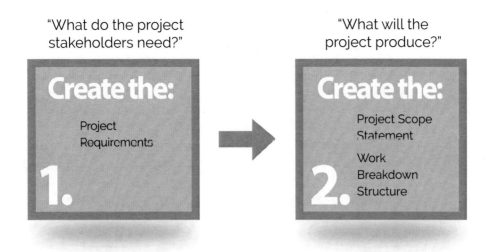

Figure 4.1: Scope Planning

of two documents: the **Project Scope Statement** and the **Work Breakdown Structure**.

WHAT DO THE PROJECT STAKEHOLDERS NEED?

The gathering of project requirements is an important first step, as it allows the project team to understand the needs and wants of the Project Sponsor (or others within the organization as indicated by the Project Sponsor). The project requirements should support the goals and objectives that were documented in the Project Charter.

Discussions with the Project Sponsor will help identify the individuals who will provide requirements for the project. A challenge for the project team is to resolve any conflicting requirements from different individuals. The Project Sponsor can be consulted if needed to provide direction and resolve any disagreements (see figure 4.2).

Project requirements may be gathered in a number of ways, and choosing an approach often depends on the number of individuals who are providing requirements. A common approach is to interview individuals within the organization. When a large number of individuals are providing requirements, approaches such as surveys, focus groups, and research may be more appropriate.

Figure 4.2: Project Requirements

When documenting requirements, it is often useful to separate them into categories such as functional requirements, performance requirements, and technical requirements, depending on the project.

The following is the Project Requirements Document template:

PROJECT REQUIREMENTS DOCUMENT	
Project Name	[This section contains the project name that should appear consistently on all project documents. Organizations often have project naming conventions.]
Functional Requirements	
[This section should list the functional requirements for the project, including any features or properties of the project's outcomes.]	
Technical/Performance Requirements	
[This section should list the technical requirements for the project (e.g., the required technology infrastructure) and any performance requirements (e.g., the minimum response time).]	

Case Study Update: Gathering the Project Requirements

Sophie sits at her desk and considers the recent Project Kickoff Meeting. While there were a few tough questions from the head of the Software Development division, it all went well. Picking up the Project Charter document, she scans the objectives for the project. She turns off her phone's ringer to prevent any interruptions.

Sophie refreshes her memory by looking at the objectives. Based on the Business Case for the project, a full product launch is required, including the support of the sales process, an update of DecoCam's website information, social media promotion, trade show materials, and the development of a promotional video.

While this is a good start, Sophie knows that these are high-level objectives. That is, the requirements for each of these objectives need additional detail in order for the scope of the project to be defined. The project has been approved with a $60,000 budget, so Sophie knows that the requirements need to fit within this budget.

In order to determine the project requirements, Sophie will need to bring a new member into her project team: a Business Analyst.

After negotiating with a couple of senior managers within the company, Sophie secures Fatehjit Kumar for a period of time. Fatehjit was one of the company's first employees and has worked in both the administrative and marketing areas of the company. He has recently moved into a Business Analyst position, and his in-depth knowledge of the company has been very useful during recent projects.

Fatehjit meets with a number of individuals within the Product Development and Marketing departments in order to understand their needs. He also reviews the approaches that were taken when similar products were launched, while checking to see the impact the approaches had on the subsequent sales activity. Fatehjit documents this information in the Project Requirements Document.

What follows is the resulting Project Requirements Document:

DECO PRODUCTIONS	**PROJECT REQUIREMENTS DOCUMENT**
Project Name	DCV4Launch—DecoCam V4 Product Launch
Functional Requirements	

1. All DecoCam product information listed on the company website and printed materials should be updated to include Version 4 and the key characteristics of this version.

(continued)

2. Promotional material should be distributed through sponsored advertisements on selected websites and through Deco Productions' social media presence.

3. A press release for this version should be created.

4. The technology blogging community should be engaged so that it covers the new release.

5. The promotional video should be professional and engaging and should demonstrate the key features of the new version.

6. Materials should be produced for upcoming trade shows and include DecoCam signs, booth giveaways branded with the DecoCam logo, and a multimedia display that will draw trade show attendees to the booth.

7. The trade show materials should be delivered and set up at each trade show.

Technical/Performance Requirements

1. The promotional video should include closed captions.

2. All promotional documents should be created in PDF format.

3. All promotional documents should be under 50 MB to ensure minimal download times.

Gather the project requirements from the project stakeholders.

WHAT WILL THE PROJECT PRODUCE?

Once the requirements are known, the **scope** of the project may be defined. The scope is the product, service, or result created during the project. During this step, two documents are produced: the Project Scope Statement and the Work Breakdown Structure.

The Project Scope Statement

When defining the scope of the project, it is important to determine the **deliverables** that will be produced during the project. Deliverables are identifiable pieces or components of the project. Defining the deliverables of a project is useful, as the project may then be viewed as a collection of smaller components rather than one large undertaking.[1]

The deliverables to be produced are based on the project requirements that were previously defined. While it is usually desirable to satisfy all of the

---

1   There are two main types of deliverables—product deliverables and project deliverables. Product deliverables are the output of the project. Examples of product deliverables could include websites, research reports, or any other product, service, or result created by a project. Project deliverables are documents created as a result of managing the project. Examples of project deliverables include the Project Charter, the Business Case, and other project documents created as a result of the project. Product deliverables are visible to the stakeholders who receive the results of the project whereas project deliverables tend to be visible only to those internal to the project (e.g., the project team). For simplicity, this text focuses on product deliverables and does not include project deliverables in the planning documents presented.

requirements, often the budget and time constraints may require trade-offs to be made. For example, certain requirements may not be included if they will cause the project budget to be exceeded. Defining the deliverables often involves a series of meetings, conversations, emails, and other communications over a period of time ranging from days to months.

In order to ensure that everyone involved in the project has access to the same information, the deliverable information should be summarized and documented in the Project Scope Statement. It is used to validate the scope with the Project Sponsor and other stakeholders. The Project Sponsor should provide specific approval for this document and therefore the scope of the project. The Project Scope Statement is a key communication tool to ensure there is a common understanding of the project scope.

In addition, thought should be given to how to measure the quality of the deliverables—by defining and documenting the specifications, standards, and characteristics of each deliverable. These should be defined as clearly and specifically as possible, as this information will be followed both when producing the deliverables and when verifying the quality of each deliverable during the Executing Phase.

The Project Scope Statement also explicitly defines what is not included in the project. For example, in the case study, the decision was made that the project team would not set up the new materials at trade shows. To ensure that everyone is aware of this decision, the Project Scope Statement should explicitly state that this work is not to be performed.

Project Scope Statements may also identify the project documents that are produced (such as the Business Case and Project Charter) and include them as deliverables. Note that this text's Project Scope Statement (for the case study) does not include the project documents.

The following is the Project Scope Statement template:

PROJECT SCOPE STATEMENT	
Project Name	[This section contains the project name that should appear consistently on all project documents. Organizations often have project naming conventions.]
Project Deliverable	**Detailed Description**
[Deliverable]	[Describe this deliverable in as much detail as possible.]
Project Exclusions	
[Indicate anything that will not be included in the scope of the project.]	

Case Study Update: Creating the Project Scope Statement

As Sophie reflects on her planning up to this point, she is feeling more confident since she has a good handle on both the needs of the project stakeholders and the project requirements.

Yet the more she thinks about the next steps, the more uneasy she feels. Sophie's natural tendency is to want to get going on the project rather than writing down the details. However, during some of her recent projects, this approach has caused problems later on. One or more of the following would usually take place:

- Even though details were discussed with the Project Sponsor and other stake-holders, memories of the discussion and decisions would fade over time. There were often disagreements about what was or was not to be included in the project.
- Team members working on the project were often confused about what they were meant to produce.
- Small details were missed, causing a number of last-minute emergencies.
- Verifying the quality of the completed deliverables was difficult, as the team members were not sure what they should be looking for.

So, for this project, Sophie decides to create a detailed Project Scope Statement. Together with Fatehjit, she frequently refers to the Project Requirements Document as they begin to define the various deliverables that will be created during the project. They frequently need to communicate with many of the stakeholders in order to determine the characteristics of each deliverable. They are also constantly aware of their overall budget and project due date. In addition, there are a number of possible deliverables that are defined as not being in the scope of their project. For example, while the Project Requirements Document included a requirement to update DecoCam printed material, it was decided that it would be more effective for the Corporate Promotions department to perform this task. To ensure this decision is documented, Fatehjit adds this decision to the Project Exclusions section of the Project Scope Statement.

The following is the Project Scope Statement for the case study project:

DECO PRODUCTIONS	**PROJECT SCOPE STATEMENT**
Project Name	DCV4Launch—DecoCam V4 Product Launch

Project Deliverable	**Detailed Description**
Website Updates	• Update the DecoCam product page to include the features of the new version. • Create an online slideshow that demonstrates the key features of the new version.
Social Media	• Develop a social media strategy and calendar for the three months following the launch of the product. • Develop the content for the planned social media posts. • Promotional documents should be in PDF format and under 50 MB.
Press Release	• Create a news story outlining the key features of the new DecoCam, including its use of advanced AI technology. • Distribute electronically to media on the same date that DecoCam V4 is available for download to the public.
Media Outreach	• Include email and phone calls to encourage publicity from major online influencers (e.g., industry magazines, top technology bloggers).
Promotional Video	• Develop a professional video that demonstrates how to use the new product. • To increase the likelihood that viewers will share the video through social media channels, the video should contain a humorous situation. • The message of the video will be the usefulness of the DecoCam Photo Assistant feature and how it will help average people take photos like a professional photographer. • The video should be no more than two minutes in length. • The video should include closed captions.
Trade Show Signage	• The signs will be on retractable banner stands. • There will be an initial creation of five stands. • They will integrate with the company's existing trade show set-up and branding. • They should provide a visual display of the product's features. • They will display information and include links to more product information. • Update the trade show supplies procedures and data files to allow for the order of additional banners.
Booth Giveaways	• These consist of a flyer that resembles a postcard. • There will be an initial creation of 2,000 postcards. • The picture side of the postcard will contain a holographic scene of an art deco building with a sign displaying the DecoCam name and logo. • The address side of the postcard will contain the necessary product and contact information. • Update the trade show supplies procedures and data files to allow for the order of additional postcards.

(continued)

Project Deliverable	Detailed Description
Multimedia Demo	• This consists of a mural showing an urban scene for visual interest. • A mobile phone will be mounted on a tripod and will run a slideshow simulating the user experience of using the DecoCam Photo Assistant feature. • Two murals will be created and two tripods with phones will be set up. • Update the trade show supplies procedures and data files to allow for the order of additional demo kits.
Project Exclusions	
Updates to DecoCam printed materials. These will be performed by the Corporate Promotions department.	
Distribution of social media posts. This will be performed by the Marketing department.	
Distribution of the DecoCam software. This will be performed by the DecoCam V4 Installation Project.	
Trade show staffing and management. Documentation and supplies for the trade shows will be created and will be available for order by the Marketing department.	
Technical support for the website content, videos, or other materials. This will be provided by the Marketing department.	

Create a Project Scope Statement that describes the project deliverables to be included and not included in the scope of the project. Ensure this document is signed off by the appropriate project stakeholder(s).

Other Supporting Documents

While the Project Scope Statement contains a description of what is (and is not) contained in the scope of the project, there are often additional details that do not fit easily into the structure of the Project Scope Statement. The Project Scope Statement may refer to other supporting documents, such as the following:

- Mural design and layout information
- Promotional video storyboard and script information
- Online slideshow design
- Other documents that support the description of the project scope

Supporting documents that describe the scope of the project may be appended to the Project Scope Statement in order to more fully describe the project scope.

The Work Breakdown Structure

In addition to the Project Scope Statement, another scope-related document is created: the Work Breakdown Structure (WBS). Whereas the Project Scope Statement describes the characteristics of each deliverable, the WBS organizes the deliverables into a hierarchy. Figure 4.3 demonstrates the appearance of a WBS in tree-diagram format.

The project itself is at the top of a WBS and is known as Level 1. The project may then be divided up into smaller pieces (deliverables), which are shown

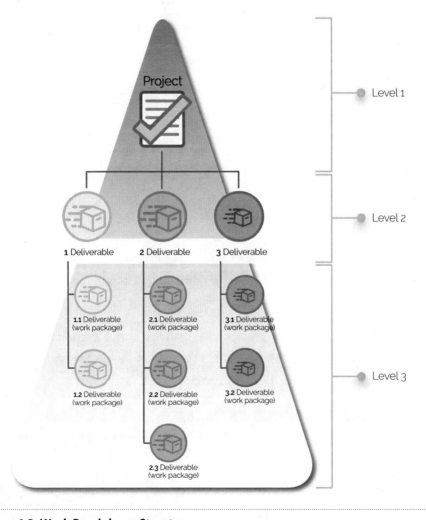

Figure 4.3: Work Breakdown Structure

in Level 2. Each Level 2 deliverable may then be divided up into yet smaller deliverables in Level 3. The deliverables that are no longer divided are also known as **work packages**.

When performing this decomposition process, it is important to understand that each level is equivalent to the level above. For example, in figure 4.3, the three deliverables in Level 2 are equivalent to Level 1 (the project), but they are broken down into more detail. Likewise, the seven deliverables (also known as work packages) in Level 3 are equivalent to the three deliverables in Level 2, again just broken down into more detail.

The WBS may also be displayed in list format. This format is often used during projects, given that it is easier to update. The WBS shown in figure 4.3 would appear as follows:

Project

1. Deliverable
    1.1   Deliverable (work package)
    1.2   Deliverable (work package)
2. Deliverable
    2.1   Deliverable (work package)
    2.2   Deliverable (work package)
    2.3   Deliverable (work package)
3. Deliverable
    3.1   Deliverable (work package)
    3.2   Deliverable (work package)

The process of dividing a project into smaller and smaller deliverables is key to the planning process, that is, viewing a project as a series of deliverables. However, it is very important to *not* include activities in the WBS—this will come later, during the discussion of the project schedule, as covered in chapter 5. Each deliverable defined should be a noun (i.e., an object) and should not include a verb (i.e., an action).

During a school project, one of the work packages identified in the WBS is Research Report. This is an appropriate name, as it is a noun. On the other hand, Write Research Report is not an appropriately named deliverable since it contains a verb. Verbs will be used when creating activities in chapter 5.

Case Study Update: Creating the Work Breakdown Structure

With the Project Scope Statement underway, the planning team (Sophie and Fatehjit) turn their attention to organizing the project. A number of deliverables have already been defined, but the question now becomes how to organize the project. Scanning the list of deliverables, they decide that the project itself may be organized into three main deliverables:

1. Trade Show Support
2. Communications
3. Promotional Video

Each of the deliverables from the Project Scope Statement is inserted under one of three deliverables above. Because of the size and complexity of the promotional video deliverable, Sophie and Fatehjit decide to break it down into two smaller deliverables as follows:

3.1   Video Plan
3.2   Video Production

As they put the finishing touch on the WBS, Sophie feels a sense of relief. The product launch is large and complex, and she wasn't quite sure where to start. But having organized the project into a hierarchy of deliverables, she can now focus on the completion of nine manageable work packages.

The completed DecoCam WBS in tree-diagram format is shown in figure 4.4.

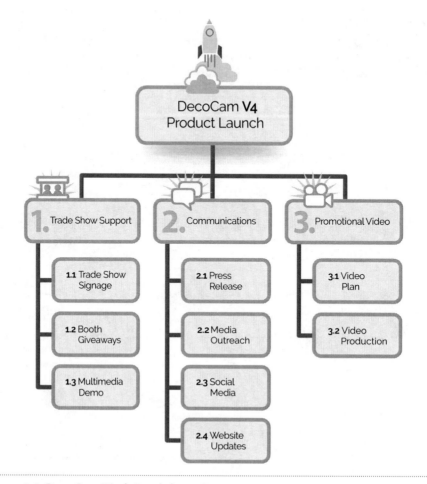

Figure 4.4: DecoCam Work Breakdown Structure

The same WBS in list format is as follows:

DecoCam V4 Product Launch

1. Trade Show Support
   1.1   Trade Show Signage
   1.2   Booth Giveaways
   1.3   Multimedia Demo
2. Communications
   2.1   Press Release
   2.2   Media Outreach
   2.3   Social Media
   2.4   Website Updates
3. Promotional Video
   3.1   Video Plan
   3.2   Video Production

There are various approaches that may be used to create a WBS:

1. A top-down approach to identify the high-level deliverables and then progressively break them down into their work packages. This is the approach used in the case study.
2. A bottom-up approach to first identify work packages and then group them together to create the structure of the WBS. This can be a useful approach when the high-level deliverables are not obvious to the project team.
3. Using a similar project's WBS as a starting point and then making changes as appropriate.
4. Using a standard WBS as defined by an organization.

When creating a WBS, a combination of any of the above approaches may be used. The goal is to develop an effective WBS that contains everything that needs to be produced during the project. This is known as the 100% rule—that all of the deliverables to be created during the project are contained in the WBS. Or, stated another way, if a deliverable is not listed in the WBS, it is not within the scope of the project.

A common area of uncertainty when creating a WBS is how to know when deliverables should no longer be decomposed or broken down into smaller deliverables. The following are two methods for determining this:

- Continue to decompose deliverables until each work package is small enough to be understood and completed by either a team or an individual.
- Use the 8/80 rule. This rule states that the work package should not be less than eight hours or greater than 80 hours. According to this rule, the decomposition of a deliverable would stop when the resulting work packages are less than eight hours, and decomposition would need to continue when a deliverable is greater than 80 hours.

The WBS also clearly demonstrates the organization of the project and serves as a guide or input to other parts of the project plan, such as the schedule and budget.

While a WBS should contain all of the deliverables to be produced, there is information that should not be included:

- Scheduling information: a WBS does not contain dates or indicate the order in which the work will be performed.
- Cost information: a WBS does not contain cost information.
- Detailed specifications: a WBS does not contain a description of the deliverables.

Similar to the Project Scope Statement, a WBS may also include the project management deliverables produced during the project, such as the Project Charter, Project Requirements Document, and Project Scope Statement. However, in practice, many Project Managers do not include project management deliverables within the WBS, as they are understood to be included within the scope of the project.

Create a Work Breakdown Structure that organizes the deliverables of the project into a hierarchy.

KEY TERMINOLOGY

Deliverable: Something that is produced during the project; the collection of all deliverables composes the scope of the project

Project Requirements Document: A planning document that describes the items and capabilities needed for project output

Project Scope Statement: A planning document that fully describes the deliverables of the project

Scope: The product, service, or result created during the project

Work Breakdown Structure: A hierarchical document listing the project deliverables to be produced during the project

Work Package: A deliverable that is at the lowest level of the WBS and is not further divided into sub-deliverables

KEY CONCEPTS

1. Gather the project requirements from the project stakeholders.
2. Create a Project Scope Statement that describes the project deliverables to be included and not included in the scope of the project. Ensure this document is signed off by the appropriate project stakeholder(s).
3. Supporting documents that describe the scope of the project may be appended to the Project Scope Statement in order to more fully describe the project scope.
4. Create a Work Breakdown Structure that organizes the deliverables of the project into a hierarchy.

DISCUSSION QUESTIONS

1. Think of a new product or service that you may be planning to purchase over the next year (e.g., phone, vacation). Make a list of the requirements for this purchase. Group your requirements into categories, such as functional, technical, and performance requirements.

2. What is the benefit of creating a Work Breakdown Structure? Why is it more effective to create a WBS and a Project Scope Statement rather than just a Project Scope Statement?

3. How much detail should be documented in the Project Scope Statement? When should you stop defining additional details?

4. Perform an online search to research how a lack of scope planning can lead to project failures. Summarize your findings.

5 Schedule Planning

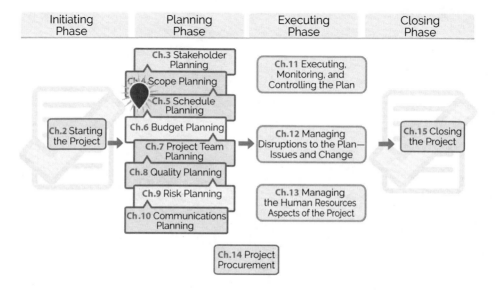

INTRODUCTION TO SCHEDULE PLANNING

Once the project scope is defined, the next step is to create a schedule. A schedule is a list of activities, arranged in logical order and containing the time that each should be started and completed. Schedules may also contain information such as the cost and required resources for each activity.

The development of a schedule is beneficial for the following reasons:

- It allows the project team to make commitments to its stakeholders about the final delivery date as well as interim deliverables.
- Everyone involved in the project is able to see their efforts within the context of the whole project and understand the connections and inter-dependencies that may exist.
- It provides an established project timeline that may be used to track the progress of the project. This established timeline is known as a **baseline**.

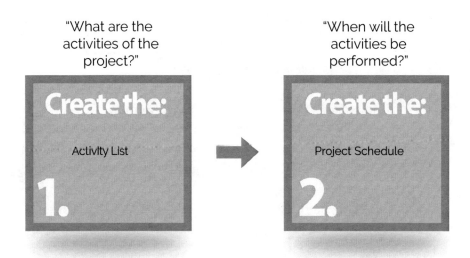

Figure 5.1: Schedule Planning

There are two main steps when planning the project timeline, as shown in figure 5.1. The first step is to create a list of the project activities required to complete the project, including the estimated duration of each activity. The next step is to arrange the activities in logical order and add the resource requirements to each activity.

WHAT ARE THE ACTIVITIES OF THE PROJECT?

During the previous chapter, we saw that a project is divided into a number of deliverables that are arranged into a hierarchy known as a Work Breakdown Structure (WBS). The deliverables at the lowest level of the WBS (i.e., not decomposed further into smaller deliverables) are called *work packages*. In order to create the project schedule, we now define the activities that will be required to create each work package. Recall that in chapter 4 we saw that all deliverables/work packages should be nouns (i.e., objects). Activities, on the other hand, are actions, and therefore activity names should start with a verb.

For example, during a school project, one of the work packages is Research Report. For this work package, two activities are defined: "perform research" and "create research report." The verb that starts each activity name (perform, create) clearly describes the action to be performed during the activity.

Depending on the work package, a larger number of detailed activities or a smaller number of general activities may be needed. To help determine the number of activities, the following criteria can be used:

- Each activity should be clear to those who will perform the activity. If it is unclear, additional sub-activities may be required.
- The **duration** of each activity (i.e., the total amount of time available for the activity) should be moderate. Extremely long activity durations (e.g., 30 days) may be challenging to manage, especially if the work is complex. Extremely short activity durations (e.g., 10 minutes) will result in a large number of activities that, in turn, increase the size and complexity of the resulting schedule.
- Each activity should have an identifiable person or group who will be responsible for its completion.

The identified activities are documented in the Activity List. The template is as follows:

ACTIVITY LIST			
Project	[This section contains the project name that should appear consistently on all project documents. Organizations often have project naming conventions.]		
Work Package	**Activity**	**Duration**	**HR Requirements**
[Name of the work package from the WBS]	[Name of the activity]	[Duration of the activity]	[Description of the human resources required to complete the activity]

Case Study Update: Creating the Activity List

It's Monday morning, and Sophie arrives early to the office, coffee in hand, ready to continue with the planning of the project. To refresh her memory, she reads through the draft WBS and Project Scope Statement that she and Fatehjit created last week.

Sophie takes a simple approach to get started. First, she considers the list of work packages that have been documented: the Trade Show Signage, Booth Giveaways, Multimedia Demo, Press Release, Media Outreach, Social Media, Website Updates, Video Plan, and Video Production. Next, she writes the name of each work package on a separate blank piece of paper. She titles another document Project Management; this is where she will reflect on the work necessary to manage this project. Then she brainstorms about each work package and begins to list its required activities. This helps her compartmentalize the work required to get each work package and the project management done. It's a big job; when she's finished, there will be 10 pieces of paper filled with activities, but Sophie knows she'll produce a better estimate and execute a better project as a result of her planning.

After about 30 minutes, Sophie completes the **Activity List** for the project.

Trade Show Signage
- Create sign graphics/text
- Order banner stands

Booth Giveaways
- Create holographic cards
- Order cards

Multimedia Demo
- Create mural for booth
- Develop demo slideshow
- Order cameras and tripods

Press Release
- Create press release
- Send press release

Media Outreach
- Create outreach list
- Perform outreach

Social Media (SM)
- Create SM strategy
- Develop SM post content

Website Updates
- Update product page
- Develop online slideshow

Video Plan
- Develop video concept
- Develop storyboard and script

Video Production
- Film video
- Edit video

Project Management
- Initiate the project
- Plan the project
- Close the project

Figure 5.2: Activity List

Using the WBS as a starting point, create an Activity List consisting of one or more activities for each work package.

Estimating Activity Duration

An important characteristic of each activity is the estimated duration. Developing accurate duration estimates can be challenging for a number of reasons:

- Given the unique nature of projects, the activity may not have been performed before, making determining its likely duration difficult.

- Unforeseen problems can cause the activity to take longer than estimated.
- The expertise of the person(s) working on the activity affects the duration. Often, their identity/ability/skill set is not known when the estimate is created.

There are a number of techniques that are helpful when creating duration estimates, including the following:

- Using the experience of past projects as a guideline for the current estimate. This may be based on the experience of the person making the estimation or through consultation with others.
- Determining the characteristics of the work that needs to be performed during the activity.

When creating activity duration estimates, the more detailed the scope of the project, the more accurate the estimates tend to be.

Given the difficulty and potential for inaccuracy when estimating duration, it is usually advisable to allow extra time in the activity for unforeseen work or issues. This is known as adding contingency to the duration. This contingency may be placed in each activity duration estimate or as a total amount at the end of the project. However, the use of contingency time may not be viewed positively by all stakeholders. Some may view it as an attempt by the project team to pad the estimates and needlessly increase the overall duration and cost of the project. Effective communication is required in order to demonstrate the use and benefit of allotting or using contingency time.

When considering activity duration, it is important to distinguish duration from the **work** involved for an activity. Whereas the duration is the length of time that an activity continues, work is the amount of effort applied to complete an activity. The determination of the amount of work for each activity will be discussed in chapter 6.

For example, a school assignment has a due date of one week from now and will likely require three hours to complete sometime during the week. This activity (completing the assignment) therefore has a duration of one week and three hours of work.

A group project (of three students) in another course has a due date of two weeks from now. The assignment will require four hours from each student in the group. This activity (completing the group project) therefore has a duration of two weeks and 12 hours of work.

The Activity List for the DecoCam V4 Product Launch project with estimated activity durations is as follows:

	ACTIVITY LIST		
DECO PRODUCTIONS			
Project	DCV4Launch—DecoCam V4 Product Launch		
Work Package	**Activity**	**Duration**	**HR Requirements**
Trade Show Signage	Create sign graphics/text	3 days	
	Order banner stands	1 day	
Booth Giveaways	Create holographic cards	2 days	
	Order cards	1 day	
Multimedia Demo	Create mural for booth	3 days	
	Develop demo slideshow	3 days	
	Order cameras and tripods	1 day	
Press Release	Create press release	2 days	
	Send press release	1 day	
Media Outreach	Create outreach list	1 day	
	Perform outreach	5 days	
Social Media	Create SM strategy	2 days	
	Develop SM post content	3 days	
Website Updates	Update product page	1 day	
	Develop online slideshow	3 days	
Video Plan	Develop video concept	3 days	
	Develop storyboard and script	7 days	
Video Production	Film video	10 days	
	Edit video	5 days	
Project Management	Initiate the project	3 days	
	Plan the project	7 days	
	Close the project	3 days	

Activity Lists do not include the start dates or end dates of the activities, and the order of the Activity List does not indicate the order in which the activities will be completed. Activity Lists may also include a detailed description of each activity, though this level of detail is not included in this text.

 Estimate the duration for each activity.

WHEN WILL THE ACTIVITIES BE PERFORMED?

Now that a list of activities has been determined, the next step is to create the schedule for the project. This involves considering the timing of the activities. This timing of activities is based on the following:

- The required sequence of activities based on the work involved, also known as determining the **dependencies** between activities
- The availability of human resources or specific equipment or technology
- Specific date requirements (e.g., a client meeting is required for a certain date)

Case Study Update: Determining When the Activities Will Be Performed

Sophie examines the 10 pieces of paper full of project activities. While she has captured the work to be done, she knows she needs to put the activities in some kind of order or sequence. The Trade Show Signage activities, for example, don't all happen at the same time. So, with a pad of sticky notes in hand, Sophie takes the Trade Show Signage work package and copies the two activities—"create sign graphics/text" and "order banner stands"—onto separate sticky notes. She does the same for the remaining pages of activities and arranges them on her office whiteboard (see figure 5.3).

Create sign graphics/text	Order banner stands	Create holographic cards	Order cards	Create mural for booth
Develop demo slideshow	Order cameras and tripods	Create press release	Send press release	Create outreach list
Perform outreach	Create SM strategy	Create SM post content	Update product page	Develop online slideshow
Develop video concept	Develop storyboard and script	Film video	Edit video	Initiate the project
Plan the project	Close the project			

Figure 5.3: Project Activities

Next, Sophie begins to rearrange the sticky notes to put them in the order that they should be performed. Her experience with previous product launches helps her determine the correct order. For example, Sophie determines that certain activities are sequential (i.e., performed in a particular order), so she arranges them as shown in figure 5.4 and draws an arrow between them.

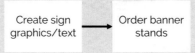

Figure 5.4: Sequential Activities

Sophie finds that there are some activities that are not related to each other and may be performed at the same time if necessary. For example, the "create SM strategy" and "develop video concept" activities do not need to be performed in any particular order. For these activities, an arrow is not drawn between them on the whiteboard (see figure 5.5).

Figure 5.5: Unrelated Activities

As Sophie arranges the sticky notes on the whiteboard, the timeline of the project is becoming clear.

Creating the Network Diagram

A useful tool for displaying the sequence of activities is a **network diagram**, which displays the project's activities as follows:

- Each activity is represented by a rectangle.
- The network diagram is read from left to right on the page.
- An arrow indicates a dependency between two activities.

Based on the required order of activities, figure 5.6 shows the network diagram for the case study project.

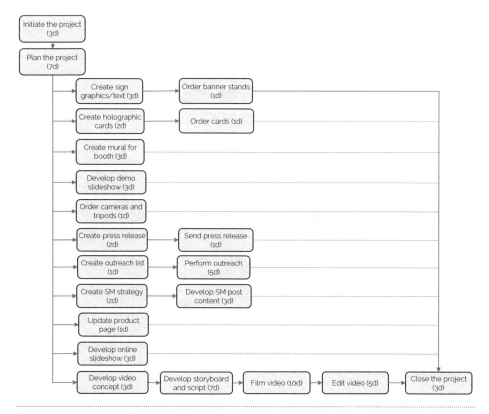

Figure 5.6: Network Diagram

Create a network diagram that demonstrates the dependencies between activities.

Case Study Update: Adding Human Resources to the Schedule

Sophie steps back from the whiteboard to review the network diagram. Her next step is to consider the human resources who will be assigned to the project. Based on the work required for this project, she writes the following requirements on her notepad:

- Graphic Designer: needed to complete the Trade Show Signage, Booth Giveaways, and Multimedia Demo work packages
- Communications Specialist: needed to complete the Press Release, Media Outreach, Social Media, and Website Updates work packages

- Marketing Specialist: needed to complete the Video Plan and Video Production work packages
- Videographer: needed to complete the Video Plan and Video Production work packages

In addition, a Business Analyst (Fatehjit Kumar) was assigned to help plan the project scope. Sophie's expertise as Project Manager will also be needed throughout the project.

As she adds each type of project role to each sticky note, she quickly realizes that there are going to be issues. Since many of the activities are scheduled to begin at the same time, after the "plan the project" activity, she will need numerous Graphic Designers and Communications Specialists. Based on her last few projects, she knows that she will only be able to secure one of each. Picking up some of the sticky notes, she starts to rearrange them into a different order.

As the human resource requirements are determined, they may be added to the Activity List:

DECO PRODUCTIONS	**ACTIVITY LIST**		
Project	DecoCam Version 4 Product Launch		
Work Package	**Activity**	**Duration**	**HR Requirements**
Trade Show Signage	Create sign graphics/text	3 days	Graphic Designer
	Order banner stands	1 day	Graphic Designer
Booth Giveaways	Create holographic cards	2 days	Graphic Designer
	Order cards	1 day	Graphic Designer
Multimedia Demo	Create mural for booth	3 days	Graphic Designer
	Develop demo slideshow	3 days	Graphic Designer
	Order cameras and tripods	1 day	Graphic Designer
Press Release	Create press release	2 days	Communications Specialist
	Send press release	1 day	Communications Specialist
Media Outreach	Create outreach list	1 day	Communications Specialist
	Perform outreach	5 days	Communications Specialist
Social Media	Create SM strategy	2 days	Communications Specialist

(continued)

Work Package	Activity	Duration	HR Requirements
	Develop SM post content	3 days	Communications Specialist
Website Updates	Update product page	1 day	Communications Specialist
	Develop online slideshow	3 days	Communications Specialist
Video Plan	Develop video concept	3 days	Marketing Specialist, Videographer
	Develop storyboard and script	7 days	Marketing Specialist, Videographer
Video Production	Film video	10 days	Marketing Specialist, Videographer
	Edit video	5 days	Marketing Specialist, Videographer
Project Management	Initiate the project	3 days	Project Manager (50%)
	Plan the project	7 days	Project Manager (50%), Business Analyst
	Close the project	3 days	Project Manager (50%)

Activities normally start as soon as they can, taking into account any dependencies or requirements to start or end on specific dates. As Sophie realized, this causes a number of activities to be scheduled to start at the same time (following the "plan the project" activity).

Using the Graphic Designer as an example, the following activities would all be scheduled to start immediately after the "plan the project" activity:

- Create sign graphics/text
- Create holographic cards
- Create mural for booth
- Develop demo slideshow
- Order cameras and tripods

Since each activity above requires a Graphic Designer's time, this would require five Graphic Designers to be available at the same time. In the case study project, Sophie determines that she will only be able to secure one Graphic Designer for her project. Similarly, four Communications Specialists will be required after the "plan the project" activity is completed, even though only one is available to the project.

This situation often occurs during the planning of a schedule where the planned order of activities causes many of the same type of human resources to be needed simultaneously. This is known as a resource overallocation and may be solved in a couple of different ways:

- Introduce additional dependencies to the network diagram to make the activities sequential. The trade-off is that this will cause a longer total duration to complete the activities because of the new dependencies.
- Schedule the human resources to spread their time (i.e., multi-task) across the activities.

Again, the trade-off is that this causes a longer total duration to complete the activities due to the multi-tasking.

Either of the above approaches or a combination of both may be used to ensure the project is scheduled according to available resources. Resolving resource conflicts through these actions is known as **resource levelling**.

Sophie decides to use the first approach listed above—that is, introducing additional dependencies based on the resource constraints. The resulting network diagram is shown in figure 5.7.

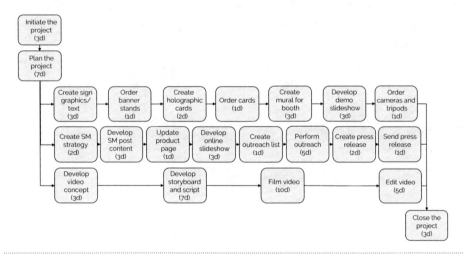

Figure 5.7: Network Diagram with Resource Constraints

Add human resource requirements to the project schedule and use resource levelling as required to resolve resource overallocations.

The main benefit of creating a network diagram is that it clearly displays the order of the activities and, in particular, the dependencies between the activities.

However, network diagrams are not effective at displaying the dates that activities are planned for and are difficult to maintain throughout the project. Because of these limitations, they are often useful for initial planning purposes but are not subsequently maintained throughout the project.

Other Project Schedule Formats

In addition to a network diagram, there are a number of schedule formats that may be used, each with its own advantages and disadvantages. The choice of a schedule format should be based on the project's characteristics, including its size, its complexity, and the likelihood that changes may occur.

The following are the three different schedule formats that may be used:

- Milestone-based
- Activity-based
- Dependency-based

The Milestone-Based Schedule

Milestones are important events that occur during a project. They are not regular activities that are measured by the duration and work involved but are instead an indicator that something significant has been completed during the project.

Milestones were first defined during the creation of the Project Charter. Additional milestones are often identified during planning.

The project's milestones are documented in a milestone-based schedule. The template is as follows:

MILESTONE-BASED SCHEDULE	
Project	[This section contains the project name that should appear consistently on all project documents. Organizations often have project naming conventions.]
Milestone	**Date**
[Name of the milestone]	[Date of the milestone]

The **milestone-based schedule** for the case study project is as follows:

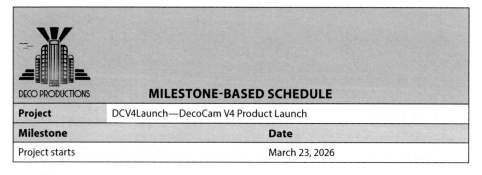

DECO PRODUCTIONS MILESTONE-BASED SCHEDULE	
Project	DCV4Launch—DecoCam V4 Product Launch
Milestone	**Date**
Project starts	March 23, 2026

Initiating Phase complete	March 25, 2026
Planning Phase complete	April 3, 2026
Trade show materials complete	April 23, 2026
Communications complete	April 29, 2026
Promotional video complete	May 8, 2026
Executing Phase complete	May 8, 2026
Project complete	May 13, 2026

Milestone-based schedules are simple to use and understand, can be easily accessed by team members and stakeholders, and will likely require minimal updates during the project. However, since activities are not contained in the schedule, they will need to be managed outside of the schedule. This may make planning for project costs and resources more difficult. Milestone-based schedules are often appropriate for small and/or simple projects.

The Activity-Based Schedule
The **activity-based schedule** contains the project's activities and includes information such as the duration, start date, and end date of each activity.

The activity information is documented in an activity-based schedule. The template is as follows:

ACTIVITY-BASED SCHEDULE			
Project	[This section contains the project name that should appear consistently on all project documents. Organizations often have project naming conventions.]		
Activity	**Duration**	**Start Date**	**End Date**
[Name of the Phase]			
[Name of the activity]	[Duration of the activity]	[Start date of the activity]	[End date of the activity]
[Name of the Phase]			
[Name of the activity]	[Duration of the activity]	[Start date of the activity]	[End date of the activity]

The activity-based schedule for the case study project is as follows:

DECO PRODUCTIONS	ACTIVITY-BASED SCHEDULE		
Project	DCV4Launch—DecoCam V4 Product Launch		
Activity	**Duration**	**Start Date**	**End Date**
Initiating			
Initiate the project	3 days	March 23, 2026	March 25, 2026
Initiating Phase complete	0 days	March 25, 2026	March 25, 2026
Planning			
Plan the project	7 days	March 26, 2026	April 3, 2026
Planning Phase complete	0 days	April 3, 2026	April 3, 2026
Executing			
Trade Show Signage			
Create sign graphics/text	3 days	April 6, 2026	April 8, 2026
Order banner stands	1 day	April 9, 2026	April 9, 2026
Booth Giveaways			
Create holographic cards	2 days	April 10, 2026	April 13, 2026
Order cards	1 day	April 14, 2026	April 14, 2026
Multimedia Demo			
Create mural for booth	3 days	April 15, 2026	April 17, 2026
Develop demo slideshow	3 days	April 20, 2026	April 22, 2026
Order cameras and tripods	1 day	April 23, 2026	April 23, 2026
Trade show materials complete	0 days	April 23, 2026	April 23, 2026
Social Media			
Create SM strategy	2 days	April 6, 2026	April 7, 2026
Develop SM post content	3 days	April 8, 2026	April 10, 2026
Website Updates			
Update product page	1 day	April 13, 2026	April 13, 2026
Develop online slideshow	3 days	April 14, 2026	April 16, 2026
Media Outreach			
Create outreach list	1 day	April 17, 2026	April 17, 2026
Perform outreach	5 days	April 20, 2026	April 24, 2026
Press Release			
Create press release	2 days	April 27, 2026	April 28, 2026
Send press release	1 day	April 29, 2026	April 29, 2026

Communications complete	0 days	April 29, 2026	April 29, 2026
Video Plan			
Develop video concept	3 days	April 6, 2026	Apr 8, 2026
Develop storyboard and script	7 days	April 9, 2026	Apr 17, 2026
Video Production			
Film video	10 days	April 20, 2026	May 1, 2026
Edit video	5 days	May 4, 2026	May 8, 2026
Promotional video complete	0 days	May 8, 2026	May 8 2026
Executing Phase complete	0 days	May 8, 2026	May 8, 2026
Closing			
Close the project	3 days	May 11, 2026	May 13, 2026
Project complete	0 days	May 13, 2026	May 13, 2026

Note that for the DecoCam project, the activities are scheduled using a five-day workweek (i.e., Monday to Friday). Other projects may schedule activities using a different approach, such as a seven-day workweek.

For certain types of projects that have fixed end dates, such as events, a **work-back schedule** may be used. A work-back schedule is a specific type of activity-based schedule in which the timing of each activity is determined by working backward from the project's end date. For example, in the case study, the project must be complete (except for the project closing) by May 8. Working backward from this date, the following things are determined:

- The video storyboard and script should be completed three weeks before this date (April 17).
- The filming of the video should be completed one week before this date (May 1).

Using this work-back method, the remainder of the activities are planned relative to the project's end date.

Activity-based schedules are often appropriate for small to medium-sized projects.

The Dependency-Based Schedule

Similarly to the activity-based schedule, the **dependency-based schedule** contains all project activities along with their durations, start dates, and end dates. Additionally, this type of schedule displays any dependencies that may be present between activities.

This type of schedule is usually created using project management software and displayed in the **Gantt Chart** format. The Gantt Chart is named after Henry Gantt, an engineer and management consultant who developed the project management tool in the 1910s.

A Gantt Chart is divided into two sections. On the left side is a spreadsheet with each row representing an activity of the project. On the right side is a timeline made up of horizontal bars that represent the duration and timing of each activity. Dependencies are represented by an arrow between activities. Milestones are represented by a diamond shape.

Figure 5.8 shows the dependency-based schedule for the case study project using the Gantt Chart format.

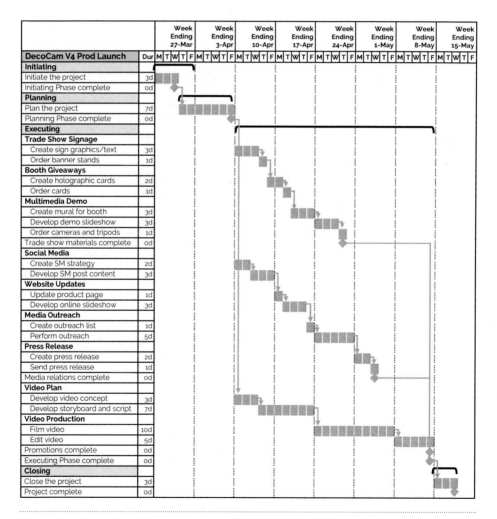

Figure 5.8: Gantt Chart

The main advantage of the dependency-based schedule is that it clearly demonstrates the timeline of the project, including the dependencies between activities. If changes are made to the timing of activities during the project, the impact on other dependent activities is displayed.

Due to the complexity of this type of schedule, more time is required for its maintenance, and project management software is usually required to view or update the schedule. This results in the schedule being less accessible to the project team and other stakeholders.

Dependency-based schedules may be appropriate for large and/or complex projects.

> There are many formats of project schedules, including network diagrams, milestone-based schedules, activity-based schedules, and dependency-based schedules.

More about Activity Dependencies

All the dependencies described up to this point are known as **Finish-to-Start** (FS) dependencies. This is the most common type of dependency, where an activity must finish before another activity can start. The majority of dependencies are FS.

There are other, less common dependency types that may occur during projects. **Start-to-Start** (SS) is a type of dependency where an activity cannot start until another activity has started. For example, the "create outreach list" and "perform outreach" activities could have been defined with an SS dependency. This would be appropriate if creating the outreach list also involved performing outreach (e.g., testing some of the names that were placed on the outreach list). This dependency type appears on a Gantt Chart in figure 5.9.

Create outreach list	1d
Perform outreach	5d

Figure 5.9: Start-to-Start Dependency

Finish-to-Finish (FF) is a type of dependency where an activity cannot finish until another activity has finished. For example, the "film video" and "edit video" activities could have been defined with a Finish-to-Finish dependency. This would be appropriate if neither could be completed without the other also being completed. This dependency type appears on a Gantt Chart in figure 5.10.

Film video	10d
Edit video	5d

Figure 5.10: Finish-to-Finish Dependency

Start-to-Finish (SF) is a type of dependency where an activity cannot finish until another activity has started. This dependency type is extremely rare and will not be demonstrated in this text.

> There are four dependency types: Finish-to-Start, Start-to-Start, Finish-to-Finish, and Start-to-Finish. Start-to-Finish dependency types are rare and are not covered in detail in this text.

Dependency Leads and Lags

In the dependencies discussed up to this point, when Activity A finishes, Activity B may start. While this is a simple way to think of activities, in real life, things are often more complex. For example, as Activity A is winding down, Activity B may be ramping up, and they may overlap to some degree. In scheduling terminology, this is known as a **lead**. Figure 5.11 demonstrates a two-day lead between the "develop storyboard and script" and "film video" activities.

Develop storyboard and script	7d
Film video	10d

Figure 5.11: Dependency with a Two-Day Lead

There may be times when a gap between activities is required. This is known as a **lag**. Lags may be included in the schedule for a number of reasons, including a required break due to the nature of the work or the unavailability of the required resources. For example, in order to send the press release at a more appropriate time, a two-day lag could be introduced between the activities "create press release" and "send press release" (see figure 5.12).

Create press release	2d
Send press release	1d

Figure 5.12: Dependency with a Two-Day Lag

Activity timing may be affected by the amount of lead or lag defined by the Project Manager.

To illustrate the different dependency types as well as lead and lag, consider the following example. As the manager of a restaurant, you need to manage each dinner as a small project. Within this project, there are various dependency types:

- When the customers receive their menus, their glasses are also filled with water; this is an example of a Start-to-Start dependency.
- Each customer's dinner arrives at the table at the same time; this is an example of a Finish-to Finish dependency.
- Once the meal is complete, the bill is given to the customers for payment; this is an example of a Finish-to-Start dependency.

Leads and lags may also be introduced:

- In order to not make the customers feel rushed after dinner, the bill is given 10 minutes after dinner completes. This is an example of a Finish-to-Start dependency with a 10-minute lag.
- The customers indicate they only have a limited time, so the bill is given 10 minutes before dinner completes. This is an example of a Finish-to-Start dependency with a 10-minute lead.

CRITICAL PATH ANALYSIS—AN OVERVIEW

For projects that use activity dependency–based schedules, it is possible to calculate the **critical path** of the project. The critical path is the longest sequence of activities in the project schedule. This sequence of activities represents the earliest planned completion time for the project.

Critical Path Analysis—A Simple Example

For a demonstration of the critical path concept, consider the network diagram in figure 5.13.

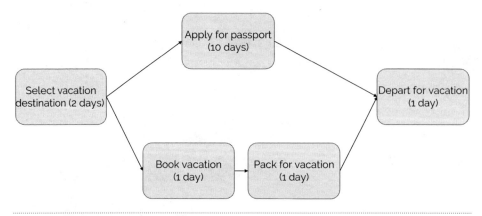

Figure 5.13: Critical Path Example

For this project, there are two paths through the network:

- Select vacation destination → apply for passport → depart for vacation (13 days)
- Select vacation destination → book vacation → pack for vacation → depart for vacation (5 days)

The first path (13 days) is the critical path since it is the longest sequence of dependent tasks and therefore represents the earliest date when this project may be completed. In other words, it would take 13 days for you to be sitting in an airport, with your tickets, suitcases, and passport in hand.

Figure 5.13 also indicates the relative importance of each activity from a time perspective. For example, on the third day, there are two activities that may be started: "apply for passport" and "book the vacation." The process of booking the vacation may be more interesting to you than the task of applying for a passport. However, because applying for the passport is on the critical path, any delay to this activity would delay the entire project. Knowledge of the critical path can help guide you to ensure the passport activity is given the higher priority.

Another concept related to the critical path is **total float**. Total float is the amount of time an activity may be delayed before it delays the project end date. By definition, all activities on the critical path have zero total float, in that a delay in any activity on the critical path will delay the end of the project. The two activities that are not on the critical path—"book vacation" and "pack for vacation"—share eight days of total float. This can be deduced by calculating that during the 10 days required for the "apply for passport" activity, two days are required to complete the "book vacation" and "pack for vacation" activities.

This leaves eight days of total float. Therefore, the two activities may be delayed up to eight days without impacting the project's completion date.

Critical Path Analysis—The Case Study Project

The critical path can now be determined for the case study project. There are three paths through the network, as follows:

- Path 1 (27 days): the path starting with "initiate the project" and "plan the project," through to the activities ranging from "create sign graphics/ text" to "order cameras and tripods," and ending with "close the project."
- Path 2 (31 days): the path starting with "initiate the project" and "plan the project," through to the activities ranging from "create SM strategy" to "send press release," and ending with "close the project."
- Path 3 (38 days): the path starting with "initiate the project" and "plan the project," through to the activities ranging from "develop video concept" to "edit video," and ending with "close the project."

As shown in figure 5.14, Path 3 is the longest and is therefore the critical path.

The time span of the critical path (38 days) also defines the total planned project duration. All tasks on the critical path (highlighted on the network diagram in figure 5.14) contain zero total float. This means that if any of the critical path tasks are delayed, all subsequent activities on the critical path will also be delayed, resulting in a delay of the project.

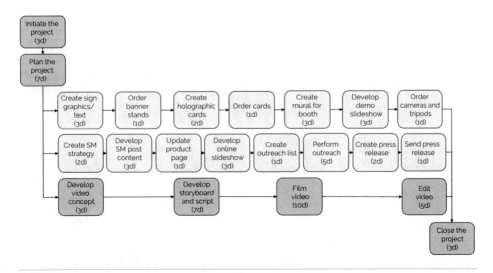

Figure 5.14: Network Diagram with Critical Path Displayed

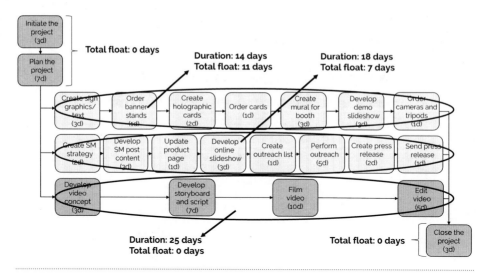

Figure 5.15: Network Diagram with Total Float Displayed

To determine the total float in the non-critical path activities, refer to the network diagram in figure 5.15. The critical path activities ranging from "develop video concept" to "edit video" in Path 3 have a total duration of 25 days. Conversely, the non-critical activities ranging from "create sign graphics/text" to "order cameras and tripods" in Path 1 have a total duration of 14 days. The amount of total float contained in these activities is 11 days (25 days minus 14 days). This means that these activities in Path 1 may be delayed by up to 11 days before delaying the completion of the project.

Using the same calculation, the activities ranging from "create SM strategy" to "send press release" in Path 2 have a total duration of 18 days, resulting in 7 days of total float (25 days minus 18 days). The activities in Path 2 may be delayed up to 7 days before delaying the completion of the project.

Figure 5.16 depicts the Gantt Chart displaying the critical path.

While determining the critical path and total float is relatively straightforward for simple schedules, it is much more difficult for larger or complex projects. For these types of projects, project management software may be used to automate the critical path calculations. The calculations required to determine the critical path may be viewed in Appendix 1: Critical Path Analysis—The Calculations.

Understanding the critical path allows the Project Manager to determine the total project duration and the impact of activity delays on the project's completion date.

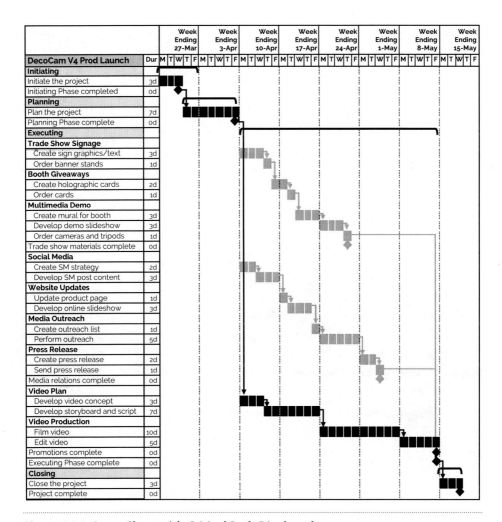

DecoCam V4 Prod Launch	Dur	Week Ending 27-Mar	Week Ending 3-Apr	Week Ending 10-Apr	Week Ending 17-Apr	Week Ending 24-Apr	Week Ending 1-May	Week Ending 8-May	Week Ending 15-May
Initiating									
Initiate the project	3d								
Initiating Phase completed	0d								
Planning									
Plan the project	7d								
Planning Phase complete	0d								
Executing									
Trade Show Signage									
Create sign graphics/text	3d								
Order banner stands	1d								
Booth Giveaways									
Create holographic cards	2d								
Order cards	1d								
Multimedia Demo									
Create mural for booth	3d								
Develop demo slideshow	3d								
Order cameras and tripods	1d								
Trade show materials complete	0d								
Social Media									
Create SM strategy	2d								
Develop SM post content	3d								
Website Updates									
Update product page	1d								
Develop online slideshow	3d								
Media Outreach									
Create outreach list	1d								
Perform outreach	5d								
Press Release									
Create press release	2d								
Send press release	1d								
Media relations complete	0d								
Video Plan									
Develop video concept	3d								
Develop storyboard and script	7d								
Video Production									
Film video	10d								
Edit video	5d								
Promotions complete	0d								
Executing Phase complete	0d								
Closing									
Close the project	3d								
Project complete	0d								

Figure 5.16: Gantt Chart with Critical Path Displayed

KEY TERMINOLOGY

Activity-Based Schedule: A schedule containing the dates of the activities defined for the project

Activity List: A list of all activities defined for the project

Baseline: An approved part of the project plan, such as the scope, cost, or schedule; it may be used as a basis for comparison when measuring the progress of the project or considering potential changes to the plan

Critical Path: The longest sequence of activities in the project schedule; this sequence of activities represents the earliest planned completion time for the project

Dependency: The required sequence of activities based on the work involved

Dependency-Based Schedule: A schedule containing the dates and dependencies of the activities defined for the project, often displayed in the Gantt Chart format

Duration: The length of time that an activity continues; does not include non-working days such as weekends or holidays

Finish-to-Finish Dependency: A type of dependency where an activity cannot finish until another activity has finished

Finish-to-Start Dependency: A type of dependency where an activity must finish before another activity can start

Gantt Chart: A chart illustrating the dependencies between activities in a project schedule, where activities are listed in rows and activity durations are represented as horizontal bars

Lag: The delay or gap of time between two dependent activities

Lead: The amount of overlap time between two dependent activities

Milestone: An important event that occurs during a project

Milestone-Based Schedule: A schedule containing the dates of the milestones defined for the project

Network Diagram: A graph that demonstrates the sequence of activities during the project; activities are represented as rectangles, and dependencies between activities are represented by arrows

Resource Levelling: The process of adjusting the timing of project activities according to the availability of the required resources

Start-to-Finish Dependency: A type of dependency where an activity cannot finish until another activity has started

Start-to-Start Dependency: A type of dependency where an activity cannot start until another activity has started

Total Float: The amount of time an activity may be delayed before it delays the project end date

Work: The amount of effort applied to complete an activity

Work-Back Schedule: A specific type of activity-based schedule in which the timing of each activity is determined by working backward from the project's end date

KEY CONCEPTS

1. Using the WBS as a starting point, create an Activity List consisting of one or more activities defined for each work package.
2. Estimate the duration for each activity.
3. Create a network diagram that demonstrates the dependencies between activities.
4. Add human resource requirements to the project schedule and use resource levelling as required to resolve resource overallocations.

5.   There are many formats of project schedules, including network diagrams, milestone-based schedules, activity-based schedules, and dependency-based schedules.

6.   There are four dependency types: Finish-to-Start, Start-to-Start, Finish-to-Finish, and Start-to-Finish. Start-to-Finish dependency types are rare and are not covered in detail in this text.

7.   Activity timing may be affected by the amount of lead or lag defined by the Project Manager.

8.   Understanding the critical path allows the Project Manager to determine the total project duration and the impact of activity delays on the project's completion date.

DISCUSSION QUESTIONS

1.   Consider the purchase of a new product that you may be planning over the next year (e.g., phone, vacation). Make a list of the activities that are needed to complete this purchase.

2.   Arrange the list of activities identified in question 1 into a logical order. Are there any activities that can be performed in parallel?

3.   The duration of an activity can be difficult to estimate. What are the factors that could cause the duration of an activity to be difficult to predict?

4.   There are three types of schedules that are defined in this chapter: milestone-based, activity-based, and dependency-based. What are some of the factors that would cause a Project Manager to choose to use each of these schedule types during a project?

5.   Provide everyday examples that demonstrate a Finish-to-Start, Start-to-Start, and Finish-to-Finish dependency.

6.   Perform an online search to research project scheduling challenges. Based on your findings, what are some of the challenges encountered during the scheduling process?

6 Budget Planning

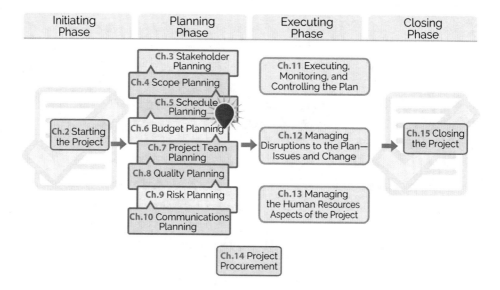

Initiating Phase	Planning Phase	Executing Phase	Closing Phase

Planning Phase:
- Ch.3 Stakeholder Planning
- Ch.4 Scope Planning
- Ch.5 Schedule Planning
- Ch.6 Budget Planning
- Ch.7 Project Team Planning
- Ch.8 Quality Planning
- Ch.9 Risk Planning
- Ch.10 Communications Planning

Initiating Phase:
- Ch.2 Starting the Project

Executing Phase:
- Ch.11 Executing, Monitoring, and Controlling the Plan
- Ch.12 Managing Disruptions to the Plan—Issues and Change
- Ch.13 Managing the Human Resources Aspects of the Project

Closing Phase:
- Ch.15 Closing the Project

Ch.14 Project Procurement

INTRODUCTION TO BUDGET PLANNING

After planning the project scope and schedule, it is time to plan for the cost of the project. Project Sponsors and other key stakeholders tend to focus on project costs because of the impact of cost overruns. Higher project costs may have one or more of the following impacts:

- A change to the project's Business Case justification, leading to the potential cancellation of the project
- Deferral of other projects due to reduced availability of funding
- Fewer funds available for expenditure within the organization
- Reduction of the company's profit (in for-profit organizations) or increased deficits and/or tax increases (in government or not-for-profit organizations)

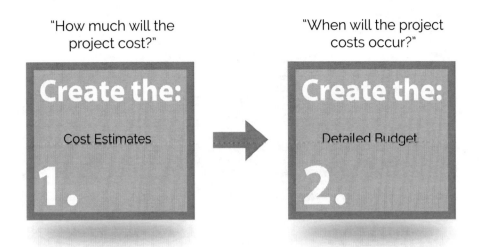

Figure 6.1: Budget Planning

Given these impacts, it is very important to carefully plan the project's costs. This helps ensure that the project's budget is consistent with the planned project scope and schedule, and also enables the costs to be managed effectively throughout the project.

There are two main steps when planning for project cost, as shown in figure 6.1.

During the first step, cost estimates are created for the planned activities and expenditures of the project. Next, the estimates are distributed over the timeline of the project.

HOW MUCH WILL THE PROJECT COST?

During the Initiating Phase, the overall budget for the project is included in the Project Charter. The budget amount tends to be a general estimate, often developed during the creation of the Business Case. Alternatively, it may represent the funds that are available for the project. During the Planning Phase, the costs of the project are estimated in detail, based on the deliverables to be produced during the project.

Costs occur during a project for a variety of reasons. Some are direct costs, meaning that they occur directly because of the activities of the project. Often the most significant direct costs result from the amount of work performed—that is, the amount of effort applied to the activities of the project. These are known as labour or salary costs. Other direct costs include the materials that are purchased, the equipment that is purchased or rented, and travel costs. There

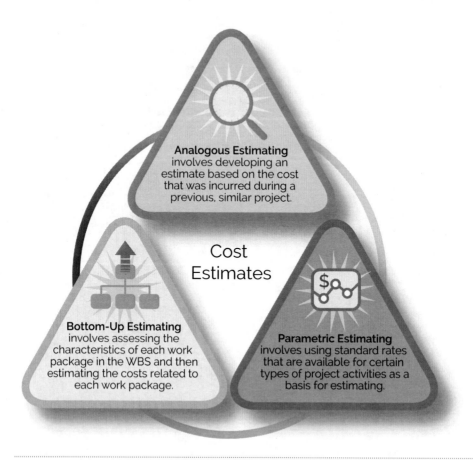

Figure 6.2: Cost Estimates

may also be indirect costs, such as the cost of the company's facilities (e.g., rent and utilities), employee benefits, and office supplies used by the project team. Figure 6.2 depicts various approaches that may be used to develop cost estimates.

Analogous Estimating

The advantage of **analogous estimating** is that it is very easy to perform and can be done early in the Planning Phase. The disadvantage is that previous cost information is required, and this may not be available for each project. Therefore, this approach is not always possible. There is also a risk that differences between the past and current project may not be known, which could reduce the accuracy of the estimate.

Parametric Estimating

Parametric estimating may be used when standard rates for project activities are available. For example, when planning a banquet, a caterer may provide a per plate cost for their services. This unit cost is then multiplied by the planned attendance in order to develop the estimate. The advantage of this approach is that it is an accurate method of cost estimating. The disadvantage is that it may only be used for certain types of costs where standard rates are available.

Bottom-Up Estimating

Because **bottom-up estimating** considers the characteristics of each work package, it is the most detailed form of estimating. The advantage of this approach is that it tends to be a relatively accurate form of cost estimating, given the high level of detail. The disadvantage is that it requires detailed scope and schedule information, and therefore this type of estimate may not be produced until later in the Planning Phase.

For all methods of cost estimating, the experience and expertise of the person performing the estimate is a significant factor. That is, greater experience and expertise tends to improve the accuracy of cost estimates.

The cost estimates for the project are entered into the Cost Estimates document. The template is as follows:

COST ESTIMATES						
Project Name	[This section contains the project name that should appear consistently on all project documents. Organizations often have project naming conventions.]					
HR Cost Estimates						
Activity	**Duration (days)**	**Resource**	**Percent-age**	**Work (days)**	**Daily Rate**	**Cost**
[Name of the activity]	[Duration of the activity]	[Description of the human resource(s) required to complete the activity]	[Required percentage of the HR]	[Duration times percentage of the HR]	[Daily rate of the HR]	[Cost of the activity]
Total HR Cost Estimates						
Other Cost Estimates						
Item	**Quantity**	**Description**			**Unit Cost**	**Cost**
[Short description of the item]	[Required quantity of the item]	[Long description of the item]			[Unit cost of the item]	[Total cost of the item]
Total Other Cost Estimates						
Total Project Cost Estimates						

Case Study Update: Creating the Cost Estimates

For Sophie, creating the cost estimates is the trickiest part of the business. From past experience, she has learned that estimating too high can cause projects to be cancelled, but estimating too low can mean she will exceed her costs later. A "guesstimate" is simply not good enough.

This time, Sophie feels confident. Thanks to her earlier work brainstorming and categorizing the work packages, she can now better assess the estimated costs of each work package and, therefore, the overall project.

Sophie decides that to perform this task, a change of scenery is in order. On the way to work, she pulls into the parking lot of her local coffee shop. After ordering a large coffee, she opens her laptop and looks at the project schedule. The majority of the costs for this project will come from the people working on the project in the form of their salaries. At Deco Productions, the Finance department has calculated what is known as a "loaded rate" for employees who work on projects. This loaded rate is an hourly rate that not only includes their salaries but also reflects overhead costs, such as benefits, building costs, and office supplies. So far, two people have been assigned to the project: Sophie (Project Manager) and Fatehjit Kumar (a Business Analyst who worked on the scope planning activities). The loaded rates for these two project roles are as follows:

- Project Manager $100/hour
- Business Analyst $80/hour

While other team members have not yet been assigned to the project, based on the work involved, Sophie knows she will need the following:

- Graphic Designer $50/hour
- Communications Specialist $60/hour
- Marketing Specialist $60/hour
- Videographer $50/hour

She considers the amount of work that will be required for each activity. For some activities, she uses her in-depth knowledge of the work involved, while for others, she considers past projects. She makes a quick call to one of the company's Graphic Designers to verify her estimates for the graphics-related work.

Sophie also includes the cost of her own time and that of Fatehjit, the Business Analyst, which she predicts will be spent during the Executing Phase. During the five weeks of execution, she estimates that about one-third of her time will be needed to manage the team, resolve issues, and communicate with the project stakeholders. She also estimates that she will need about one day per week of Fatehjit's time to answer the project team's questions about the project scope and provide Quality Control for the completed deliverables.

Next, Sophie creates a list that outlines the amount of materials and equipment the project will need:

- Trade show banner stands (5)
- Holographic cards for the trade show booth (2,000)
- Murals for the multimedia demo (2)
- Camera and tripods for the multimedia demo (2)

As she records this information, she checks the current price of each item by referring to a number of suppliers' websites. Finally, she considers any additional costs that may be incurred during the project.

One hour, one large coffee, and two maple donuts later, Sophie has settled on a total cost estimate for the project and heads into work.

The following are the cost estimates produced for the project. In the HR cost estimates section, the estimated duration of each activity is listed. Based on the estimated amount of effort, human resources are assigned to each activity with a percentage allocation. For example, during the "plan the project" activity (seven-day duration) the following is allocated:

- 50% of a Project Manager is assigned, resulting in 3.5 days of work
- 100% of a Business Analyst is assigned, resulting in seven days of work

DECO PRODUCTIONS   **COST ESTIMATES**

Project Name		DCV4Launch—DecoCam V4 Product Launch				
HR Cost Estimates						
Activity	**Duration (days)**	**Resource**	**Per-centage**	**Work (days)**	**Daily Rate**	**Cost**
Initiate the project	3	Project Manager	50	1.5	$800	$1,200
Plan the project	7	Project Manager	50	3.5	$800	$2,800
	7	Business Analyst	100	7	$640	$4,480
Create sign graphics/text	3	Graphic Designer	100	3	$400	$1,200
Order banner stands	1	Graphic Designer	100	1	$400	$400

(continued)

Activity	Duration (days)	Resource	Per-centage	Work (days)	Daily Rate	Cost
Create holographic cards	2	Graphic Designer	100	2	$400	$800
Order cards	1	Graphic Designer	100	1	$400	$400
Create mural for booth	3	Graphic Designer	100	3	$400	$1,200
Develop demo slideshow	3	Graphic Designer	100	3	$400	$1,200
Order cameras and tripods	1	Graphic Designer	100	1	$400	$400
Create SM strategy	2	Communications Specialist	100	2	$480	$960
Develop SM post content	3	Communications Specialist	100	3	$480	$1,440
Update product page	1	Communications Specialist	100	1	$480	$480
Develop online slideshow	3	Communications Specialist	100	3	$480	$1,440
Create outreach list	1	Communications Specialist	100	1	$480	$480
Perform outreach	5	Communications Specialist	100	5	$480	$2,400
Create press release	2	Communications Specialist	100	2	$480	$960
Send press release	1	Communications Specialist	100	1	$480	$480
Develop video concept	3	Marketing Specialist	100	3	$480	$1,440
Develop storyboard and script	7	Marketing Specialist	100	7	$480	$3,360
Film video	10	Videographer	100	10	$400	$4,000
	10	Marketing Specialist	100	10	$480	$4,800
Edit video	5	Videographer	100	5	$400	$2,000
	5	Marketing Specialist	100	5	$480	$2,400
Monitor and control	25	Project Manager	34	8.5	$800	$6,800
	25	Business Analyst	20	5	$640	$3,200
Close the project	3	Project Manager	50	1.5	$800	$1,200
Total HR Cost Estimates						**$51,920**

Other Cost Estimates				
Item	**Quantity**	**Description**	**Unit Cost**	**Cost**
Banner stands	5	Banner stands for trades show	$200	$1,000
Holographic cards	2,000	Cards for trade show booth giveaways	$1	$2,000
Murals	2	Murals for trade show multimedia demo	$100	$200
Cameras and tripods	2	Cameras and tripods for trade show multimedia demo	$700	$1,400
Total Other Cost Estimates				**$4,600**
Total Project Cost Estimates				**$56,520**

Once the detailed estimates are created for the project, they should be compared to the budget for the project that was documented in the Project Charter. In the case study, the detailed estimate is less than the original budget amount. This is a desirable position to be in at this point in the project. During the project, actual costs may increase by up to $3,480 before the original budget is exceeded. This is known as a **budget contingency**.

If the detailed estimates exceed the Project Charter budget, discussions with the Project Sponsor would need to take place. Possible solutions include modifying the project scope and/or increasing the funds available to the project. If any changes occur, the Project Charter would need to be updated, as well as the WBS, Project Scope Statement, and project schedule.

Develop cost estimates for the human resource, material, equipment, and other requirements.

WHEN WILL THE PROJECT COSTS OCCUR?

In order to accurately plan for the timing of project costs, an activity-based or dependency-based schedule is required. Using this schedule as a guide, the estimated costs are distributed across the timeline of the project in order to create the Detailed Budget (see figure 6.3).

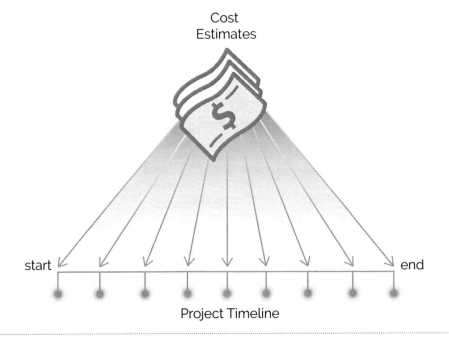

Figure 6.3: Detailed Budget

This cost information is entered into the Detailed Budget. The template is as follows:

DETAILED BUDGET									
Project Name	[This section contains the project name that should appear consistently on all project documents. Organizations often have project naming conventions.]								
	[Period 1]	**[Period 2]**	**[Period 3]**	**[Period 4]**	**[Period 5]**	**[Period 6]**	**[Period 7]**	**[Period 8]**	**Total**
HR Costs									
[Name of the activity]									
Other Costs									
[Description of the item]									
Total Planned Costs									

In the above template, columns are added or removed as needed, depending on the number of time periods required for the project. The processes described in this section would generally be performed for projects with a long duration and/or high costs. For projects with a short duration and/or low costs, this level of cost planning is generally not required.

Case Study Update: Creating the Detailed Budget

Sophie reviews the total cost estimate of the project. She is relieved that it is less than the $60,000 budget, giving her a small contingency fund. However, she also knows from experience that costs often are higher than estimated and that they will need to be managed closely throughout the project.

To do so, in addition to the amount of the estimated costs, she will need to know when they are planned to occur. For example, if $30,000 is spent by the halfway point of the project, does this mean that the project will meet its budget? What if more of the costs will be incurred near the end of the project? This could indicate that the project will be over budget.

Opening her laptop, Sophie creates a spreadsheet:

- For each row, she lists an activity of the project.
- For each column, she lists a week of the project (eight in total).

Sophie focuses first on the human resource costs. Using the project schedule and the planned costs that are contained in the detailed estimates, she begins to fill in the cells of the spreadsheet.

For example, for the week ending March 27, her calculations would be as follows:

- The "initiate the project" activity is planned to start and finish in three days. The Project Manager (Sophie) plans to spend 50% of her time on this activity. Because her daily rate is $800, this results in a total planned cost of $1,200 ($400/day × 3 days). This amount is placed under the March 27 column.
- The first two days of the "plan the project" activity are also planned to start during this week. There are two resources assigned to this activity: 50% of the Project Manager's time and 100% of the Business Analyst's time. This results in a total planned cost of $2,080 ($400/day × 2 days for the Project Manager + $640/day × 2 for the Business Analyst).

Sophie continues to calculate the planned cost for each of the remaining seven weeks of the project schedule.

Next, she considers the other (non-HR) costs and determines when these costs will likely occur. Based on the schedule, the banner stands ($1,000) will be ordered during the week ending April 10, the cards ($2,000) during the week ending April 17, and the cameras and tripods during the week ending April 24. Material costs for the murals will occur during the week ending April 17. Sophie inserts a row for each of these.

Once complete, she double-checks her work to ensure that the total cost in her new spreadsheet ($56,520) matches the total of the cost estimates she developed earlier. Once the planned costs for all weeks are calculated, the Detailed Budget is complete.

The following is the **Detailed Budget** for the case study project:

DECO PRODUCTIONS

DETAILED BUDGET

Project Name	DCV4Launch—DecoCam V4 Product Launch								
	Week ending 27-Mar	Week ending 3-Apr	Week ending 10-Apr	Week ending 17-Apr	Week ending 24-Apr	Week ending 1-May	Week ending 8-May	Week ending 15-May	Total
HR Costs									
Initiate the project	$1,200								**$1,200**
Plan the project	$2,080	$5,200							**$7,280**
Create sign graphics/ text			$1,200						**$1,200**
Order banner stands			$400						**$400**
Create holo-graphic cards			$400	$400					**$800**
Order holo-graphic cards				$400					**$400**
Create mural for booth				$1,200					**$1,200**
Develop demo slideshow					$1,200				**$1,200**
Order cam-eras and tripods					$400				**$400**
Create SM strategy			$960						**$960**
Develop SM post content			$1,440						**$1,440**
Update prod-uct page				$480					**$480**
Develop on-line slideshow				$1,440					**$1,440**
Create out-reach list				$480					**$480**

Task	1	2	3	4	5	6	7	8	Total
Perform outreach					$2,400				**$2,400**
Create press release						$960			**$960**
Send press release						$480			**$480**
Develop video concept			$1,440						**$1,440**
Develop storyboard and script			$960	$2,400					**$3,360**
Film video					$4,400	$4,400			**$8,800**
Edit video							$4,400		**$4,400**
Monitor and control			$2,000	$2,000	$2,000	$2,000	$2,000		**$10,000**
Close the project								$1,200	**$1,200**
Other Costs									
Banner stands			$1,000						**$1,000**
Holographic cards				$2,000					**$2,000**
Murals				$200					**$200**
Cameras and tripods					$1,400				**$1,400**
Total Planned Costs	$3,280	$5,200	$9,800	$11,000	$11,800	$7,840	$6,400	$1,200	**$56,520**

While every project will have its own unique distribution of costs, the Detailed Budget shown above is typical of how costs are incurred during a project. In the early stage of the project (first week), costs are relatively low. This corresponds to the Initiating Phase. Costs tend to increase during the Planning Phase and the start of the Executing Phase (second and third week). As the Executing Phase continues (weeks 4 to 7), the costs continue to rise rapidly, peaking about three-fourths of the way through the project and then beginning to fall as the work nears completion. During the Closing Phase (final week), the costs are relatively low.

The Detailed Budget shown above reports the costs for each week of the project. For projects with a longer duration, costs may be reported on a monthly basis, as indicated in the following Detailed Budget.

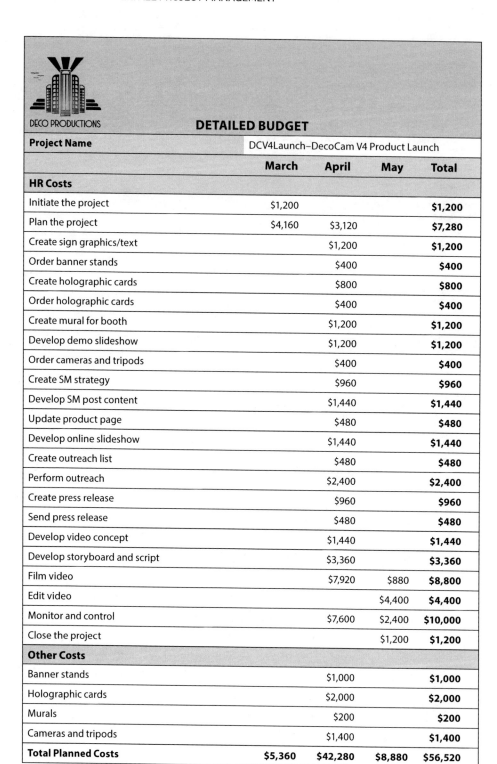

DECO PRODUCTIONS   **DETAILED BUDGET**

Project Name	DCV4Launch–DecoCam V4 Product Launch			
	March	**April**	**May**	**Total**
HR Costs				
Initiate the project	$1,200			**$1,200**
Plan the project	$4,160	$3,120		**$7,280**
Create sign graphics/text		$1,200		**$1,200**
Order banner stands		$400		**$400**
Create holographic cards		$800		**$800**
Order holographic cards		$400		**$400**
Create mural for booth		$1,200		**$1,200**
Develop demo slideshow		$1,200		**$1,200**
Order cameras and tripods		$400		**$400**
Create SM strategy		$960		**$960**
Develop SM post content		$1,440		**$1,440**
Update product page		$480		**$480**
Develop online slideshow		$1,440		**$1,440**
Create outreach list		$480		**$480**
Perform outreach		$2,400		**$2,400**
Create press release		$960		**$960**
Send press release		$480		**$480**
Develop video concept		$1,440		**$1,440**
Develop storyboard and script		$3,360		**$3,360**
Film video		$7,920	$880	**$8,800**
Edit video			$4,400	**$4,400**
Monitor and control		$7,600	$2,400	**$10,000**
Close the project			$1,200	**$1,200**
Other Costs				
Banner stands		$1,000		**$1,000**
Holographic cards		$2,000		**$2,000**
Murals		$200		**$200**
Cameras and tripods		$1,400		**$1,400**
Total Planned Costs	**$5,360**	**$42,280**	**$8,880**	**$56,520**

The benefits of creating a Detailed Budget include the following:

- It facilitates the effective monitoring of project costs. As actual project costs are incurred during the project, they may be compared to the planned costs. This leads to more effective management of project costs, as potential cost overages are more likely to be detected earlier in the project.
- It identifies the required cash flow. For example, in the Detailed Budget, the timing of other expenses (e.g., murals, cards, cameras, and tripods) can be easily determined, thus making it easier for the organization to arrange for funds to be available.

Create a Detailed Budget that shows the distribution of the estimated costs over the timeline of the project.

KEY TERMINOLOGY

Analogous Estimate: An estimate based on the cost that was incurred during a previous, similar project

Bottom-Up Estimate: An estimate based on the characteristics of each work package in the WBS and Project Scope Statement

Budget Contingency: The difference between the total approved Project Budget and the current cost estimate

Detailed Budget: A planning document showing the timing of all planned costs for the project

Parametric Estimate: An estimate based on the available standard rates

KEY CONCEPTS

1. Develop cost estimates for the human resource, material, equipment, and other requirements.
2. Create a Detailed Budget that shows the distribution of the estimated costs over the timeline of the project.

DISCUSSION QUESTIONS

1. Think of a project from your personal, work, or school activities where the actual costs incurred were higher than you originally anticipated. Describe the reasons why your cost estimates were inaccurate.

2. Provide an example where each of the three estimating techniques—analogous, parametric, and bottom-up—would be appropriate.

3. In order to ensure the project does not go over budget, a Project Manager doubles the cost estimates. What are the potential problems that this approach may create?

4. Perform an online search to research different reasons for cost overruns. Based on your findings, summarize the five most common reasons for cost overruns.

7 Project Team Planning

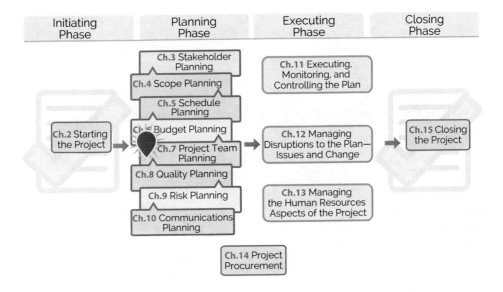

| Initiating Phase | Planning Phase | Executing Phase | Closing Phase |

Ch.3 Stakeholder Planning

Ch.4 Scope Planning

Ch.5 Schedule Planning

Ch.6 Budget Planning

Ch.2 Starting the Project

Ch.7 Project Team Planning

Ch.8 Quality Planning

Ch.9 Risk Planning

Ch.10 Communications Planning

Ch.11 Executing, Monitoring, and Controlling the Plan

Ch.12 Managing Disruptions to the Plan—Issues and Change

Ch.13 Managing the Human Resources Aspects of the Project

Ch.15 Closing the Project

Ch.14 Project Procurement

INTRODUCTION TO PROJECT TEAM PLANNING

During the planning for the project schedule in the case study, the number and skills of the people required for the project were identified. These included a Business Analyst, Graphic Designer, Communications Specialist, Marketing Specialist, and Videographer. Other than the Business Analyst, the team had not yet been assigned to the project.

During the next stage of project planning, the processes to plan for the project team members will be examined. When planning for the project team, it is useful to think of the project as a temporary organization that happens to reside within a permanent organization. It will need an organizational structure, an ability to bring people into and out of the temporary organization, and roles for the team members to perform. The organization and processes related to remote project teams—that is, when the project team is spread across multiple geographic locations, including international locations—will also be examined.

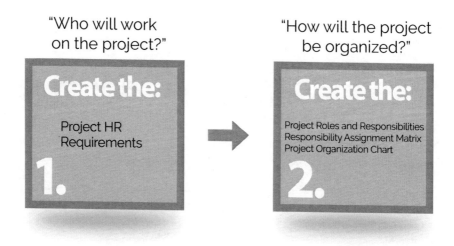

"Who will work on the project?"

Create the:

Project HR Requirements

1.

"How will the project be organized?"

Create the:

Project Roles and Responsibilities
Responsibility Assignment Matrix
Project Organization Chart

2.

Figure 7.1: Project Team Planning

There are two main steps when planning for project human resources, as shown in figure 7.1.

WHO WILL WORK ON THE PROJECT?

Once the Project Manager is assigned to a project, a key task is to ensure that project team members are identified and acquired during the project. Up to this point in the project planning, the project schedule has been developed by estimating the human resources and work effort needed for each activity. Putting this information together, the resource needs on a week-by-week basis may be determined.

Human resources are generally acquired from the following three sources:

- Internal staff (already employed by the organization)
- New hires (to be hired by the organization in order to work on the project)
- Contract workers (to be hired on contract to work on the project)

The use of internal human resources involves acquiring team members for a certain period of time as required by the project. They may be assigned to the project full-time or for a certain percentage of their time. Internal staff members are more likely to be familiar with the organization and be known to the Project Manager. The experience gained during the project will stay within the organization and may be applied to future projects. However, there is a limited number of internal staff, and they may be allocated to other projects. Additionally, they may not possess the skill level necessary for the project.

In some cases, the human resources required for a project are not available within the organization. One option is to hire a new employee or multiple employees to work on the project. Given the amount of time needed to hire a new employee (weeks, or in some cases even months), a great deal of lead time is necessary to ensure new hires are available when needed for a project. New hires can provide the organization with the opportunity to acquire new skill sets for the project; they also increase the number of potential resources available to the project. The downside is the long lead time needed for the hiring process. The new hire will also be unfamiliar with the organization, which can result in them taking a longer amount of time to become productive during the project.

A third source of human resources are contract workers who are brought into the organization in order to work on the project. Depending on the type of human resources required, the amount of lead time may vary. For example, lower skilled or abundant human resources may be acquired in a few days, while higher skilled or less abundant human resources may be acquired in a few weeks or more. Each of the above sources has advantages and disadvantages. Contract workers increase the number of potential resources available to the project and can generally be acquired more quickly than new hires. However, they may be unfamiliar with the organization, and the experience gained by the contract worker will leave the organization once their time on the project ends.

The human resources required for a project may be acquired by either the Project Manager, a Resource Manager, or combination of both. A Resource Manager is a person within an organization whose responsibilities include acquiring the human resources needed for projects. A representative from the organization's Human Resources area may also be involved, particularly when human resources are acquired from outside the organization.

The human resource requirements should be included in the Project HR Requirements document. The following is the template:

PROJECT HR REQUIREMENTS								
Project Name	[This section contains the project name that should appear consistently on all project documents. Organizations often have project naming conventions.]							
Resource Type	[Period 1]	[Period 2]	[Period 3]	[Period 4]	[Period 5]	[Period 6]	[Period 7]	[Period 8]
[Description of resource]								

In the template, columns are added or removed as needed, depending on the number of time periods required for the project.

Case Study Update: Creating the Project HR Requirements

As Sophie develops the project schedule, she naturally begins to think about the human resource needs of her project. Deco Productions always has a number of overlapping projects underway at any one point in time, so it can be challenging to get the workers she wants assigned to her project.

In the Deco Productions organization, all of the project workers report to a Resource Manager (Anand Bhandari). Anand's responsibility is to work with each Project Manager to ensure that each project receives the human resources necessary to complete their project. This is a challenging process, as the various projects often require the same type of human resources at the same time. This often involves a great deal of discussion, negotiation, and, in some cases, adjustments to the project timeline.

Sophie knows from experience that in order to ensure that Anand assigns the required human resources to her project, she needs to demonstrate when she needs each type of resource. It is not sufficient to talk generally about when team members are required. With the company's increased focus on cost reduction, Sophie is expected to provide spreadsheets detailing her resource needs. She opens her laptop and examines her schedule. Looking at each week of the schedule, she notes the human resource time required and records this information in a resource spreadsheet.

Once complete, Sophie sends Anand a link to the spreadsheet and then heads to his office. After her detailed planning, she is feeling good about their meeting.

The following is the **Project HR Requirements** document for the case study project:

DECO PRODUCTIONS

PROJECT HR REQUIREMENTS

Project Name	DCV4Launch—DecoCam V4 Product Launch							
Resource Type	**Week ending 27-Mar**	**Week ending 3-Apr**	**Week ending 10-Apr**	**Week ending 17-Apr**	**Week ending 24-Apr**	**Week ending 1-May**	**Week ending 8-May**	**Week ending 15-May**
Project Manager	2.5 days	2.5 days	1.7 days	1.7 days	1.7 days	1.7 days	1.7 days	1.5 days
Business Analyst	2 days	5 days	1 day	1 day	1 day	1 day	1 day	

Graphic Designer	5 days	5 days	4 days		
Communications Specialist	5 days	5 days	5 days	3 days	
Marketing Specialist	5 days	5 days	5 days	5 days	5 days
Videographer			5 days	5 days	5 days

Acquire the human resources needed to complete the project.

HOW WILL THE PROJECT BE ORGANIZED?

Project Roles and Responsibilities

As human resources are acquired, the project team begins to form. It is important that each team member understands their role on the project and their project responsibilities. Therefore, the roles and responsibilities of each team member should be documented.

The following is the **Project Roles and Responsibilities** template:

PROJECT ROLES AND RESPONSIBILITIES		
Project Name	[This section contains the project name that should appear consistently on all project documents. Organizations often have project naming conventions.]	
Name	**Role**	**Responsibilities**
[Team member name]	[Their role or job title]	[Detailed description of their project responsibilities and job duties]

Case Study Update: Creating the Project Roles and Responsibilities

Leaving Anand's office, Sophie feels good about the people who have been assigned to her project. As expected, Fatehjit Kumar will continue through the Executing Phase of the project. Chris Sandburg is assigned to be the Graphic Designer. Sophie has had a good working relationship with Chris over the years, so this is a big plus for the project. A relatively new employee, Sarah Pierce, is assigned to be the project's Communications Specialist. Sophie is less familiar with her, but she thinks Sarah will be a good fit. Another plus is the assignment of Maddy Wen as the Marketing Specialist for the project. Sophie perceives that the one potential negative assignment to the project is that of

(continued)

Eli Briggs as the project's Videographer. Eli has been a challenge to work with on past projects. Sophie makes a mental note to find ways to motivate Eli during this project.

Now that her team is in place, Sophie begins to document the key responsibilities of each team member. Since many of the responsibilities are inherent in the role and do not vary significantly from project to project, she is able to use previous Roles and Responsibilities documents from other projects as a starting point. However, as each project is unique, she ensures that any additional or modified responsibilities are included.

The following is the Roles and Responsibilities document for the case study project:

DECO PRODUCTIONS   **PROJECT ROLES AND RESPONSIBILITIES**

Project Name	DCV4Launch—DecoCam V4 Product Launch	

Name	Role	Responsibilities
Arun Singh	Project Sponsor	• Provides funding for the project • Provides overall direction and approves major changes for the project • Provides final sign-off for the project • Communicates the project's progress to the senior management of Deco Productions
Sophie Featherstone	Senior Project Manager	• Has overall responsibility for the project's completion • Creates and maintains the project plans • Approves minor changes and determines which changes will require Project Sponsor approval • Manages the project team and assists each team member to resolve issues • Communicates project updates and other information to the Project Sponsor
Fatehjit Kumar	Business Analyst	• Completes the project scope–related documents • Communicates project updates and any issues to the Project Manager • Clarifies the project scope to the project team as requested • Performs Quality Control for all completed deliverables
Chris Sandburg	Graphic Designer	• Responsible for the completion of all work packages related to the trade show • Communicates project updates and any issues to the Project Manager • Provides graphic design consulting to the rest of the project team as required

Sarah Pierce	Commu-nications Specialist	• Responsible for the completion of all work packages related to media relations, social media, and updates to the website • Communicates project updates and any issues to the Project Manager • Provides communications consulting to the rest of the project team as required
Maddy Wen	Marketing Specialist	• Responsible for the completion of the promotional video • Provides direction to the Videographer • Communicates project updates and any issues to the Project Manager • Provides marketing consulting to the rest of the project team as required
Eli Briggs	Videogra-pher	• Responsible for the completion of video-related activities, under the direction of the Marketing Specialist • Communicates project updates and any issues to the Marketing Specialist

Define the roles and responsibilities of each team member.

Responsibility Assignment Matrix

Another planning tool that may be used to clarify the planned involvement of people within the project is known as a **Responsibility Assignment Matrix (RAM)**.

One type of RAM is known as a **RACI Chart**. The acronym RACI stands for Responsible, Accountable, Consulted, and Informed. The template is as follows:

RACI CHART							
	[Name]	[Name]	[Name]	[Name]	[Name]	[Name]	[Name]
[Project work package or activity]	R/A/C/I	R/A/C/I	R/A/C/I	R/A/C/I	R/A/C/I	R/A/C/I	R/A/C/I
R—Responsible A—Accountable C—Consulted I—Informed							

A RACI Chart contains the following four codes that are used to describe each person's involvement in the project:

- R—Responsible: the person or people who will actually perform the work
- A—Accountable: the person who will ensure the work is completed successfully

- C—Consulted: the person or people who will have input into the work being performed; those responsible for the work would normally consult with this person
- I—Informed: the person or people who will be informed regarding the work

When defining the involvement, there may be multiple people responsible, consulted, or informed. However, for each line (i.e., work package or activity) in the RACI Chart, only one person should be accountable. That is, accountability should not be shared.

Case Study Update: Creating the Responsibility Assignment Matrix

Sophie calls together her new project team to discuss the project and their roles. While the Roles and Responsibilities document is informative to the team, the team members have additional questions, such as "Do I need to let anyone know when I'm done my work?" and "Who makes sure that work is complete?"

To help clarify this information, Sophie leads a discussion with the team. Using the RACI Chart, she places the name of the Project Sponsor or one of the project team members at the top of each column. For each high-level deliverable, the team discusses who should make sure the work is completed, who should complete the work, who should be consulted, and who should be informed.

RACI Charts may be developed at any level of detail, either for the entire project or for subsets of the project. For the case study project, it was developed for each high-level deliverable.

DECO PRODUCTIONS	RACI CHART						
	Arun	Sophie	Fatehjit	Chris	Sarah	Maddy	Eli
Trade Show Support	C	C	C	A, R	I	I	
Communications	I	C	C	I	A, R	I	
Promotional Video	C	C	C		I	A, R	R
Project Management	C	A, R	R	I	I	I	I
R—Responsible A—Accountable C—Consulted I—Informed							

A RACI Chart provides useful information to the people working on the project. For example, the above RACI Chart illustrates the following regarding the promotional video deliverable:

- Maddy will ensure the video is completed according to the schedule (accountable) and will also perform the work (responsible).
- Eli will perform the work under Maddy's direction (responsible).
- Maddy will seek out input from Arun, Sophie, and Fatehjit as required (consulted).
- Because of Sarah's communication role, Maddy will update her periodically about the progress of promotional video work (informed).
- Maddy does not need to interact with Chris, as the promotional video does not affect Chris's work on the project.

For the management of the project, the following responsibilities are determined:

- Sophie will ensure project management is performed (accountable) and also perform the work (responsible).
- Fatehjit will also perform some project management activities (responsible).
- Sophie will interact with Arun as required to gain his input (consulted).
- Sophie will keep the rest of the project team aware of the progress of the project (informed).

Define the involvement of team members by defining who is accountable, responsible, consulted, and informed for the deliverables of the project.

Project Organization Chart

Companies often create hierarchical charts to demonstrate their internal organization. For example, a company's organization chart may list all departments and the people who work in each one. This helps stakeholders understand how the work of the company is being performed as well as the roles and relationships of the team members.

As projects can be considered temporary organizations that exist within companies, creating a **Project Organization Chart** can be useful for the same reasons.

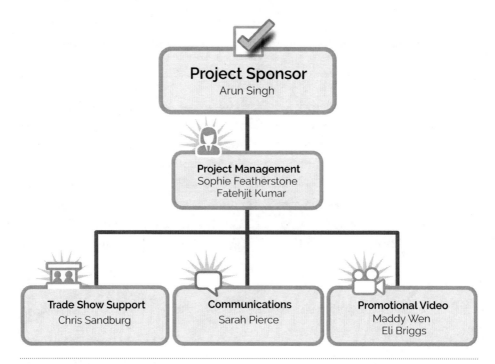

Figure 7.2: Project Organization Chart

The organization chart for the case study project is shown in figure 7.2. This Project Organization Chart demonstrates the following organizational information:

- At the top of the chart is Arun, the Project Sponsor, who has overall accountability for the project.
- Reporting to Arun is Sophie, the Project Manager, who is accountable for the management of the project. Fatehjit, the Business Analyst, reports to Sophie.
- There are three main parts of the project: Trade Show Support, Communications, and the Promotional Video. The team member(s) are listed for each.

Create a Project Organization Chart demonstrating the organization of the project.

REMOTE PROJECT TEAMS

With advances in communications technology, remote work has become increasingly common in many organizations. A remote project team is one in which some or all of the project team members spend time working at a remote location, normally their homes. In some instances, remote project team members spend all of their working hours at their remote location, while in other instances they may split their working hours between their remote location and a central office (e.g., working two days per week at a central office).

Benefits of Remote Project Teams

Being able to draw from a wide geographic area allows for greater access to human resources, as organizations are not limited to the immediate area of their central office. This can reduce the potential for resource constraints, resulting in increased project output. Team members often value the work-life balance of working from home, which leads to increased levels of job satisfaction and greater employee retention.

Remote work may increase the productivity of team members because they are able to focus on their work without the distractions that often occur within office environments (e.g., unwanted interruptions from others in the office). Team members are not required to spend time commuting to and from the central office and may instead spend this time on project activities.

Remote work may also result in reduced costs for the project. Having remote team members requires a smaller space in the central office, leading to reduced office costs such as rent and insurance.

Challenges of Remote Project Teams

With a central office arrangement, communication often happens naturally as a result of working in a shared space. For example, a team member can drop by a colleague's desk for an informal discussion that may lead to an exchange of vital information. Within remote project teams, this type of informal discussions may occur less frequently as team members are physically separated and the opportunity for spontaneous discussions is reduced. (While technology exists for remote "drop-ins" and chats, the lack of co-location can still inhibit spontaneous communication and connection.)

A reduction in communication can reduce familiarity among team members and ultimately the trust that exists among them. The reduction of in-person interactions via group meetings, shared office space, and social outings can lead to reduced bonding of the project team. This reduction in communication and trust can then cause reduced levels of collaboration, particularly for creative and design activities.

Within shared workspaces, the Project Manager is able to "walk around" a project team in order to observe the work and mood of the team, a management principle described by Thomas J. Peters and Robert H. Waterman Jr. (2004, p. 122) as Management by Walking Around. This approach helps the Project Manager understand how the project is progressing. Within remote project teams, this ability to interact informally with the team is reduced, and therefore effectively managing the project team may be more challenging.

Depending on their location, team members may be working in different time zones. This can reduce the availability of team members to communicate synchronously through phone, video, or chat applications, leading to reduced communication.

Strategies for Managing Remote Project Teams

Despite the challenges of remote project teams, given their advantages and the availability of high-speed communications and video conferencing systems, the use of remote project teams in some form is likely here to stay. It is therefore important to consider strategies to ensure the effective use of remote project teams.

- Clearly define roles and responsibilities. Remote project team members may lack the visual cues and ongoing feedback regarding their role on the project. While it is important to document the roles and responsibilities for all project teams (see the Project Roles and Responsibilities section earlier in this chapter), it is vital that this is documented and clearly communicated to remote project team members.
- Set up regular and ongoing communication. Remote project teams will require an even greater focus on regular, ongoing communication given that they have fewer opportunities for informal communication than in-person teams do. Communication may be in the form of daily check-in meetings, periodic team meetings, or weekly Project Status Reports. Without regular, ongoing communication, the risk that remote project team members will begin to feel isolated from the project increases.
- Clearly define goals and deadlines. While this is important for all project teams, remote project team members tend to work more independently, so it is vital that they understand what needs to be accomplished and by when. Goals and deadlines should be discussed during regular communication.
- Foster a team culture. Approaches to encourage team members to get to know each other and build relationships should be developed. Some examples include setting up social channels on the organization's communication systems for casual conversations, sharing personal updates during meetings, and organizing virtual team-building activities.

- Set up periodic in-person meetings. Creating the opportunity for remote project team members to periodically meet each other in-person tends to increase their familiarity with each other, which then benefits their ongoing remote work. This may take the form of encouraging remote team members to periodically come into the physical office or holding in-person events such as social outings or formal meetings and conferences.
- Develop inclusive scheduling solutions. For some remote project teams, project team members may be in different time zones. Whenever possible, meetings should be scheduled during times convenient to all team members. While there may be times when early morning or late evening meetings are unavoidable for certain team members, efforts should be made to minimize the impact to the remote project team members.
- Use video conferencing and collaboration tools effectively. There are many tools available to allow remote project teams to interact effectively, including video conferences and collaboration tools such as chat and electronic whiteboards. Guidelines and best practices should be established to ensure they are used effectively.
- Consider diverse cultures. With dispersed teams it is common for projects to include team members from diverse cultures. When establishing project communication guidelines, Project Managers need to consider principles of inclusivity to ensure all team members feel heard and respected. (See the Challenges of International Project Teams section later in this chapter.)

Remote project teams present both benefits and challenges. It is therefore important to consider strategies for success.

INTERNATIONAL PROJECT TEAMS

Some remote project teams may have project team members located in other countries. International project teams are also remote project teams, so the benefits, challenges, and strategies discussed above also apply to international project teams.

In this section, the additional benefits and challenges of and strategies for managing international project teams will be considered. Choosing to manage international project teams is an important strategic decision for an organization, as managing such teams often involves coordination across multiple time zones, languages, cultures, and legal systems.

Benefits of International Project Teams

As discussed during the section regarding remote project teams, the use of international project teams increases the pool of potential human resources for a project. The use of international project team members may also result in lower costs for the organization to hire those members located in countries with lower labour costs. International project teams may also provide opportunities for increased team learning, as team members from different countries bring their diverse experience and perspectives to the team.

While having project team members in different time zones may cause challenges (see the Remote Project Teams section), there may also be opportunities for projects to be worked on continuously. See the following for an example.

For a project, teams are located in San Francisco, Tokyo, and London. Given each city's time zone, a continuous workflow may be used for project work as shown in figure 7.3.

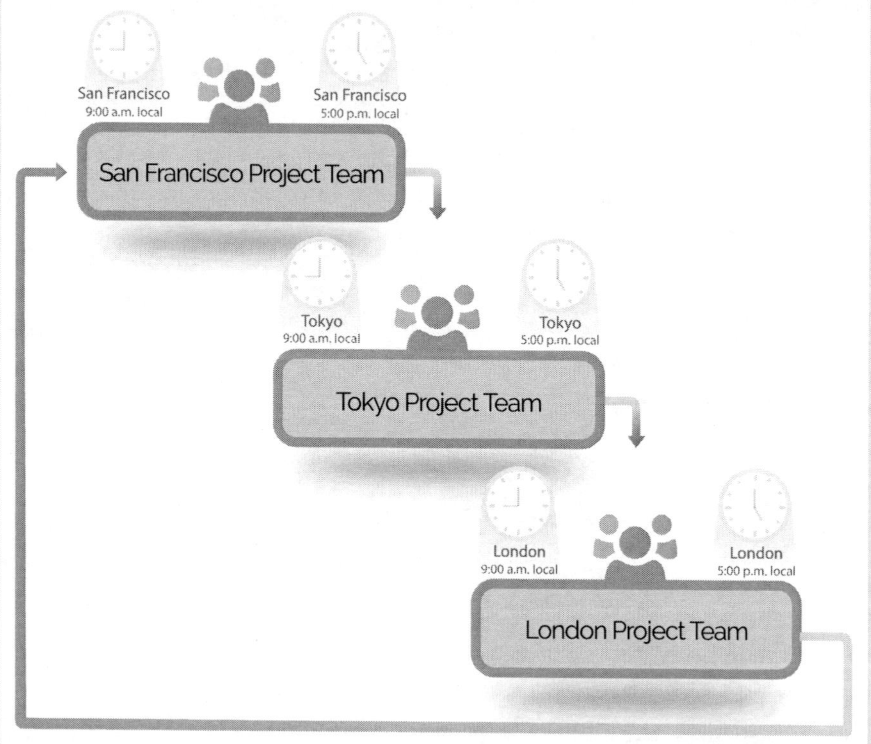

San Francisco
9:00 a.m. local

San Francisco
5:00 p.m. local

San Francisco Project Team

Tokyo
9:00 a.m. local

Tokyo
5:00 p.m. local

Tokyo Project Team

London
9:00 a.m. local

London
5:00 p.m. local

London Project Team

Figure 7.3: Project Teams in Different Time Zones

As each team works on the project, at 5:00 p.m., the work is passed to the next team, who are at the start of their workday (9:00 a.m.).

Challenges of International Project Teams

While international project teams offer significant benefits, there are also challenges to overcome. Each country has its own unique culture, which for a project means different approaches to communication, business etiquette, and personal interactions. If team members lack awareness of these cultural differences, misunderstanding and conflict may arise.

Miscommunication may occur due to language differences among countries and can lead to problems occurring within the project. Individual project team members may also face challenges integrating with the rest of the project team if they are not conversant in the dominant language being used on the team.

Each country will have legal and regulatory systems that require additional effort from team members to conduct business effectively. In certain countries, political instability, crime, or cybersecurity concerns may pose security risks. As well, there may be additional costs due to the potential for increased travel or currency fluctuations.

Strategies for Managing International Project Teams

In addition to the strategies for managing remote teams, the following are strategies to consider when planning for international project teams:

- Foster awareness of cultural differences. The awareness of cultural differences should be addressed through strategies such as cultural awareness training and the promotion of open communication within the project teams.
- Overcome language barriers. Guidelines should be created to define the language(s) to be used throughout the project. For example, a common language could be required during team meetings. In addition, the use of multilingual staff and translation software may be used.
- Understand and manage legal and regulatory differences. The organization may need to build expertise in this area as well as work with local consultants and employees.
- Manage security risks. For countries with security risks, appropriate security protocols should be developed in order to manage this risk for project team members.
- Manage additional costs. Travel costs may be reduced through the use of video conferencing and communications systems. In instances where currency fluctuations present a significant risk to the project, financial products such as currency-hedged funds may be used to manage this risk.

In addition to the challenges and opportunities presented by being remote, globally dispersed project teams face unique circumstances. It is therefore important to consider strategies for international project team success.

Case Study Update: Remote/International Project Teams

Sophie surveys her project team, noting that Chris is visiting from the Deco Productions office in Morocco. This is not a surprise, as the Morocco office has a very effective graphic design department and tends to provide design services to many of Deco Productions projects.

While some of her project team has worked with the Morocco office on previous projects, others have not. At the next project team meeting, Sophie will discuss how to best communicate with remote team members as well as some of the differing cultural norms across the two offices. Given the different time zones, she will also ensure that project team meetings are held at a time within each office's normal business hours whenever possible. She makes a note to schedule some additional check-in meetings with Chris throughout the project as she will have less contact with him than with the rest of the project team.

While including remote project team members presents some additional challenges, the benefits of gaining access to the Morocco team's graphic design expertise more than compensates for these challenges.

KEY TERMINOLOGY

Project HR Requirements: A planning document indicating the type of human resources needed and the amount of time they are required for a project

Project Organization Chart: A hierarchical chart that demonstrates the organization of the project and how the areas of responsibility interrelate

Project Roles and Responsibilities: A planning document containing a description of the key project roles

RACI Chart: A specific type of Responsibility Assignment Matrix; the acronym RACI stands for Responsible, Accountable, Consulted, and Informed

Responsibility Assignment Matrix: A planning tool used to clarify the planned involvement of people within the project

KEY CONCEPTS

1. Acquire the human resources needed to complete the project.
2. Define the roles and responsibilities of each team member.
3. Define the involvement of team members by defining who is accountable, responsible, consulted, and informed for the deliverables of the project.
4. Create a Project Organization Chart demonstrating the organization of the project.
5. Remote project teams present both benefits and challenges. It is therefore important to consider strategies for success.
6. In addition to the challenges and opportunities presented by being remote, globally dispersed project teams face unique circumstances. It is therefore important to consider strategies for international project team success.

DISCUSSION QUESTIONS

1. Think of a project from your personal, work, or school activities in which people working on the project were disorganized or confused about their role. Describe how the Roles and Responsibilities document, RACI Chart, or Project Organization Chart may have helped during this project.
2. Perform an online search to research the following question: "How long does the hiring process take?" According to your findings, what is the average length of the hiring process? What are the implications of this when planning for human resources on a project?
3. The Roles and Responsibilities document and the Responsibility Assignment Matrix are both used to define the responsibilities of the project team. Describe how these two documents differ.
4. Should the Project Manager be involved in the acquisition of new team members, or should this be left to the Resource Manager?
5. Describe how technology may be used to enhance the communication and collaboration within remote and international project teams.

8 Quality Planning

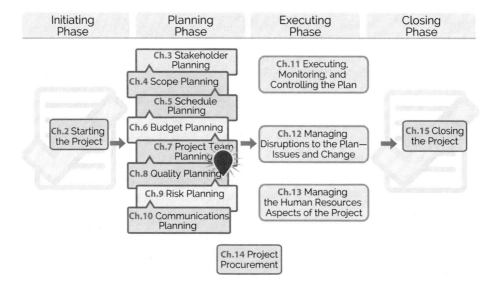

| Initiating Phase | Planning Phase | Executing Phase | Closing Phase |

Ch.3 Stakeholder Planning

Ch.4 Scope Planning

Ch.5 Schedule Planning

Ch.6 Budget Planning

Ch.7 Project Team Planning

Ch.8 Quality Planning

Ch.9 Risk Planning

Ch.10 Communications Planning

Ch.11 Executing, Monitoring, and Controlling the Plan

Ch.2 Starting the Project

Ch.12 Managing Disruptions to the Plan— Issues and Change

Ch.13 Managing the Human Resources Aspects of the Project

Ch.14 Project Procurement

Ch.15 Closing the Project

INTRODUCTION TO QUALITY

Project **quality** is closely associated with the scope of a project. While the scope indicates what a project will produce, its quality is measured by how the product of the project performs. While the word *quality* is used frequently during projects and everyday conversation, there are many definitions of this concept. This text will follow the definition created by J. M. Juran and J. A. De Feo (2010, p. 5), who described quality as follows: "To be fit for purpose, every good and service must have the right features to satisfy the customer needs and must be delivered with few failures."

This definition acknowledges the importance of effective scope planning in order to have the right features to satisfy the customer. It also describes the importance of verifying the completed deliverables to ensure that the output of the project is reliable.

Project quality means having the right features to satisfy customer needs, delivered with few failures.

A key theme of quality management is that quality should be designed into the product rather than relying on inspection to find defects. W. Edwards Deming (2000, p. 29) argued that "quality comes not from inspection, but from improvement of the production process." The focus of project quality management should be on the development of sound processes, from the start of the project and throughout all of its phases. The greater the focus placed on improving the ongoing processes of the project, the less inspection and rework that will be required—that is, the prevention of defects is achieved rather than relying on inspection of the final product. An important aspect of quality management is promoting a culture of continual improvement at both the organization and project level.

Quality should be designed into the product rather than relying on inspection.

Quality management consists of the following three main processes:

1. **Quality Planning**: The activities performed to develop a quality plan for the project, including the identification of quality standards that will be followed. Quality Planning takes place during the Planning Phase of the project and will be covered in this chapter.
2. **Quality Assurance**: The activities performed to prevent defects and errors during the project. Quality Assurance will be covered in chapter 11.
3. **Quality Control**: The activities performed to verify the quality of the project deliverables. Quality Control will be covered in chapter 11.

There is one main step when planning for project quality, as shown in figure 8.1.

"What are the
quality standards
for the project?"

Create the:

Quality
Management
Plan

1.

Figure 8.1: Quality Planning

WHAT ARE THE QUALITY STANDARDS FOR THE PROJECT?

Quality standards consist of the requirements, specifications, or characteristics that are used to ensure that the output of the project meets the desired level of quality. They may be as follows:

- Quality standards that are related to the product, service, or result of the project, that is, the detailed specifications for the project deliverables. These standards are documented in the Project Scope Statement.
- Quality standards of the organization to be followed by the project. These standards define the way the project operates and are documented in the **Quality Management Plan**.

In addition to quality standards, the Quality Management Plan may include such information as the approach to be taken for Quality Assurance and Quality Control, and the quality-related roles in the organization during the project.

A key consideration when defining a quality standard, whether in the Project Scope Statement or the Quality Management Plan, is to ask oneself "How will this standard be measured?"

Consider a school assignment that requires a written essay. If the quality standard indicates that the essay should be a "significant length," it would be very difficult to know whether you achieved this standard. What does *significant* really mean in this context? If the quality standard were instead that the essay should be 2,500 words, then measuring whether you met the standard would be much more straightforward.

The example above demonstrates the use of **metrics**. Metrics are numerical values that are used to make objective quality measurements. For example, determining whether a numerical standard of 2,500 words has been met is more effective than trying to meet a more general standard, such as writing an essay of "significant length."

However, it is unlikely that an essay will be exactly 2,500 words—in fact, it would be unusual if it were. Therefore, a **tolerance** may be defined. A tolerance is the maximum allowable variance from the standard or specifications of the project. If a tolerance of 200 words is defined, then an essay that has between 2,300 and 2,700 words would meet the standard, while an essay of 2,000 words or 3,000 words would not.

When defining quality standards, there may be confusion between the goals and objectives of the project (defined in the Project Charter) and the quality standards. These differ as follows:

- Goals describe what the project is designed to achieve, and objectives describe the specific and measurable outcomes of the project.
- Quality standards describe the characteristics of the project's deliverables and the way the project operates.

For the example above, the goal may be to pass the course, while the objectives may be to submit the assignment on time and to achieve a minimum grade of 80%. These should not also be repeated as quality standards. A valid quality standard, as indicated above, is that the completed essay is 2,500 words, plus or minus 200 words.

There are additional sections of the Quality Management Plan:

- Quality Assurance: this section describes the Quality Assurance activities and methods that will be performed during the project.
- Quality Control: this section describes the Quality Control activities and methods that will be performed during the project.
- Quality Roles: this section describes the quality-related roles for the project, including the identification of the personnel who will perform these roles.

The Quality Management Plan template is shown here:

QUALITY MANAGEMENT PLAN	
Project Name	[This section contains the project name that should appear consistently on all project documents. Organizations often have project naming conventions.]
Quality Standards	
[Category Standards] 1. [Standard #1] 2. [Standard #2] 3. [Standard #3] **[Category Standards]** 4. [Standard #4] 5. [Standard #5] 6. [Standard #6]	
Quality Assurance	
[This section describes how Quality Assurance will be performed during the project.]	
Quality Control	
[This section describes how Quality Control will be performed during the project.]	
Quality Roles	
[This section describes the quality-related roles for the project.]	

Case Study Update: Creating the Quality Management Plan

Now that her project team planning is complete, Sophie turns her attention to the next element of the plan: project quality. She starts by asking herself a simple question: "How will quality be achieved for this project?"

She sets out to list the features that will set the project apart and help ensure that it is a quality project. Given the creation of graphics and videos, there is a fair amount of technology involved. Sophie knows that technology failures tend to reflect on the overall project quality, even if they are minor, so she begins by writing "Technical Standards" on a sheet of paper.

Next, she considers the amount of written text that will be produced, such as in the press release and for the holographic cards, mural, and updates to the website. Since even a single spelling or grammatical error reduces the perception of quality, she writes "Writing Standards" as another subheading on the sheet.

Sophie knows that social media will be used significantly during the product launch. This is something that can be of great benefit to the project but can also be detrimental if mistakes are made. She adds "Social Media Standards" to the sheet. She also understands how important communication is to the success and quality of the project. She writes "Communication Standards" as the last subheading.

For each subheading, she starts to list the standards that should be met for the project. Some standards are defined by the Deco Productions organization, while others are standards defined for this project.

Next, Sophie considers the Quality Assurance activities for the project. She plans to hold biweekly quality audit meetings to review and improve the ongoing processes of the project. She also plans to promote an environment of continual improvement within the project. A comprehensive test plan will also be developed to ensure that all the deliverables meet the project's standards.

She decides that inspection will be the primary method of Quality Control for the project. Each deliverable produced will be verified using the comprehensive test plan.

Finally, Sophie considers the quality-related roles for the project. As the Project Manager, she will ensure that all aspects of the Quality Management Plan are completed. Fatehjit will be accountable for creating the comprehensive test plan and will be accountable for the Quality Control activities.

The following is the Quality Management Plan for the case study project.

DECO PRODUCTIONS	**QUALITY MANAGEMENT PLAN**
Project Name	DCV4Launch—DecoCam V4 Product Launch
Quality Standards	

Technical Standards
1. All image files will be in PNG format and a minimum of 20 megapixels.
2. All video files will be 4K and in MP4 format.
3. All images displayed must be verified to ensure that there is no copyright infringement.

Writing Standards
4. The press release will use Canadian Press (CP) style.
5. The press release will be 250 words, with a tolerance of plus or minus 50 words.
6. All written material that will be viewed by anyone outside of the company will contain zero spelling or grammatical errors.

Social Media Standards
7. All social media content produced will meet the company's social media policy in terms of content, frequency, and approved social media platforms.

Project Communication Standards
8. All emails must be responded to within 24 hours.
9. Meeting agendas for all formal project meetings are required 24 hours in advance of the meeting.
10. Minutes for all formal project meetings are required within 48 hours of the meeting's completion.
11. The status of the project (updated schedule and budget) must be reported to the Project Sponsor on a weekly basis.

(continued)

Quality Assurance
During the project, quality audit meetings will be scheduled on a biweekly basis. During the meetings, the project's processes will be reviewed and updated as required. All project team members will attend. An environment of continual improvement will be fostered. Team members will be encouraged to examine their processes and make improvements on an ongoing basis. A comprehensive test plan will be created. In this plan, test cases will be created in order to verify all deliverables of the project.
Quality Control
The primary method of Quality Control will be inspection. All deliverables will be inspected according to the test plan. The test plan will be executed once the deliverables are complete. If any changes are subsequently made to a deliverable, the applicable test cases will be performed again.
Quality Roles
Sophie Featherstone will have primary accountability for the quality of the project. This includes ensuring that all Quality Assurance and Quality Control activities are completed. Fatehjit Kumar will be accountable for creating the Quality Assurance Plan and ensuring all deliverables are verified during Quality Control.

Quality Planning results in the creation of the Quality Management Plan, which describes the quality standards, the approach to Quality Assurance and Quality Control, and the quality-related roles for the project.

KEY TERMINOLOGY

Metric: A numerical value used to make objective quality measurements

Quality: A product's fitness for its purpose, defined as having the right features and being delivered with few errors

Quality Assurance: The activities performed to prevent defects and mistakes during the project

Quality Control: The activities performed to verify the quality of the deliverables

Quality Management Plan: A planning document that describes the quality standards to be followed during the project

Quality Planning: The activities performed to identify the quality standards that will be followed during the project

Quality Standard: The requirements, specifications, or characteristics that are used to ensure that the output of the project meets the desired level of quality

Tolerance: The maximum allowable variance from the standard or specifications of a project

KEY CONCEPTS

1. Project quality means having the right features to satisfy customer needs, delivered with few failures.

2. Quality should be designed into the product rather than relying on inspection.

3. Quality Planning results in the creation of the Quality Management Plan, which describes the quality standards, the approach to Quality Assurance and Quality Control, and the quality-related roles for the project.

DISCUSSION QUESTIONS

1. Scope and quality are both related to the output of the project. What is the difference between these two concepts?

2. What are some of the ways that a Project Manager can encourage project team members to continually improve the processes of the project?

3. Think of a project from your personal, work, or school experience in which the quality of the results was not as you had anticipated. What were the causes of the lower-quality output?

4. Dr. W. Edwards Deming and Dr. Joseph Juran are known as "quality gurus," which is a term used to describe individuals who have made a significant contribution to quality management. Perform an online search to research quality gurus. Choose one not cited in this chapter and described this person's approach to quality.

9   Risk Planning

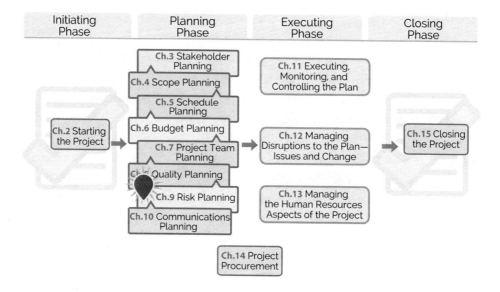

Initiating Phase	Planning Phase	Executing Phase	Closing Phase

Ch.3 Stakeholder Planning

Ch.4 Scope Planning

Ch.5 Schedule Planning

Ch.6 Budget Planning

Ch.7 Project Team Planning

Ch.8 Quality Planning

Ch.9 Risk Planning

Ch.10 Communications Planning

Ch.11 Executing, Monitoring, and Controlling the Plan

Ch.2 Starting the Project

Ch.12 Managing Disruptions to the Plan— Issues and Change

Ch.15 Closing the Project

Ch.13 Managing the Human Resources Aspects of the Project

Ch.14 Project Procurement

INTRODUCTION TO RISK PLANNING

During projects, there are uncertain situations that, if they occur, could cause a negative or positive impact to the project's outcomes. These are known as **risks**; negative risks are referred to as threats, and positive risks are referred to as opportunities. This text will focus on the management of threats to the project.

Too often overlooked, the management of risk is an essential component of successful project management. The complexity of a project environment provides many situations where things could go wrong. The limited amount of time available for the project puts pressure on the project team and may lead to problems. Given this environment, it is important to take a systematic approach to the management of risk.

One of the challenges of measuring the success of risk management is that when a potential problem is averted, nothing visible occurs. It is difficult to determine whether the problem was averted due to effective risk management or whether it would have been avoided regardless.

Imagine that a plane is rerouted from its normal flight path because the air traffic controller spots a large flock of birds. When the potential crisis is averted, there is no way to be 100% sure that the change in flight path prevented a bird from entering the plane's engine, as the birds may have ended up flying away even if the plane's flight path had not changed. However, the air traffic controller's decisiveness represents diligent risk management, given the information known at the time and the potential negative impact that could have occurred if no action had been taken.

That being said, the benefits of project risk management should become apparent over time. Projects that exercise sound risk management practices should be observed to experience fewer problems and setbacks as compared to projects that ignore or practice limited risk management.

Figure 9.1 shows the two main steps involved when planning for project risk.[1]

Figure 9.1: Risk Planning

---

1   An initial step of risk planning, creating the Risk Management Plan, may also be performed. This plan defines how the risk management activities will be performed during the project. This text does not include the Risk Management Plan but instead focuses on the development of the Risk Register.

WHAT CAN GO WRONG DURING THE PROJECT?

The first step is to consider everything that could possibly go wrong during the project. An idea should not be ignored because "it will never happen." Often, the risk that was least expected ends up causing problems.

Team members and other stakeholders should be involved in the discussion, as they may be aware of additional risks. The scope of the project should be considered in order to identify potential problems. The documentation from previous projects may also be reviewed for additional ideas.

This work will result in a list of risks for the project. However, not all risks pose an equal threat. While some risks may cause severe problems if they occur, others may be only minor issues (see figure 9.2).

Figure 9.2: Risk Severity

Each identified risk should be assessed in order to determine its severity level. This allows the risks to be put in order from the highest level of severity to the lowest. When assessing risk, there are two factors that should be estimated:

- The probability that the risk will occur
- The impact to the project if the risk does occur

Determining the probability of a risk is challenging, as it is difficult to predict the future with complete accuracy. However, through judgment and experience, a reasonable estimate is usually possible. A qualitative method (e.g., high, medium, or low) or a quantitative method (e.g., 10%, 20%) may be used to express the probability.

The second factor is the impact to the project if the risk does occur. Possible impacts include the following:

- Project delays
- Higher costs
- Dissatisfied project stakeholders
- Lower quality

Determining the impact of a risk is also challenging as there are many variables that affect what happens during a project. Again, through judgment and experience, a reasonable estimate of the impact is usually possible. A qualitative method (e.g., high, medium, or low) or a quantitative method (e.g., the financial cost to the project) may be used to express the impact.

There are various factors to consider when determining whether to use a qualitative or quantitative method. Quantitative methods are more precise, allowing for an effective comparison of risks. For example, a risk that is estimated to have a probability of 50% is more severe than a risk that is estimated at 40%. However, team members are not always comfortable estimating quantitative probabilities and impacts.

Since qualitative methods are more general, team members tend to be more comfortable assigning assessments such as medium or low. The downside of this approach is that it is less precise. For example, if two risks are estimated to have a medium probability and a medium impact, it is difficult to determine which one is more severe.

K. Heldman (2005, pp. 136–141) created an approach that incorporates both qualitative and quantitative aspects. Using this method, the probability of each identified risk will be assessed according to table 9.1.[2]

Table 9.1: Probability Table

Probability	Probability Factor	Description
Likely	0.8	Occurs frequently during projects. Conditions are present for its occurrence during the project.
Possible	0.5	Occurs sometimes during projects. Some conditions are present for its occurrence during the project.
Unlikely	0.2	Does not generally occur during projects. Conditions are not present for its occurrence during the project.

---

2   The probability categories, factors, and descriptions contained in this probability table may be customized for different organizations. This is provided as one example.

Using this method, the probability of each identified risk will be assessed with a probability factor of 0.8, 0.5, or 0.2. Note that the probability factor does not equate to the probability of the risk occurring. For example, the likely category does not indicate that there is an 80% chance that the risk will occur. Instead, using this system, a risk assessed as likely is considered to be four times more likely to occur than a risk assessed as unlikely.

The impact of each identified risk will be assessed according to table 9.2, in which the result will have an impact factor of 10, 8, 5, or 2.[3]

Table 9.2: Impact Table

Impact	Impact Factor	Description
Critical	10	The occurrence of the risk would be catastrophic for the project, with significant impact to the organization's finances, performance, or reputation.
Severe	8	The occurrence of the risk would be severe for the project, with a high impact to the organization's finances, performance, or reputation.
Moderate	5	The occurrence of the risk would be a moderate issue for the project but is unlikely to significantly impact the organization's finances, performance, or reputation.
Low	2	The occurrence of the risk would be negligible for the project and would not impact the organization's finances, performance, or reputation.

Once the probability and impact of a risk are assessed, the severity of the risk may be determined. Figure 9.3 shows a probability-impact matrix, which includes the probability on one axis and the impact on the other axis.

The highest risks are in the upper-right quadrant (high probability, high impact), while the lowest risks are in the lower-left quadrant (low probability, low impact). The other two quadrants indicate medium risk.

---

3   The impact categories, factors, and descriptions contained in this impact table may be customized for different organizations. This is provided as one example.

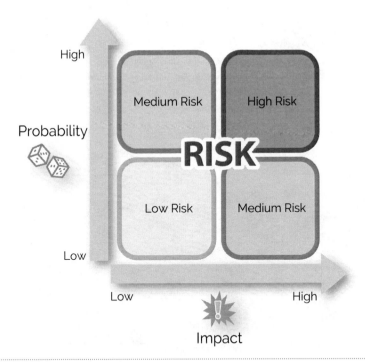

Figure 9.3: Probability-Impact Matrix

Based on an assessment of the probability and impact, a risk score can be calculated by multiplying the probability factor by the impact factor. This creates a range of risk scores from 0.4 (unlikely probability and low impact) to 8 (likely probability and critical impact). The assessed risks may then be placed into the following **Risk Register** template:

RISK REGISTER					
Project Name	[This section contains the project name that should appear consistently on all project documents. Organizations often have project naming conventions.]				
#	**Risk**	**Risk Description**	**Probability Factor**	**Impact Factor**	**Risk Score**
[1, 2, etc.]	[Name of the risk]	[Full description of the risk]	[Likely (0.8), Possible (0.5), or Unlikely (0.2)]	[Critical (10), Severe (8), Moderate (5), or Low (2)]	[Probability factor multiplied by impact factor]

(continued)

#	Risk	Risk Description	Risk Response Type	Risk Response Plan	Contingency Plan	Probability Factor	Impact Factor	Risk Score
			[Accept/Mitigate/ Avoid/Transfer/ Escalate]	[Detailed description of how the selected risk response type will be implemented. Not required if the "accept" response type is selected.]	[Detailed description of the contingency plan. Includes the conditions that would cause the contingency plan to be triggered.]			

The Risk Register should be displayed in descending order from the highest risk score to the lowest (i.e., the most critical risks are displayed first). Note that the risk number is a number assigned to each risk as a unique identifier, much like a student number identifies a student or a part number identifies a part. Therefore, since the Risk Register is sorted by risk score, the numbers in the risk number column will not normally appear in order.

Case Study Update: Identifying and Analyzing Project Risks

Sophie has gathered her project team together to plan for possible risks. The project's remote team member (Chris) is also attending the meeting through video conferencing. Sophie calls the meeting to order.

"I've called the meeting today so that we, as a team, can plan for what could go wrong during the DecoCam V4 Product Launch project. We've had a lot of problems on other projects recently. I think if we put some additional focus on risk management, we can reduce the number of problems for this project."

Fatehjit, the team's Business Analyst, leans forward in his chair. "I hear you, Sophie, but many things that have happened in the past were outside of our control. What could we do about it anyway?"

"Fair enough, Fatehjit," Sophie replies. "But even for these issues, it would be useful for us to have a backup plan. And I bet there are many potential problems that are well within our control—we want to prevent them from ever happening."

Sophie then hands out a few blank cards to each team member and asks Chris to take out a few blank cards in his office. She asks each person to write down as many potential problems as they can. While the team may be tempted to eliminate ideas, it is best to allow for an open flow of ideas and not filter anything at this point.

Within a few minutes, completed cards are scattered across the table. Sophie writes each risk on the whiteboard:

1. Team member leaves the project.
2. Written materials contain errors.
3. Product launch is moved to an earlier date.
4. New requirements are received.
5. Trade show material costs are higher than expected.
6. Delivery of trade show materials is delayed.
7. The promotional video is late.
8. Promotional video's language translations are incorrect.
9. Social media posts attract inappropriate replies.
10. Multimedia demo causes disorientation to customers.

Sophie and the project team proceed to discuss and plan for each risk in detail. This includes creating a longer description of each risk as well as selecting the probability factor and impact factor of each risk. They calculate the risk score for each risk and put these in order from the highest score to the lowest.

The following is the Risk Register that was created for the case study project:

DECO PRODUCTIONS	**RISK REGISTER**				
Project Name	DCV4Launch—DecoCam V4 Product Launch				
#	**Risk**	**Risk Description**	**Probability Factor**	**Impact Factor**	**Risk Score**
8	Promotional video's language translations are incorrect.	Incorrect translation of the video to French and Spanish results in customer complaints and negative publicity.	Likely (0.8)	Severe (8)	6.4
	Risk Response Type	**Risk Response Plan**	**Contingency Plan**		

(continued)

#	Risk	Risk Description	Probability Factor	Impact Factor	Risk Score
2	Written materials contain errors.	Errors are found in the written materials, such as the press release and website updates.	Possible (0.5)	Critical (10)	5.0
	Risk Response Type	**Risk Response Plan**	**Contingency Plan**		

#	Risk	Risk Description	Probability Factor	Impact Factor	Risk Score
6	Delivery of trade show materials is delayed.	Delivery of trade show materials is delayed.	Likely (0.8)	Moderate (5)	4.0
	Risk Response Type	**Risk Response Plan**	**Contingency Plan**		

#	Risk	Risk Description	Probability Factor	Impact Factor	Risk Score
1	Team member leaves the project.	A team member leaves the project for a prolonged period of time for any reason, such as leaving the company or illness.	Possible (0.5)	Moderate (5)	2.5
	Risk Response Type	**Risk Response Plan**	**Contingency Plan**		

#	Risk	Risk Description	Probability Factor	Impact Factor	Risk Score
9	Social media posts attract inappropriate replies.	The social media posts created for the product launch attract inappropriate replies that result in negative publicity.	Possible (0.5)	Moderate (5)	2.5
	Risk Response Type	**Risk Response Plan**	**Contingency Plan**		

#	Risk	Risk Description	Probability Factor	Impact Factor	Risk Score
3	Product launch is moved to an earlier date.	The release date of DecoCam V4 is moved up, necessitating an earlier product launch date.	Unlikely (0.2)	Critical (10)	2.0
	Risk Response Type	**Risk Response Plan**	**Contingency Plan**		

#	Risk	Risk Description	Probability Factor	Impact Factor	Risk Score
7	The promotional video is late.	The promotional video takes longer than expected and is not available for the product launch.	Unlikely (0.2)	Severe (8)	1.6

Risk Response Type	Risk Response Plan	Contingency Plan

#	Risk	Risk Description	Probability Factor	Impact Factor	Risk Score
4	New requirements are received.	New requirements are received after planning is complete, causing changes to the project's deliverables.	Possible (0.5)	Low (2)	1.0

Risk Response Type	Risk Response Plan	Contingency Plan

#	Risk	Risk Description	Probability Factor	Impact Factor	Risk Score
10	Multimedia demo causes disorientation to customers.	The multimedia demo's virtual reality causes disorientation and dizziness to some customers.	Unlikely (0.2)	Moderate (5)	1.0

Risk Response Type	Risk Response Plan	Contingency Plan

#	Risk	Risk Description	Probability Factor	Impact Factor	Risk Score
5	Trade show material costs are higher than expected.	When ordering the trade show materials (e.g., the banner stand), the actual costs are higher than originally budgeted.	Unlikely (0.2)	Low (2)	0.4

Risk Response Type	Risk Response Plan	Contingency Plan

These risks may also be plotted on the probability-impact matrix, as shown in figure 9.4.

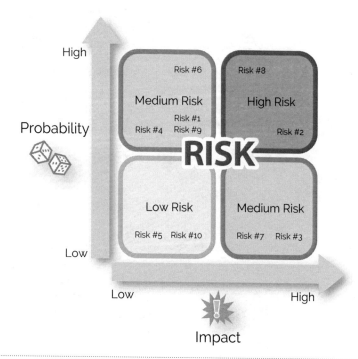

Figure 9.4: Probability-Impact Matrix (with Risks Displayed)

 Identify and analyze the project risks according to their probability and impact.

HOW CAN THE RISKS BE MANAGED?

The list of risks identified in the previous section could cause significant problems to the project. It is clear that the project would be much more successful if the risks did not occur. Rather than leaving this to chance, the Project Manager should make a **risk response plan** to manage the identified risks before they occur.

There are five types of risk response plans:

- **Risk acceptance**: the possibility that the risk will occur is accepted, and therefore no action is taken until the risk occurs.
- **Risk mitigation**: actions are defined that reduce the probability or impact of the risk.
- **Risk avoidance**: the conditions that cause the risk are removed from the project scope, eliminating any possibility of the risk.
- **Risk transfer**: the impact of the risk is transferred to another entity outside of the project. The most common examples are transferring the

risk to an individual (e.g., providing a waiver) or an organization (e.g., purchasing insurance).

- **Risk escalation**: the risk is determined to be outside of the scope of the project and is communicated to the appropriate individual or area of the organization for resolution. It is important that they accept the risk escalation before this risk response is complete.

Note that if risk management processes are not performed, all risks will default to the risk acceptance response type.

For each of the risk response types other than avoidance, a portion of the original probability and impact may still remain. This is known as **residual risk**. The following describes the residual risk for each of the risk response types:

- Risk acceptance: since no actions are taken, the residual risk will be equal to the original identified risk.
- Risk mitigation: the residual risk will be equal to the reduced probability and impact that remain once the defined actions are performed.
- Risk avoidance: the residual risk will be zero, given that the scope was changed to eliminate the risk.
- Risk transfer: the residual risk will be equal to any remaining impact that remains after the risk transfer. For example, if insurance is purchased, a deductible may need to be paid if the risk occurs.
- Risk escalation: the amount of residual risk will depend on the nature of the escalation. If the risk that was escalated is completely removed from the scope of the project, then the residual risk is zero. However, if there is any impact to the project as a result of this escalation, then this would be the residual risk.

Given the presence of residual risk, some risks will occur during a project. The next step is to determine the actions to perform if a risk occurs. These actions are referred to as **contingency plans**.

Those new to risk management may question why contingency plans are needed. Couldn't they just be planned if and when the risk occurs? Why spend all this effort for something that may not happen?

Reasons for contingency planning include the following:

1. Determining the best course of action when problems are occurring, and perhaps even in a crisis situation, is difficult. Considering the

risk in advance without the pressure of the problem allows for a more measured plan.

2.   A contingency plan helps identify processes that should be created in advance and that would be too late to create once the problem occurs. For example, bringing a first aid kit to a project involving a physical activity would be helpful in case of injury.

The five risk response types are often confused with each other. Before the case study project is revisited, the following example will be explored in order to differentiate each of the five types.

Consider that, as part of your employment, you were able to purchase a new phone and expense it to your company. However, you are concerned that you may lose it. You assess the probability of this occurrence as unlikely, though the impact would be severe.

There are five possible risk response strategies available to you:

- Accept the risk: if you happen to lose the phone, you will deal with the problem at that point.
- Mitigate the risk: develop careful procedures when using your phone, such as always keeping the phone in the same location and making a point to always check that the phone is in this location before travelling. You could also download a "phone finder" application to help recover your phone if it gets lost.
- Avoid the risk: you can choose not to own a company phone.
- Transfer the risk: you could purchase phone replacement insurance from your service provider.
- Escalate the risk: you could ask your manager to determine how to resolve the possible loss of the phone.

Notice that each risk response strategy has advantages and disadvantages. Acceptance takes the least effort but does not reduce the probability or impact of the risk. Mitigation reduces the severity of the risk but takes additional effort and the risk may still occur. Avoidance completely eliminates the risk, but it is the most restrictive option. Transference often requires an ongoing cost (in this example, an insurance premium would be paid). Escalation is not always possible for many risks.

Case Study Update: Creating Risk Response and Contingency Plans

Sophie looks at the list of risks and prepares to address the project team.

"I don't want any of these risks to occur during the project. So is there anything we can do now to make them less of an issue later on?"

The team decides that no additional actions are needed for the low-priority risks. For the other risks, they make a list of additional actions they could perform that will help lessen the seriousness of the risks. For one risk—Risk #8, the translation of the promotional video to other languages—they decide that the risk of problems is too high, and they recommend that the requirement be removed from the project's scope. Another risk—Risk #3—is escalated to Arun for discussion with the senior management team.

Next, the team considers each risk as well as what actions should be taken if the risk occurs and what would trigger these actions during the project.

Sophie records the minutes of the meeting, ensuring that the activities discussed are accurately documented.

The following is the updated Risk Register for the case study project:

DECO PRODUCTIONS   **RISK REGISTER**

Project Name	DCV4Launch—DecoCam V4 Product Launch				
#	Risk	Risk Description	Probability Factor	Impact Factor	Risk Score
8	Promotional video's language translations are incorrect.	Incorrect translation of the video to French and Spanish results in customer complaints and negative publicity.	Likely (0.8)	Severe (8)	6.4

Risk Response Type	Risk Response Plan	Contingency Plan
Avoid	This requirement should be removed from the project due to the negative publicity that may occur if errors are made. Further work to improve the organization's translation capabilities should be performed.	The risk is avoided. No contingency plan.

(continued)

#	Risk	Risk Description	Probability Factor	Impact Factor	Risk Score
2	Written materials contain errors.	Errors are found in the written materials, such as the press release, and website updates.	Possible (0.5)	Critical (10)	5.0

	Risk Response Type	Risk Response Plan	Contingency Plan		
	Mitigate	Strict attention must be paid to the quality processes throughout the project.	Printed materials will be recalled and reproduced. The electronic material will be immediately corrected. This plan is triggered if the error is reported.		

#	Risk	Risk Description	Probability Factor	Impact Factor	Risk Score
6	Delivery of trade show materials is delayed.	Delivery of trade show materials is delayed.	Likely (0.8)	Moderate (5)	4.0

	Risk Response Type	Risk Response Plan	Contingency Plan		
	Mitigate	Schedule trade show materials to be delivered at least one week before they are required.	Call suppliers to investigate the cause of the delay and determine ways to expedite the delivery. Inform the trade show team of the possible delay. This plan is triggered if materials are more than two days late from their original delivery date.		

#	Risk	Risk Description	Probability Factor	Impact Factor	Risk Score
1	Team member leaves the project.	A team member leaves the project for a prolonged period of time for any reason, such as leaving the company or illness.	Possible (0.5)	Moderate (5)	2.5

	Risk Response Type	Risk Response Plan	Contingency Plan		
	Mitigate	Ensure all project documentation and files are saved in the shared folder. Ensure all team members provide weekly progress updates.	Reassign work to other team members. Work with the Resource Manager to replace the missing team member as soon as possible. This plan is triggered in either of the following scenarios: 1. Team member is absent for more than three consecutive days. 2. Team member resigns.		

#	Risk	Risk Description	Probability Factor	Impact Factor	Risk Score
9	Social media posts attract inappropriate replies.	The social media posts created for the product launch attract inappropriate replies that result in negative publicity.	Possible (0.5)	Moderate (5)	2.5

Risk Response Type	Risk Response Plan	Contingency Plan
Accept	This risk is accepted, as the team cannot control the replies to social media posts.	Remove any offensive posts according to the company's social media policy. This plan is triggered if an inappropriate reply is detected. Replies to social media posts should be monitored at least twice per day.

#	Risk	Risk Description	Probability Factor	Impact Factor	Risk Score
3	Product launch is moved to an earlier date.	The release date of DecoCam V4 is moved up, necessitating an earlier product launch date.	Unlikely (0.2)	Critical (10)	2.0

Risk Response Type	Risk Response Plan	Contingency Plan
Escalate	Notify Arun to discuss this risk with the senior management team.	Contact the Resource Manager to determine if an additional videographer is available. Await the response from the Project Sponsor. This plan is triggered if the product launch date is moved.

#	Risk	Risk Description	Probability Factor	Impact Factor	Risk Score
7	The promotional video is late.	The promotional video takes longer than expected and is not available for the product launch.	Unlikely (0.2)	Severe (8)	1.6

Risk Response Type	Risk Response Plan	Contingency Plan
Mitigate	Weekly checkpoints are planned in order to review the progress of the video.	Add another videographer from another area of the company. This plan is triggered if the video falls behind schedule by five days or more.

#	Risk	Risk Description	Probability Factor	Impact Factor	Risk Score
4	New requirements are received.	New requirements are received after planning is complete, causing changes to the project's deliverables.	Possible (0.5)	Low (2)	1.0

Risk Response Type	Risk Response Plan	Contingency Plan
Accept	This risk is accepted, as the project scope has been planned effectively and additional requirements gathering is not recommended.	Requested changes will be assessed and either approved or rejected according to the project's change management process. This plan is triggered if a new requirement is requested.

(continued)

#	Risk	Risk Description	Probability Factor	Impact Factor	Risk Score
10	Multimedia demo causes disorientation to customers.	The multimedia demo's virtual reality causes disorientation and dizziness to some customers.	Unlikely (0.2)	Moderate (5)	1.0

Risk Response Type	Risk Response Plan	Contingency Plan
Transfer Mitigate	Create signs indicating that the demo may cause disorientation or dizziness and that people should use the demo at their own risk. Mitigate by ensuring that people must be seated when viewing the demo.	Stop the multimedia demo and provide assistance as necessary. This plan is triggered if a trade show participant displays signs of disorientation or dizziness.

#	Risk	Risk Description	Probability Factor	Impact Factor	Risk Score
5	Trade show material costs are higher than expected.	When ordering the trade show materials (e.g., the banner stand), the actual costs are higher than originally budgeted.	Unlikely (0.2)	Low (2)	0.4

Risk Response Type	Risk Response Plan	Contingency Plan
Accept	This risk is accepted, as the trade show material costs are a small percentage of the overall project budget.	Investigate alternative suppliers if available. Otherwise, the budget will be adjusted for the higher cost. This plan is triggered if the trade show material costs are 10% or more over budget.

Determine the risk response and contingency plan for each risk.

KEY TERMINOLOGY

Contingency Plan: The actions to be performed in the event that the defined risk occurs

Residual Risk: The amount of risk remaining after risk response actions have been completed

Risk: An uncertain situation that, if it occurred, could cause a negative impact (threat) or positive impact (opportunity) to the project

Risk Acceptance: The possibility that the risk will occur is accepted, and therefore no action is taken until the risk occurs

Risk Avoidance: The conditions that cause the risk are removed from the project scope, eliminating any possibility of the risk

Risk Escalation: The risk is determined to be outside of the scope of the project and is communicated to the appropriate individual or area of the organization for resolution

Risk Mitigation: Actions are defined that reduce the probability or impact of the risk

Risk Register: A planning document that contains all identified risks for the project and includes their probability factor, impact factor, risk score, risk response plan, and contingency plan

Risk Response Plan: The actions to be performed prior to the occurrence of a defined risk; the five types of risk response plans are risk acceptance, risk mitigation, risk avoidance, risk transfer, and risk escalation

Risk Transfer: The impact of the risk is transferred to another entity outside of the project

KEY CONCEPTS

1. Identify and analyze the project risks according to their probability and impact.
2. Determine the risk response and contingency plan for each risk.

DISCUSSION QUESTIONS

1. Risk response plans and contingency plans are often misunderstood. What is the difference between these two risk management concepts?
2. What is the difference between the risk avoidance and risk mitigation response strategies?
3. Think of a project from your personal, work, or school experience during which problems occurred. Could these risks have been identified earlier in the project? Could the risk response plans discussed in this chapter (i.e., accept, mitigate, avoid, transfer, and escalate) have been used?
4. Perform an online search to research common project management risks. Summarize five common risks and their possible risk response plans.

10 Communications Planning

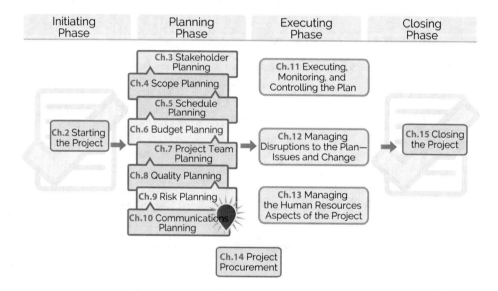

| Initiating Phase | Planning Phase | Executing Phase | Closing Phase |

- Ch.3 Stakeholder Planning
- Ch.4 Scope Planning
- Ch.5 Schedule Planning
- Ch.6 Budget Planning
- Ch.7 Project Team Planning
- Ch.8 Quality Planning
- Ch.9 Risk Planning
- Ch.10 Communications Planning

- Ch.2 Starting the Project

- Ch.11 Executing, Monitoring, and Controlling the Plan
- Ch.12 Managing Disruptions to the Plan— Issues and Change
- Ch.13 Managing the Human Resources Aspects of the Project

- Ch.15 Closing the Project

- Ch.14 Project Procurement

INTRODUCTION TO COMMUNICATIONS PLANNING

In order for a project to be successful, people need to work together to achieve the project's objectives. This requires the exchange of relevant information between people inside the project and people outside the project at the appropriate time. To do this effectively, communications planning and coordination are required.

Project teams will often decide to communicate "when required" instead of developing a communications plan. This usually means that there is less communication between team members on a project, which can lead to an increased number of problems. More time is then spent on solving the problems, and less time is spent on the communications that were to be performed "when required." This becomes a vicious cycle that leads to underperformance.

Unfortunately, communications planning may have negative connotations for those who see it as resulting in long, needless meetings and increased bureaucracy. Therefore, the challenge for the Project Manager is to develop a clear and practical communications plan. Regardless of whether a planned communication is a meeting, report, presentation, or email, care should be taken that each communication is necessary and adds to the performance of the project.

Figure 10.1 shows the three main steps of planning for project communications.

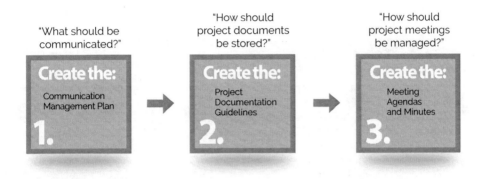

Figure 10.1: Communications Planning

WHAT SHOULD BE COMMUNICATED?

Determining the content of a formal communications plan can be challenging. The plan is not intended to document all of the informal communications that naturally take place during a project. Not only would this be a large and time-consuming task, but planning for this level of detail would also be impractical.

When developing a communications plan for the project, the information needs of the project stakeholders, and how best to satisfy these needs, should be taken into account. The communications plan should contain details regarding the following communications, which are planned to take place during the project:

- Communication of project information: this includes meetings, reports, emails, and information posted online. Communications of this type include the distribution of information, the collection of requirements, and the resolution of issues.
- Communication of project status information: this often includes a number of reports and meetings.

The communications are then documented in a **Communication Management Plan**. When creating this plan, consider the information needs of the project stakeholders. The goal should be to ensure that each stakeholder has access to the information they need to perform their role effectively. The Stakeholder Engagement Plan should also be consulted, and any planned communications included in this document should be considered for possible inclusion in the Communication Management Plan.

The template for the Communication Management Plan is as follows:

COMMUNICATION MANAGEMENT PLAN			
Project Name	[This section contains the project name that should appear consistently on all project documents. Organizations often have project naming conventions.]		
Communication Name	**Description**	**Audience**	**Timing**
[Short name of the communication]	[Full description of the communication, including the purpose and the communication medium to be used]	[People or group to receive or attend to the communication]	[Date or frequency of the communication]

Case Study Update: Creating the Communication Management Plan

Sophie begins to think about the communications that should occur during the project. How much communication is needed? It would be nice to have frequent meetings, but when would the work itself get done? Should there be more face-to-face interaction or more information posted online? How often should the information be produced? All these questions pass through Sophie's mind as she considers how to plan the communications.

She then asks herself, "Who is it that the project needs to communicate with?" The answer is clear: the project stakeholders. With this insight, she pulls out the Stakeholder Register and lists each stakeholder on a blank sheet of paper. She considers the different reasons why she might have to communicate with them, such as providing a status update or a review of daily work tasks. She then proceeds to list the reasons under each stakeholder name.

Sophie considers different communication media, such as video meetings, in-person meetings, emails, and written reports, and asks herself which one would be the most effective for each of the requirements on her list. Next, she considers the timing. When should one-time communications occur? How often should recurring communications occur?

As Sophie finishes this process, she reviews the results of her work: a document outlining the various communications that will be performed during the project. While she knows that effective communication will be an ongoing challenge, she's feeling a lot more confident now that she has a plan.

The following is the Communication Management Plan for the case study project:

DECO PRODUCTIONS	COMMUNICATION MANAGEMENT PLAN		
Project Name	DCV4Launch—DecoCam V4 Product Launch		
Communication Name	**Description**	**Audience/ Attendees**	**Timing**
Project Kickoff Meeting	Meeting to review the Project Charter for the project and obtain formal approval to proceed to the Planning Phase	Casey Serrador Arun Singh Sophie Featherstone	March 25, 2026
Distribution of the Project Charter	Project Charter sent as email by Sophie Featherstone	Project Managers of the other V4 projects	March 27, 2026
Scope Review Meeting	Video meeting to formally review the project plans and obtain approval to proceed to the Executing Phase	Casey Serrador Arun Singh Project team	April 3, 2026
Daily Project Team Huddle	Daily 15-minute video meeting of the product launch team to review the current status of the project and outstanding issues	Project team	Daily, beginning April 6, 2026
Project Status Report	Weekly status report. Email sent by Sophie Featherstone.	Arun Singh Project Managers of the other V4 projects	Weekly: Thursdays by noon
Project Status Review Meeting	Weekly review of all DecoCam V4 projects	Arun Singh Project Managers of the other V4 projects	Weekly: Fridays at 1:00 p.m.

(continued)

Communication Name	Description	Audience/ Attendees	Timing
Quality Audit Meeting	Meeting to create and update project processes in order to increase project quality	Project team	Biweekly: Mondays at 1:00 p.m.
Company Announcement	An announcement of the new product launch (this information will be included in the weekly message board)	Deco Productions employees	May 8, 2026
Lessons Learned	Meeting to review the lessons of the project in order to improve future projects	Arun Singh Project team Anand Bhandari	May 11, 2026
Final Project Meeting	Final review of the project's results	Casey Serrador Arun Singh Project team	May 13, 2026

Create a plan for the project communications based on the information needs of the project stakeholders.

HOW SHOULD PROJECT DOCUMENTS BE STORED?

Project documentation consists of design documents, schedules, budgets, quality plans, risk information, status reports, issues, meeting agendas and minutes, presentations, and many other documents. The creation of documentation guidelines will make it easier to find and update these documents throughout the project. The guidelines will also help ensure that the documentation is kept current and that the project team is viewing and updating the latest version of each document.

The guidelines should address the following:

- Where will the documents be stored?
- How will the documents be organized?
- What is the naming convention for documents?
- What documents require multiple versions?

In some instances, the project's organization may already have established communication guidelines for projects.

Storage Location, Organization, and Access Control

The storage location for both electronic and hard copy project documents should be determined. Consider factors such as whether the documents will be backed up and whether a secure passcode is required for all or certain documents.

In order to organize the stored documents, categories or folders should be considered. Possible categories or folders include project phases (e.g., Planning) and project or document types (e.g., Status Reports).

Naming Conventions

When saving documents, project team members often create file names that are meaningful only to themselves and do not consider other team members or projects. For example, if a team member creates a document containing the Work Breakdown Structure and names the file "WBS," how will this file be differentiated from the other versions of the document created during the project or from the Work Breakdown Structures from other projects? Team members should use a file naming convention that will be clear to everyone. The naming convention may include information such as the project name or code, the document name, the version (if applicable), and the date.

Since files are usually sorted in alphanumeric order, the structure of the naming convention should be created with this in mind.

Document Versions

For certain documents, multiple versions may be required in order to view the history of major updates to each document.

In these instances, a separate copy of each version is stored, with the latest version representing the current state of the document. The majority of project documents do not typically require separate versions.

The template for the **Project Documentation Guidelines** document is as follows:

PROJECT DOCUMENTATION GUIDELINES	
Project Name	[This section contains the project name that should appear consistently on all project documents. Organizations often have project naming conventions.]
Storage Location and Organization	
[This section describes the location of project documents and how they are organized.]	
Naming Conventions	
[This section describes the naming conventions for all project files.]	
Document Versions	
[This section indicates which documents require multiple versions.]	

Case Study Update: Creating the Project Documentation Guidelines

Sophie knows from past experience that effective communication is vital for her project. More often than not, whenever one of her projects has underperformed, the root cause was a problem with the way people communicated with each other.

During her last project, it was difficult for her project team to find the latest project documents. A great deal of time and effort was spent figuring out where documents were stored, and in some cases mistakes were made because an incorrect document was used. This time, Sophie plans to set out the guidelines at the start of the project.

Sophie plans to store all documents on the project website using a new document management system recently purchased by Deco Productions. Folders will be set up to logically organize the documents, and the company standard for project file names will be used. Lastly, Sophie will designate the documents that will require versions to be maintained.

What follows is the Project Documentation Guidelines for the case study project:

DECO PRODUCTIONS	**PROJECT DOCUMENTATION GUIDELINES**
Project Name	DCV4Launch—DecoCam V4 Product Launch

Storage Location and Organization

All project documents will be stored on the secure project website. Sophie Featherstone will be the administrator and will grant Read or Read/Write access to the project team and certain project stakeholders as needed.

Documents will be filed in the following folders:

- Initiating
- Scope
- Schedule
- Budget
- Team/HR
- Quality
- Risk
- Communication
- Meeting Agenda and Minutes
- Status Reports
- Issues
- Changes
- Closing

Naming Conventions
All document file names will be as follows: Project ID - Document Name - Version (if required) - Date of Report (YYYYMMDD) Examples: • DCV4Launch-ProjectCharter-1.0-20260325 • DCV4Launch-ProjectStatusReport-20260424
Document Versions
Document versions will be maintained for the Project Charter and Project Scope Statement. For all other project documents, only the latest version will be saved. Major changes to the document will result in a new version number (e.g., 2.0, 3.0). Minor changes will result in a new decimal (e.g., 2.1, 2.2).

Create guidelines to demonstrate how the project should store and organize project documents, how these documents should be named, and whether document versions are required.

HOW SHOULD PROJECT MEETINGS BE MANAGED?

The Communication Management Plan will usually refer to a number of meetings that will occur during the project. They should be run as effectively as possible, and therefore meeting protocols should be established for the project. These should include the following:

- Creating a **meeting agenda**
- Following the agenda during the meeting
- Documenting the meeting discussion, decisions, and **actions items** in the **meeting minutes**

When considering meeting protocols, it is important to acknowledge that not every gathering of two or more project team members warrants an agenda and meeting minutes. There are many informal meetings that naturally occur during a project that do not require this level of documentation. For these meetings, less formal methods of documentation, such as an email summary or an update of planning documents, are sufficient. The additional rigour of agendas and meeting minutes should be reserved for formal meetings, which are usually defined in the Communication Management Plan.

Meeting Agenda

The meeting agenda should include the details of the meeting (e.g., meeting name, location), who is invited to the meeting, and a list of the topics for the meeting. For some meetings, the first item on the agenda may be a review of the previous meeting's minutes or action items. The agenda should be sent prior to the meeting, preferably at least a day or two earlier.

The following is the template for the Meeting Agenda document:

MEETING AGENDA		
Project Name	[This section contains the project name that should appear consistently on all project documents. Organizations often have project naming conventions.]	
Meeting Name	[This section contains the name of the meeting.]	
Meeting Facilitator	[This section contains the name of the person who will facilitate the meeting.]	
Meeting Details	[This section contains the meeting date, start and end time, and location (room number or virtual meeting details).]	
Meeting Invitees	[This section contains a list of people invited to the meeting]	
Agenda		
Topic	**Presented By**	**Time Allotted**
[Description of the agenda item, including whether the item is for information, discussion, or decision]	[Name of the person who will lead the discussion]	[Amount of time allotted to this item]

Case Study Update: Creating a Meeting Agenda

Sophie scans the Communication Management Plan and sees that the next meeting is the Scope Review Meeting, so she starts to work on the agenda. She decides to invite Arun and the project team.

Thinking about the meeting, she lists the topics to be included. For each topic, she includes the person who will present the topic and the amount of time to be allotted, making sure there is enough time to cover each topic and leave a few minutes at the end of the meeting in case any topics require a little more time. She knows from past experience that this sometimes happens during meetings.

Once the agenda is complete, she saves the information in the Meeting Agenda document and sends it to the meeting attendees a few days before the meeting.

The following document is the Meeting Agenda for the case study project:

DECO PRODUCTIONS	**MEETING AGENDA**	
Project Name	DCV4Launch—DecoCam V4 Product Launch	
Meeting Name	Scope Review Meeting	
Meeting Facilitator	Sophie Featherstone	
Meeting Details	April 3, 2026 10:00 a.m.–11:30 a.m. Video login password: 07260802	
Meeting Invitees	Arun Singh, Sophie Featherstone, Maddy Wen, Chris Sandburg, Sarah Pierce, Fatehjit Kumar, Eli Briggs	
Agenda		
Topic	**Presented By**	**Time Allotted**
1. Introduction—an overview of the planning process to date will be provided	Sophie	10 minutes
2. Walkthrough of the trade show scope	Chris	20 minutes
3. Walkthrough of the communications scope	Sarah	20 minutes
4. Walkthrough of the promotional video scope	Maddy	20 minutes
5. Project scope sign-off	Sophie	10 minutes

Running the Meeting and Meeting Minutes

During the meeting, the meeting facilitator should ensure that the agenda is followed throughout the meeting. Before beginning the meeting, the agenda should be reviewed, and additional items may be added to the agenda based on the feedback from the meeting attendees. Someone should also be designated to record the minutes of the meeting. This includes a summary of the discussion, decisions that were made, and any required action items.

As the meeting progresses, sometimes a new topic unrelated to the agenda is raised by someone attending the meeting. Discussion of this topic could result in some agenda items not being covered during the meeting or the meeting exceeding its allotted time. To address this, the meeting facilitator can move the topic to a "parking lot." This then "parks" the topic to be discussed at a later time. Once all agenda items are completed, and if time permits, the parking lot items may be discussed. Alternatively, they can be added to the Parking Lot section of the meeting minutes and potentially be added to a future meeting's agenda.

Meeting minutes provide two important benefits:

- They provide important documentation of discussions and decisions that take place during the project. Without the minutes being recorded, important details may be forgotten or changed, which then leads to further problems.
- They may be reviewed by those not able to attend the meeting.

The following is the template for the Meeting Minutes document:

MEETING MINUTES		
Project Name	[This section contains the project name that should appear consistently on all project documents. Organizations often have project naming conventions.]	
Meeting Name	[This section contains the name of the meeting.]	
Meeting Facilitator	[This section contains the name of the person who will facilitate the overall meeting.]	
Meeting Date	[This section contains the meeting date.]	
Meeting Attendees	[This section contains a list of people who attended the meeting.]	
Minutes		
Topic	**Summary of Discussion/Decision**	
[Description of the agenda item]	[Contains a summary of the meeting discussion and any decisions that were made. Action items resulting from this topic will be recorded in the Action Items area below.]	
Action Items		
Description of Action	**Assigned To**	**Date Required**
[Description of the action to be taken following the meeting]	[Name of the person assigned to this action item]	[Date that this action should be completed]
Parking Lot		
[Description of the new topic raised during the meeting and moved to the parking lot]		

Case Study Update: Conducting Effective Project Meetings

As the Scope Review Meeting is about to start, Sophie confirms with Fatehjit that he will record the minutes of the meeting and lets him know that Eli will be unable to attend, as he was invited to another meeting. She then starts the meeting.

"Good morning, everyone, and welcome to this key milestone meeting. Special thanks for the project team for their hard work in getting the scope defined in such a short period of time. Before we begin the meeting, are there any additional topics to add to the agenda?"

The team agrees that there are no additional items, and Sophie begins the meeting. She guides the meeting to cover each agenda topic and keeps her eye on the time to ensure that each topic stays within the time allotted. As each topic is concluded, the key discussions, decisions, and action items are summarized so that Fatehjit can ensure this information is recorded accurately in the meeting minutes.

During the meeting, Maddy mentions that she read about a new video processing software system that has just been released. She begins to talk about how this could improve the quality of the new promotional video that she and Eli are creating. Since this is not an agenda item for the current meeting, Sophie recommends that the discussion of the new video processing system be added to the meeting's parking lot. This satisfies Maddy, as she knows from past experience that Sophie will follow up on the parking lot items after the meeting and ensure that they are effectively handled.

Following the meeting, Sophie and Fatehjit meet to review the meeting minutes. Based on this discussion, they make a few adjustments to the information, and then Sophie files both the agenda and the meeting minutes in the Meeting Agenda and Minutes folder, as defined in the Project Documentation Guidelines.

Another successful meeting has been concluded. Checking the Communication Management Plan, Sophie begins work on the next agenda.

The following document is the Meeting Minutes for the case study project:

DECO PRODUCTIONS	**MEETING MINUTES**
Project Name	DCV4Launch—DecoCam V4 Product Launch
Meeting Name	Scope Review Meeting
Meeting Facilitator	Sophie Featherstone
Meeting Date	April 3, 2026
Meeting Attendees	Arun Singh, Sophie Featherstone, Maddy Wen, Chris Sandburg, Sarah Pierce, Fatehjit Kumar

(continued)

Minutes	
Topic	**Summary of Discussion/Decision**
1. Introduction—an overview of the planning process to date	• Sophie reviewed the key project milestones. • Overall, the project remains on schedule.
2. Walkthrough of the trade show scope	• Chris provided a description of the trade show deliverables. • Arun asked whether the banners would be large enough. Chris will investigate further. • Arun also confirmed that the project team should not be responsible for set-up at the trade show.
3. Walkthrough of the communications scope	• Sarah provided a description of the communications deliverables. • Sophie suggested that the press release should contain additional information about the current DecoCam product. Fatehjit indicated that the Project Scope Statement would be updated.
4. Walkthrough of the promotional video scope	• Maddy provided a description of promotional video deliverables, including a demo of the storyboard. • Maddy also played a 30-second demo video to demonstrate the look and feel of the final product. • Arun suggested showing this demo to Casey.
5. Project scope sign-off	• Arun provided his sign-off for the project and thanked the team for their efforts to date.

Action Items		
Description of Action	**Assigned To**	**Date Required**
Determine whether the banner size currently defined in the Project Scope Statement is adequate.	Chris	April 7, 2026
Book a meeting with Casey to show her the demo video.	Sophie	April 10, 2026

Parking Lot
There is a new video processing system that could be considered for the promotional video. See Maddy for more information.

Plan for effective project meetings that include the use of project agendas and meeting minutes.

KEY TERMINOLOGY

Action Item: An activity identified during a meeting to be completed at a later date

Communication Management Plan: A planning document that contains all the planned communications for a project; the plan includes the name, description, intended audience, and the date or frequency of the communications

Meeting Agenda: A document containing a list of topics to be accomplished during a meeting

Meeting Minutes: A document containing a summary of the discussion, decisions, and defined action items that occurred during a meeting

Project Documentation Guidelines: A planning document that contains guidelines for the documentation of a project; the guidelines describe the storage location, preferred organization method, and naming conventions for project files and indicate which documents require multiple versions

KEY CONCEPTS

1. Create a plan for the project communications based on the information needs of the project stakeholders.
2. Create guidelines to demonstrate how the project should store and organize project documents, how these documents should be named, and whether document versions are required.
3. Plan for effective project meetings that include the use of project agendas and meeting minutes.

DISCUSSION QUESTIONS

1. Describe the possible problems that may occur during a project if communications are not planned in advance.
2. In the case study example, the press release and outreach activities were included in the project schedule but not in the Communication Management Plan. Should these activities also have been included in the Communication Management Plan?
3. Think of a project from your personal, work, or school experience during which problems occurred. Could any of these problems have been averted or reduced through more effective communication?
4. Perform an online search to research project communication best practices. Summarize your findings.

11

Executing, Monitoring, and Controlling the Plan

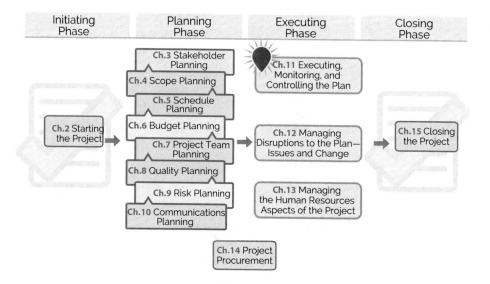

| Initiating Phase | Planning Phase | Executing Phase | Closing Phase |

Ch.3 Stakeholder Planning

Ch.4 Scope Planning

Ch.11 Executing, Monitoring, and Controlling the Plan

Ch.5 Schedule Planning

Ch.2 Starting the Project

Ch.6 Budget Planning

Ch.7 Project Team Planning

Ch.12 Managing Disruptions to the Plan— Issues and Change

Ch.15 Closing the Project

Ch.8 Quality Planning

Ch.9 Risk Planning

Ch.13 Managing the Human Resources Aspects of the Project

Ch.10 Communications Planning

Ch.14 Project Procurement

INTRODUCTION TO THE EXECUTING PHASE

With the completion of the project plans, another phase gate decision is required. If approved, the project leaves the Planning Phase and enters the Executing Phase. The purpose of the Executing Phase is to produce the deliverables of the project by carrying out the project plans.

The creation of the project's product, service, or result takes place during this phase. The project team increases in size with the team members added to the project as planned in the HR Requirements document.

There is also a change in atmosphere as the project moves from planning to executing. Whereas planning usually involves a small number of people creating written plans and documents, executing involves a larger number of people creating the actual deliverables. It is the action-oriented time of the project that includes the completion of the work, the management of the team, the resolution of issues, and ongoing communication with the project stakeholders.

INTRODUCTION TO EXECUTING, MONITORING, AND CONTROLLING THE PLAN

After the Planning Phase, the next step is to create the deliverables of the project. This involves the following:

- Performing the activities of the schedule
- Producing the deliverables
- Maintaining the budget
- Monitoring the risks
- Creating the communications
- Managing the quality of the deliverables

Monitoring and controlling each of these aspects of the project will be discussed in the sections that follow. However, it is important to recall that an action taken to control one aspect of the project often impacts other aspects. For example, if actions are taken to speed up activities for a project that has fallen behind schedule, this usually impacts the project's scope, cost, resources, and other aspects. For more information, see the Project Constraints section in chapter 1.

Organizations that manage large, complex projects often employ a methodology called **Earned Value Management** (EVM) to measure the project's performance. This methodology is presented in Appendix 2: An Overview of Earned Value Management.

PERFORMING THE ACTIVITIES OF THE SCHEDULE

The actions taken during the Executing Phase should follow the project schedule to ensure that all activities are completed. For example, the portion of the case study project schedule related to the Trade Show Signage is shown in figure 11.1.

DecoCam V4 Product Launch	Dur	27-Mar	3-Apr	10-Apr
Initiating				
Initiate the project	3d			
Initiating Phase complete	0d			
Planning				
Plan the project	7d			
Planning Phase complete	0d			
Executing				
Trade Show Signage				
Create sign graphics/text	3d			
Order banner stands	1d			

Figure 11.1: Project Schedule (Trade Show Signage)

As indicated in chapter 5, when creating a schedule, a baseline may be established. As activities are completed during the Executing Phase, their progress may be compared to the baseline. It is important to do so, as the project schedule tends to be the most dynamic of all the project planning documents. The timing and duration of activities will often vary from the original plan for a variety of reasons, including the following:

- The work takes longer than expected.
- The person working on the activity is unavailable or has reduced availability.
- The scope of the project has increased.
- External factors were not predicted.

If the project begins to fall behind schedule, approaches such as process improvement, overlapping activities, adding more resources to activities, outsourcing project work, or reducing the scope of the project can shorten the duration of a project.

Process Improvement

When a reduced amount of time is available, this can motivate the project team to devise innovative approaches that result in less time and effort being spent to complete the required work. While there are limitations to this approach, often efficiencies may be gained through process improvement.

Overlapping Activities

During the original planning, tasks are often planned to be sequential, as this is the simplest approach to completing the work. If the project begins to fall behind schedule, the timing of activities may be changed to increase the level of overlap. Activities may be scheduled to overlap slightly (i.e., by a few days or a short amount of time) or completely (i.e., occurring at the same time).

Increasing the overlap of activities tends to increase the cost of the project. Because an increasing amount of work is done in parallel rather than sequentially, increased communication and coordination are required to complete the work. There is also the potential for more rework, as changes made in one activity may affect work already completed in another activity. The increased complexity of overlapping activities may also negatively affect the quality of the project.

The overlapping of activities in order to shorten the duration of a project is also known as **fast-tracking**.

Adding More Resources to Activities

Another approach is to add more resources to activities in order to complete them earlier. This can take the form of additional human resources or increased work hours of the people already assigned to the activities.

As with overlapping activities, adding resources will usually increase the cost of the project. While the activities will be completed sooner, the additional communication, coordination, and potential for rework (due to increased numbers of workers and longer hours) will likely increase the cost of the project. The quality may also suffer, as the higher number of workers often leads to an increased likelihood of miscommunications and other errors.

Adding additional resources to activities in order to shorten the duration of a project is also known as **crashing**.

Outsourcing Project Work

Another method of adding resources to the project is to outsource work to another organization. This work remains within the overall scope of the project but is performed outside of the project team.

Outsourcing project work is also known as **project procurement** and is covered in detail in chapter 14.

Reducing the Scope of the Project

Eliminating scope from the project can also cause the project to be completed earlier. This would be a significant change to the project and would likely require the approval of the Project Sponsor.

Other than process improvements, each of the methods listed above involves trade-offs that the Project Manager would need to carefully consider. In each case, the impact to the project's cost, scope, and quality would be balanced against the shortened project schedule.

 Complete the activities of the project according to the schedule, making adjustments as needed.

PRODUCING THE DELIVERABLES

The Project Scope Statement and Quality Management Plan provide a description of the deliverables to be produced and the desired level of quality to be achieved during the project. The following are excerpts from the Project Scope Statement and Quality Management Plan for the press release deliverable.

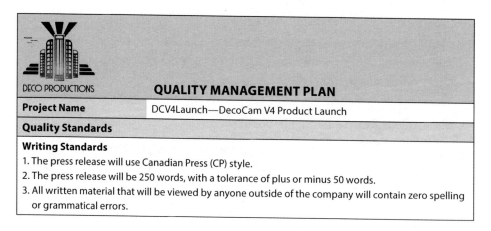

DECO PRODUCTIONS	**PROJECT SCOPE STATEMENT**
Project Name	DCV4Launch—DecoCam V4 Product Launch
Project Deliverable	**Detailed Description**
Press Release	• Create a news story outlining the key features of the new DecoCam, including its use of advanced AI technology. • Distribute electronically to media on the same date that DecoCam V4 is available for download to the public.

DECO PRODUCTIONS	**QUALITY MANAGEMENT PLAN**
Project Name	DCV4Launch—DecoCam V4 Product Launch
Quality Standards	

Writing Standards
1. The press release will use Canadian Press (CP) style.
2. The press release will be 250 words, with a tolerance of plus or minus 50 words.
3. All written material that will be viewed by anyone outside of the company will contain zero spelling or grammatical errors.

The project team should create the press release exactly as described above. After each deliverable contained in the Project Scope Statement has been created, the full scope of the project will be complete.

Adherence to the Project Scope Statement helps reduce the possibility of **scope creep** occurring during the project. Scope creep is the gradual and uncontrolled growth of a project's scope. It tends to occur in small additions to the project scope, with each addition being seen as insignificant and unlikely to impact the cost, schedule, or other aspects of the project. Over time, these small additions accumulate and can represent a significant addition to the project scope.

> Produce the project deliverables according to the Project Scope Statement and Quality Management Plan.

MONITORING THE BUDGET

The costs that were previously estimated during planning will be incurred during the Executing Phase. In some cases, the costs may be equal to what was planned, but usually there will be either a positive or negative variance. For example, the team members may take more or less time than estimated to complete the activities. Additionally, the cost of the required materials may work out to be more or less than the estimate. Unexpected problems will usually increase costs, while unforeseen opportunities may lower costs.

All expenditures should be managed carefully during the project. For example, in the case study, the cost of each camera and tripod set was estimated to be $700. If the cost quoted by a supplier turns out to be $1,500, further action may be required.

In addition to managing costs as they occur, costs incurred should be tracked and compared to the budget. The following demonstrates the Detailed Budget of the case study at the end of the third week.

DECO PRODUCTIONS	**DETAILED BUDGET**								
Project Name	DCV4Launch—DecoCam V4 Product Launch								
	Week ending 27-Mar	Week ending 3-Apr	Week ending 10-Apr	Week ending 17-Apr	Week ending 24-Apr	Week ending 1-May	Week ending 8-May	Week ending 15-May	**Total**
Initiating									
Initiate the project	$1,200								**$1,200**
Planning									
Plan the project	$2,080	$5,200							**$7,280**

(continued)

	Week ending 27-Mar	Week ending 3-Apr	Week ending 10-Apr	Week ending 17-Apr	Week ending 24-Apr	Week ending 1-May	Week ending 8-May	Week ending 15-May	Total
Executing									
Create sign graphics/text			$1,200						**$1,200**
Order banner stands			$400						**$400**
Create holographic cards			$400	$400					**$800**
Order holographic cards				$400					**$400**
Create mural for booth				$1,200					**$1,200**
Develop demo slideshow					$1,200				**$1,200**
Order cameras and tripods					$400				**$400**
Create SM strategy			$960						**$960**
Develop SM post content			$1,440						**$1,440**
Update product page				$480					**$480**
Develop online slideshow				$1,440					**$1,440**
Create outreach list				$480					**$480**
Perform outreach					$2,400				**$2,400**
Create press release							$960		**$960**
Send press release							$480		**$480**
Develop video concept			$1,440						**$1,440**
Develop storyboard and script			$960	$2,400					**$3,360**

	Week ending 27-Mar	Week ending 3-Apr	Week ending 10-Apr	Week ending 17-Apr	Week ending 24-Apr	Week ending 1-May	Week ending 8-May	Week ending 15-May	Total
Film video					$4,400	$4,400			$8,800
Edit video							$4,400		$4,400
Monitor and control			$2,000	$2,000	$2,000	$2,000	$2,000		$10,000
Other Costs:									
Banner stands			$1,000						$1,000
Holographic cards				$2,000					$2,000
Murals				$200					$200
Cameras and tripods					$1,400				$1,400
Closing									
Close the project								$1,200	$1,200
Total Planned Costs	$3,280	$5,200	$9,800	$11,000	$11,800	$7,840	$6,400	$1,200	$56,520
Total Actual Costs	$4,200	$5,000	$9,900						$19,100
Variance	($920)	$200	($100)						($820)

At the end of the third week, the plan was to have spent $18,280 ($3,280 + $5,200 + $9,800). However, the actual amount spent is $19,100 ($4,200 + $5,000 + $9,900). This means that the project is $820 over budget after three weeks. If this trend were to continue, the team could exceed its overall budget for the project.

The Project Manager should review the costs to date in order to determine the likelihood that this trend will continue during the remainder of the project and if any actions should be taken.

Monitor the Detailed Budget by comparing the planned costs to the actual costs incurred, making adjustments as required.

MONITORING THE RISKS

As the project proceeds, conditions may change, which could either increase or decrease the level of risk.

The Risk Register should be monitored during the execution of the project in order to do the following:

- Add new risks that become apparent
- Determine whether the probability or impact has changed for any of the risks
- Determine whether the risk response plans remain appropriate and are being performed as needed
- Determine whether the contingency plans remain appropriate and whether they should be put into action

The following demonstrates the Risk Register for the two risks related to the trade show materials.

DECO PRODUCTIONS	RISK REGISTER	
Project Name	DCV4Launch—DecoCam V4 Product Launch	
# Risk	**Risk Description**	**Risk Analysis**
6 Delivery of trade show materials is delayed.	Delivery of trade show materials is delayed.	• Probability: Likely (0.8) • Impact: Moderate (5) • Risk Score: 4.0
Risk Response Type	**Risk Response Plan**	**Contingency Plan**
Mitigate	Schedule trade show materials to be delivered at least one week before they are required.	Call suppliers to investigate the cause of the delay and determine ways to expedite the delivery. Inform the trade show team of the possible delay. This plan is triggered when materials are more than two days late from their original delivery date.
# Risk	**Risk Description**	**Risk Analysis**
5 Trade show material costs are higher than expected.	When ordering the trade show materials (e.g., the banner stand), the actual costs are higher than originally budgeted.	• Probability: Unlikely (0.2) • Impact: Low (2) • Risk Score: 0.4
Risk Response Type	**Risk Response Plan**	**Contingency Plan**
Accept	This risk is accepted, as the trade show material costs are a small percentage of the overall project budget.	Investigate alternative suppliers if available. Otherwise, the budget will be adjusted for the higher cost. This plan is triggered when the trade show material costs are 10% or more over budget.

For Risk #6, the Project Manager ensures the delivery date is scheduled as planned (one week before the trade show materials are required). If the delivery were late by two days or more, the Project Manager would invoke the contingency plan.

For Risk #5, the Project Manager reviews the material costs. If they are higher than the budgeted amount by 10% or more, the contingency plan is put into action.

This constant level of attention will help ensure that the Risk Response Plan remains current and relevant.

> Monitor the project risks to ensure that the risk response plans and contingency plans are performed as required.

CREATING THE COMMUNICATIONS

During the execution of the project, the Communication Management Plan should be periodically consulted to ensure that the planned communications are being carried out. These may be one-time communications (e.g., the company announcement on May 8) or recurring communications (e.g., the Project Status Report every Thursday at noon).

The effectiveness of the project's communications should be continually reviewed and assessed. This may result in adjustments to the Communication Management Plan to improve the level of communication.

> Monitor the project communications for effectiveness and make adjustments as required.

Case Study Update: Executing, Monitoring, and Controlling the Plan

With the project now in full swing, Sophie settles into her task of ensuring that all the deliverables of the project are created as planned. The design of the trade show banners has just been completed and has been reviewed by the Marketing department. Based on their feedback, a few minor adjustments were made, and the order was submitted on time.

(continued)

The project has been proceeding on schedule so far, though one of Sophie's team members (Eli) was sick for a couple of days, which caused some delays on his activities. Through a combination of adding some overtime hours and assigning Fatehjit to one of Eli's activities, the project was put back on schedule.

Sophie notices that the costs are running higher than expected after the first three weeks. She will look into this immediately, as she does not want the project to go over budget.

After opening the Risk Register, she scans each risk. One of the highest risks is that the written material produced by the project contains spelling or grammatical errors. She notices that the plan is to mitigate the risk through strict attention to quality processes in this area. She makes a mental note to add this to tomorrow's project team meeting agenda. Since Eli has been sick, Sophie considers whether she should increase the probability for Risk #7 ("The promotional video is late"). She updates the probability from "unlikely" to "possible." She will pay close attention to this risk over the next couple of weeks.

She has also been steadily working through the Communication Management Plan by making sure all of the planned communications have been scheduled. All are in place so far except for the final two communications (i.e., the company announcement and the Final Project Meeting), which will occur later in the project.

Overall, Sophie is feeling good about the progress of the project.

REPORTING THE STATUS OF THE PROJECT

Throughout a project, the progress made often varies from the project plan. At any time, the project may be ahead of or behind schedule and under or over budget, and more or less of the project scope may be completed. It is the nature of the planning process that there is some level of variance between the planned progress and the actual progress of the project.

However, it is important that the Project Manager and project stakeholders are aware of this variance. An accurate assessment of the project's current status allows the Project Manager to implement corrective measures as needed.

The status of the project is documented in a **Project Status Report**. For most projects, a weekly status report is recommended. The Project Status Report enhances the communication between the project team and the stakeholders. Many stakeholders are not involved in the day-to-day activities of the project, so the Project Status Report serves as their main window into the project.

The Project Status Reporting Process

The Project Status Report is produced by the Project Manager in consultation with the project team. To produce this report, the following steps need to be completed:

1. List the activities that the team members worked on during the past week, even if the work was not completed.
2. List the activities that the team members plan to work on during the next week of the project. Note that the same activity may be listed in steps 1 and 2. For example, if an activity started during the past week and will continue into next week, then it would be listed in each section.
3. List the current project issues. The Project Manager should review the list of outstanding issues and determine those issues that should be included on the status report. Some issues may not be significant enough to share with stakeholders outside of the project team.
4. List the recent changes to the project. Changes that have been made to the project since the last status report should be listed.
5. Based on the completion of the first four steps, identify the overall status of the project. While projects often have various positive and negative occurrences, it is important to report the overall condition of the project to provide clarity to the Project Sponsor and other stakeholders. A common method is to select one of following colours to describe the status of the project:
    *   Green: the project is on schedule to achieve its objectives according to the project plan.
    *   Yellow: the project is underperforming, and there is some risk that the project will not achieve its objectives according to the plan.
    *   Red: the project is experiencing significant problems, and there is a high level of risk that the project will not achieve its objectives according to the plan.

The template for the Project Status Report is as follows:

PROJECT STATUS REPORT	
Project Name	[This section contains the project name that should appear consistently on all project documents. Organizations often have project naming conventions.]
For Week Ending	[Date of the report]

(continued)

Project Status	[Green 🙂 , Yellow 😐 , or Red ☹]
Status Description	[Provide an overview of the project's current status. If the status is yellow or red, indicate the following: • The reason(s) why the status is yellow or red • The planned action(s) that will bring the project back to a green status]
Activities—During the Past Week	
[List all activities that the team members worked on during the past week of the project.]	
Activities—Planned for Next Week	
[List all activities that the team members will work on during the next week of the project.]	
Project Issues	
[List any issues that are significant and should be shared with the audience of this report. If any related work has been done or decisions have been made, a summary should be provided.]	
Project Changes	
[List any project changes that have been approved since the last report.]	

Case Study Update: Reporting the Status of the Project

Sophie is running late this morning, as it took a little longer than expected to drop her daughter off at daycare. Without bothering to take off her coat, she hurriedly signs in to the video meeting for the daily project team huddle.

On Thursday mornings, the main purpose of the meeting is to determine the current status of the project so that Sophie can complete the weekly Project Status Report.

Sophie reviews the work of the past week listed on the schedule. Each team member reports whether the work was completed or if any work remains to be done. Likewise, the work scheduled for the coming week is reviewed. Various comments are made regarding the viability of the plan and the possible adjustments needed. Sophie keeps notes on what is said throughout the meeting.

Next, any outstanding issues are reviewed, which often generates some lively discussion among the team. Afterward, Sophie ensures that the team is aware of any changes to the project plans that were approved during the past week.

Finally, she asks, "Is the project where it needs to be in order to complete successfully?" Sophie encourages the team to be completely transparent when reporting status updates. She wants her team to be as accurate as possible in their reporting, and she certainly does not want them to cover up any problems that may occur. While a yellow or red status is not desirable, as it attracts the attention of the Project Sponsor and other stakeholders, it allows Sophie to request additional resources if needed. In turn, the management of Deco Productions needs this early warning system in order to respond with assistance as required.

As the discussion goes on, it becomes clear that the project currently has a yellow status. The unresolved budget issue and the need to hire a new actor for the promotional video are both significant concerns.

As the discussion proceeds, Sophie updates the Project Status Report on her laptop. As documented in the Communication Management Plan, she needs to send this report to the Project Sponsor and other DecoCam V4 Project Managers by noon in preparation for the Project Status Review Meeting on Friday.

Sophie likes to involve the project team in the creation of the Project Status Report, not only because they are providing the information for the status updates, but also because it benefits the team to understand the current status of the project as a whole. Following the meeting, Sophie makes sure that any required updates are made to the project plans based on the team meeting. She then makes a few final edits to the Project Status Report and sends it to Arun and the other Project Managers. A quick glance at her watch shows that the time is 11:55 a.m. Smiling to herself, she is reminded why Thursday mornings are always busy.

Based on this work, the following Project Status Report is produced.

DECO PRODUCTIONS	**PROJECT STATUS REPORT**
Project Name	DCV4Launch—DecoCam V4 Product Launch
For Week Ending	Friday, April 10, 2026
Project Status	Yellow 😐
Status Description	The work of the project is proceeding well, with all tasks currently on schedule. The project is reporting a yellow project status for two main reasons: 1. The project is currently $820 over budget. 2. This first issue listed below (i.e., video concept taking longer than expected) could potentially delay the completion of the promotional video. The source of the budget increase is being investigated—more information to come. A high priority has been placed on reducing the duration of the work required to create the storyboard and script.

(continued)

Activities—During the Past Week
Create sign graphics/text
Order banner stands
Create holographic cards
Create social media strategy
Develop social media post content
Develop video concept
Develop storyboard and script
Activities—Planned for Next Week
Create holographic cards
Order holographic cards
Create mural for booth
Update product page
Develop online slideshow
Create outreach list
Develop storyboard and script
Project Issues
The development of the video concept took longer than expected, which has delayed the start of the storyboard and script. Sophie is reviewing options to shorten the duration of the work required to create the storyboard and script.
The demo version from the Development project is late—this is usually sent as part of the media outreach. More information has been requested from the Development project's Project Manager.
The Deco Productions company logo on the trade show banner is too small. No progress has been made on this issue.
The trade show banner stand selected is not available. No progress has been made on this issue.
Project Changes
The software required to create the multimedia demo was upgraded.

Project Dashboards

Project Dashboards may also be used to communicate the status of a project. At any point in time during a project, there may be aspects that are going very well (e.g., the schedule) and other aspects that are not going well (e.g., the budget). Project Dashboards provide summary information about these different aspects, which provides the stakeholders greater insight into the performance of the project.

Project Dashboards display certain key performance indicators for a project in graphical format:

- The status (green, yellow, or red) of the overall project and of each major deliverable

- The risk level for the overall project and for each major deliverable
- The status of the project's activities
- The status of the budget
- The status of project issues

There are many variations of Project Dashboards. Figure 11.2 shows a sample for the case study project.

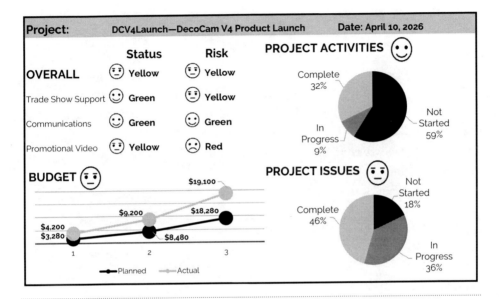

Figure 11.2: Project Dashboard

Report the status of the project on a periodic basis.

PROJECT QUALITY DURING THE EXECUTING PHASE

During the Planning Phase, the quality standards for the project were defined and recorded in the Quality Management Plan. During the Executing Phase, the quality of the project is managed and the project deliverables are verified in order to ensure that they meet these standards.

Two main functions accomplish this: Quality Assurance and Quality Control. While they are presented as separate functions, during projects they are often performed by the same individuals or team members, who may perform both functions repeatedly over a period a time.

Quality Assurance

Quality Assurance involves creating and updating project processes in order to effectively manage the quality of the project. This may be accomplished through a number of methods, such as conducting quality audits and continual process improvement. For example, a process could be established requiring all written material to be verified using a new spelling- and grammar-checking software application.

This aspect of Quality Assurance is ongoing—a never-ending quest to improve the way the project is performed. Quality Assurance is driven by the key quality concept of striving for issue prevention over inspection.

Of course, some level of inspection is usually required. Therefore, test cases for verifying the completed project deliverables are also developed. When creating these test cases, the project planning documents should be consulted, including the Project Requirements Document, Project Scope Statement, and Quality Management Plan. The test cases are documented in the **Quality Assurance Plan**.

The template for the Quality Assurance Plan is as follows:

QUALITY ASSURANCE PLAN		
Project Name	[This section contains the project name that should appear consistently on all project documents. Organizations often have project naming conventions.]	
Test Cases		
Deliverable	**Test Cases**	**Performed By**
[Work package from the WBS]	[A full description of the test(s) that should be performed to verify the quality of the work package]	[The name of the person(s) who should perform the test(s)]

Case Study Update: Performing Quality Assurance

Sophie has a small sign propped on her desk with the popular adage "Anything that can go wrong will go wrong." When she bought the sign at a novelty store a couple of years ago, she thought Murphy's law was just a funny quote. Now, after a few projects, she knows that it tends to be all too true.

For this reason, she puts a great deal of focus on Quality Assurance during her projects. As she planned in the Quality Management Plan, she holds biweekly quality audit meetings in order to create and improve project processes. Sophie is a great believer in creating effective processes that help to prevent problems from occurring. While Deco Productions has a standard list of Quality Assurance processes, she's always looking to enhance them for her project. For example, at one of the quality audit meetings, the following process improvements were identified:

- Deco Productions has recently acquired improved spelling- and grammar-checking software. The editing process for all written material will be updated to include running this new software.
- A new schedule process will be implemented. Whenever Sophie updates the schedule, a copy of the schedule will be placed in the project team's discussion forum. This will help ensure that each team member has the most up-to-date information.
- A new process will be introduced to the daily team huddle. Each team member will provide an informal demonstration of their deliverables as they are developed. This will lead to an increased awareness of each deliverable, resulting in fewer defects caused by communication problems.

Fatehjit also begins work on the Quality Assurance Plan that will be used to verify all of the deliverables produced during the project. Using the WBS as a guide, he scans the Project Scope Statement and Quality Management Plan as he develops the test cases. In a few instances, he also contacts the team member responsible for the deliverable in order to clarify his understanding.

The Quality Assurance Plan for the case study project is as follows:

DECO PRODUCTIONS	QUALITY ASSURANCE PLAN	
Project Name	DCV4Launch—DecoCam V4 Product Launch	
Test Cases		
Deliverable	**Description**	**Performed By**
Trade Show Signage	1. Spelling/grammar of all text contains no errors. 2. Graphics appear according to company standards. 3. Information on the banner is accurate (e.g., names, links, dates). 4. Banner stand meets the size requirements.	Fatehjit

(continued)

Deliverable	Description	Performed By
Booth Giveaways	1. Spelling/grammar of all text contains no errors. 2. Graphics appear according to company standards. 3. Information on the giveaway is accurate (e.g., names, links, dates).	Fatehjit
Multimedia Demo	1. Multimedia demo instructions contain no spelling/grammatical errors. 2. Multimedia demo instructions accurately describe the demo. 3. Repeated use of the demo does not cause dizziness or other physical effects.	Fatehjit
Social Media	1. Spelling/grammar of all text contains no errors. 2. All names and titles are correct.	Fatehjit
Website Updates	1. Spelling/grammar of all text contains no errors. 2. All names and titles are correct.	Fatehjit
Press Release	1. Spelling/grammar of all text contains no errors. 2. Information in the press release is accurate (e.g., names, links, dates). 3. Meets CP style standards.	Fatehjit
Video Plan	1. Storyboard includes all video requirements. 2. Script is complete for each storyboard frame.	Fatehjit
Video Production	1. Video is viewable on all major devices. 2. Spelling/grammar of all text contains no errors. 3. Information in the video is accurate (e.g., names, links, dates).	Maddy

Quality Assurance involves creating and updating project processes and plans to effectively manage the quality of the project.

Quality Control

During **Quality Control**, the deliverables are verified according to the test cases defined in the Quality Assurance Plan.

After the deliverables are created, the Quality Control processes are performed. Records are maintained regarding the success or failure of each test. If there is a failure, the defect is communicated to the appropriate project team member(s) to be resolved. Once the correction is made, the Quality Control processes are repeated to test the updated deliverable. This cycle is repeated until no defects are found.

If any subsequent changes are made to the deliverable, then the Quality Control processes would need to be repeated to ensure that a defect was not introduced because of the change.

Case Study Update: Performing Quality Control

As the deliverables are completed and each team member verifies their own work, Fatehjit gets involved to perform the tests defined in the Quality Assurance Plan. Fatehjit is responsible for most of the Quality Control for the project, though he and Maddy will jointly test the deliverables related to the video.

Over the years, Fatehjit has developed a keen eye for defects, particularly spelling errors. While the team's work in this area has been very good, they are always amazed at how he can quickly locate a misplaced letter or punctuation error that was not identified by the spelling- and grammar-checking software.

Fatehjit and Maddy make sure they keep detailed records of the tests performed and are aware of any changes that occur after a deliverable has been verified. Even the smallest change can affect the quality of a deliverable at any point in the project.

As Quality Control nears completion, the team grows increasingly confident about the overall quality of their product.

Quality Control involves the verification of the project deliverables to ensure they meet the defined quality standards.

KEY TERMINOLOGY

Crashing: Adding additional resources to activities in order to shorten the duration of a project

Earned Value Management: A project management methodology that integrates schedule, cost, and scope information in order to measure project performance

Fast-Tracking: The overlapping of activities in order to shorten the duration of a project

Project Dashboard: A report that provides a series of indicators that graphically summarize the current performance of a project

Project Procurement: The portion of project work that is performed externally by another organization

Project Status Report: A report that provides a description of the project's current status

Quality Assurance Plan: A document containing the processes that will be implemented to improve the level of project quality and a description of the tests that will be performed to verify the quality of the deliverables

Quality Control: The activities performed to verify the quality of the project deliverables according to the Quality Assurance Plan

Scope Creep: The gradual and uncontrolled growth of a project's scope

KEY CONCEPTS

1. Complete the activities of the project according to the schedule, making adjustments as needed.

2. Produce the deliverables according to the Project Scope Statement and Quality Management Plan.

3. Monitor the Detailed Budget by comparing the planned costs to the actual costs incurred, making adjustments as required.

4. Monitor the project risks, ensuring that the risk response plans and contingency plans are performed as required.

5. Monitor the project communications for effectiveness and make adjustments as required.

6. Report the status of the project on a periodic basis.

7. Quality Assurance involves creating and updating project processes and plans to effectively manage the quality of the project.

8. Quality Control involves the verification of the project deliverables to ensure they meet the defined quality standards.

DISCUSSION QUESTIONS

1. You are at the midpoint of a project and have used only 30% of your budget. Does this mean that you will be under budget at the end of the project?

2. Think of a project from your personal, work, or school experience in which the work started to fall behind schedule and was at risk of being late. What did you do to get the work back on schedule?

3. When indicating the overall status of the project, the colour green, yellow, or red is selected. Should combinations of colours also be allowed? For example, a status between yellow and red could be labelled as orange. Discuss the pros and cons of this approach.

4. Project Status Reports are usually produced on a weekly basis. Should they be produced more frequently or less frequently? Discuss the pros and cons of each option.

5. Perform an online search to research different Project Dashboard formats. Make a list of the information contained in these dashboards. What information do you think is the most important to include?

6. Perform an online search to research examples of Project Status Reports. List any additional information not mentioned in this text that may be included in the report.

7. One of your team members comes to you with an idea for continual improvement. His idea is that rather than having a second person test the quality of an output, simply having everyone verify their own output would be more efficient. How would you respond to this idea?

8. Quality Assurance and Quality Control are closely related concepts. Perform an online search to research "Quality Assurance versus Quality Control." Summarize your findings.

12 Managing Disruptions to the Plan—Issues and Change

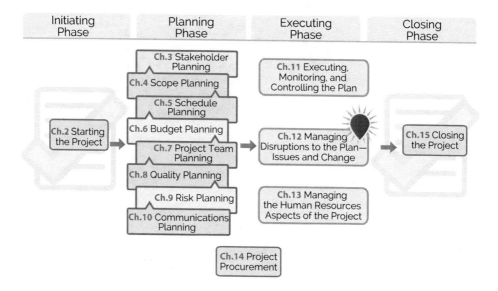

| Initiating Phase | Planning Phase | Executing Phase | Closing Phase |

Ch.3 Stakeholder Planning

Ch.4 Scope Planning

Ch.5 Schedule Planning

Ch.2 Starting the Project

Ch.6 Budget Planning

Ch.11 Executing, Monitoring, and Controlling the Plan

Ch.7 Project Team Planning

Ch.8 Quality Planning

Ch.9 Risk Planning

Ch.10 Communications Planning

Ch.12 Managing Disruptions to the Plan— Issues and Change

Ch.15 Closing the Project

Ch.13 Managing the Human Resources Aspects of the Project

Ch.14 Project Procurement

INTRODUCTION TO MANAGING DISRUPTIONS TO THE PLAN

Ideally, the execution of the project would consist of systematically completing each aspect of the project plan. All aspects of the plan would have been planned thoroughly, all estimates would be accurate, no one would change their mind, and nothing in the business environment would change during the project. Unfortunately, this is not the reality of most projects. Instead, as projects are executed, they are constantly being bombarded by disruptions to the previously completed plan. These disruptions include the following:

- Planning errors or omissions
- Project work taking longer than expected
- New information becoming available to the project
- Project team performance problems
- New or changing stakeholders
- New or changing technology
- Changes in the business environment

If they are not attended to, disruptions such as these will cause the project to underperform, as each disruption will cause the project to divert from its plan. As a result, the plan will become more difficult to manage successfully.

To prepare for this environment, it is vital to maintain sound processes to address project disruptions as they occur. There are two main processes: managing project issues and managing project change.

MANAGING PROJECT ISSUES

A project **issue** is a condition or situation that, if left unresolved, will reduce the performance or effectiveness of the project. In order to successfully complete the project, it is important that the Project Manager documents, prioritizes, and resolves issues effectively.

Recall that in chapter 9, project risks were discussed, including how to plan for their possible occurrence. However, issues and risks are not the same. An issue is something that is presently occurring during the project, whereas a risk is something that may occur in the future. If a risk does occur, it becomes an issue.

Documenting Issues

At any time, there are often many issues that are occurring for a project, especially for large or complex projects.

In order to manage the project effectively in this environment, a list of issues called an **Issue Log** is created. Not only does this provide a record of current issues, but it also provides a history of issues previously resolved by the project team. Issue Logs vary in terms of the information gathered for each issue, but at a minimum should contain a description of the issue, its priority, its current status, and a unique identifier. The Issue Log template is as follows:

ISSUE LOG				
Project Name	[This section contains the project name that should appear consistently on all project documents. Organizations often have project naming conventions.]			
Issue #	**Description**		**Priority**	**Status**
[1, 2, etc.]	[Full description of the issue with as much detail as needed or references to other documents. May include the name of the team member who has been assigned to resolve the issue. Once the issue is completed, this field should be updated to include the details of the resolution.]		[High/ Medium/ Low]	[Not started/ Started/ Completed/ NPW]

Assigning numbers to each issue is useful for instances when you may need to refer to a specific issue. For example, the project budget may have many related issues, and numbering the issues reduces the likelihood of confusing them.

Guidelines should be set for each priority value. For example, the high-priority designation could be used for critical issues that must be resolved immediately. The medium-priority designation could be used for important issues to be addressed only after all high-priority issues are resolved. Low-priority issues are relatively minor issues that may be addressed once all high- and medium-priority issues are resolved.

The status of each issue should be kept current. The normal progress of an issue would move from not started, to started, to completed. NPW stands for "not proceeded with" and should be used for issues that will not be addressed during the project.

Document project issues in an Issue Log.

Prioritizing Issues

It is useful to create the Issue Log using spreadsheet software that can filter and sort the issues according to their priority and/or status.

For example, the Project Manager could filter the spreadsheet to only show the not started issues and then sort them from high to low priority. This would clearly demonstrate the priority of issues that are not currently started.

Resolving Issues

In order to resolve issues, a problem-solving approach should be used. Depending on the size and complexity of an issue, this process may be performed formally, with written documentation and analysis (for large issues), or quickly and informally, with minimal documentation (for small issues). The steps in figure 12.1 describe a systematic problem-solving process.

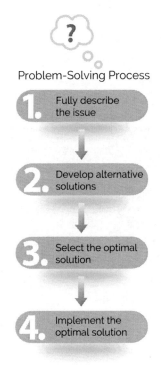

Figure 12.1: Problem-Solving Process

1. Fully Describe the Issue
In order to resolve the issue, it is important to fully describe the nature of the issue in as much detail as possible.

2. Develop Alternative Solutions
Depending on the nature of the issue, there are often many alternative solutions available. At this stage, it is important that different alternatives are considered and the team does not get locked into a single solution. For example, even in situations where an error occurs, at least two alternatives usually exist: correct the issue or do nothing (i.e., live with the issue).

Creative solutions should be considered at this point. Problems often cause the team to look at the project in different ways, which may help them to generate innovative solutions.

The costs and benefits of each alternative should be estimated. Some alternatives may solve the issue effectively but may cause an increase in the project budget or a delay in the project schedule. Other alternatives may solve the issue but may increase the risk for the project.

3. Select the Optimal Solution

In some instances, choosing the most appropriate solution to resolve an issue is straightforward. In cases where the choice is less obvious, a number of approaches may be used to select the optimal solution, including the following:

- Comparison of the costs and benefits: this approach tends to be useful when the costs and benefits are quantifiable and allow for an effective comparison.
- Weighted average: for this method, a set of criteria is developed for making the decision and a weight is assigned to each criterion. Then a score is assigned to each potential solution based on those weightings.

The following example illustrates how to assign weighted scores to potential project solutions. In the example, there are three different criteria: cost, timeliness, and effectiveness of the solution. The weights that are assigned are 20%, 30%, and 50% respectively. Two alternatives are ranked from 1 (poor) to 10 (best) for each of the criteria. Table 12.1 summarizes the results.

Table 12.1: Weighted Averages

	Cost (20%)		Time (30%)		Effective (50%)	
	Score	Weighted Score	Score	Weighted Score	Score	Weighted Score
Alternative 1	5	1.0	6	1.8	9	4.5
Alternative 2	8	1.6	6	1.8	5	2.5

The total weighted scores are as follows:

- Alternative 1: 1.0 + 1.8 + 4.5 = 7.3
- Alternative 2: 1.6 + 1.8 + 2.5 = 5.9

Therefore, based on the weighted averages, Alternative 1 would be the optimal solution to the issue.

If the selected alternative is within the project's approved budget, timeline, and scope, then the process will move on to step 4. However, if the selected alternative represents an increase to the approved budget, a delay to the timeline, or a change to the project scope, then additional approval may be required.

4. Implement the Optimal Solution

Once an optimal solution is selected, and in situations where the optimal solution is a correction or adjustment to the approved plans of the project, the actions required to implement this solution should be scheduled and performed. However, if the optimal solution involves a change to the approved plans of the project, then additional approval is required before the issue can be resolved. For more detail, see the Managing Project Change section later in this chapter.

During the resolution of issues, multiple issues often occur simultaneously, and there may be limited time to research different alternatives. Often the determination of alternatives and the optimal solution depends primarily on the expertise, experience, and intuition of the Project Manager and the project team. This highlights the importance of project planning and the creation of effective project plans. The planning process tends to immerse the Project Manager and project team in the details of the project, which is very useful when quick and effective decisions are needed to resolve issues.

Case Study Update: Resolving Issues

They start as a trickle, become a steady stream, and turn into a tsunami: problems! To Sophie, it seemed like every day something new was going wrong. The problems were coming from all angles. The execution of the project has just started, and already the following problems have occurred:

- The Deco Productions company logo on the trade show banner is too small.
- The trade show banner stand is not available.
- The price of the giveaways is 40% more than budgeted.
- The demo version from the Development project team is late—demos are usually sent as part of the media outreach.
- The first version of the multimedia demo isn't working as planned—the user experience is not very effective.
- The main actor signed for the promotional video was diagnosed with pneumonia and may need to be replaced.

During past projects, Sophie tried to solve each problem as it appeared. While this worked for small projects early in her career, on larger projects she became overwhelmed with issues and couldn't solve them as they arose. She would start to lose track of the status

(continued)

of the problem, which further compounded the issue. Now this seems to be happening again on this project.

Luckily, Sophie has developed a process that helps her manage the torrent of problems that often occur. As each issue is identified, she records the key information in an Issue Log that she keeps in a spreadsheet on her laptop before she tries to solve it. This has helped her to keep track of each issue and to prioritize them so that she and the team are working on the most important issues first.

For small, frequent issues, Sophie has learned to trust her instincts. She's found that with the knowledge gained during the planning of the project, along with past experience, she's able to solve most problems quickly and effectively. For larger issues, she uses a formal method of determining the alternatives and then selecting the optimal solution.

Sophie has found that problems and issues can be very disruptive to the project team. Some team members assume the worst and develop a negative outlook for the project, which can affect the morale of the entire team. To minimize this, Sophie encourages each team member to follow the problem-solving process. Taking a systematic approach to resolving issues tends to reduce the negative emotions by focusing the team on alternatives and solutions.

The six new issues that were added to the project's Issue Log are shown here. Note that these are in addition to the existing issues of the project.

DECO PRODUCTIONS			**ISSUE LOG**	
Project Name	DCV4Launch—DecoCam V4 Product Launch			
Issue #	**Description**		**Priority**	**Status**
13	The Deco Productions company logo on the trade show banner is too small.		Medium	Not started
14	The trade show banner stand is not available.		Medium	Not started
15	The price of the giveaways is 40% more than budgeted. • Chris verified that the original estimate was too low. No further action to be taken.		Low	NPW
16	The demo version from the Development project team is late—demos are usually sent as part of the media outreach. • Sophie requested more information from the Project Manager of the Development project team. Sarah will consider alternatives once this information is received.		Medium	Started

17	The first version of the multimedia demo isn't working as planned—the user experience is not very effective. • Decision made to upgrade the demo software to a newer version. • Chris tested the new version and resolved the issue.	High	Completed
18	The main actor signed for the promotional video was diagnosed with pneumonia and may need to be replaced. • Decision made to hire a new actor. • Maddy is working with the Resource Manager to hire a new actor.	High	Started

Using spreadsheet software, the Issue Log can be easily sorted according to the priority and/or status columns. For example, the Issue Log could be sorted from high- to low-priority issues.

 Resolve issues in priority order using a systematic problem-solving approach.

MANAGING PROJECT CHANGE

Once a project's plans are approved, any potential additions or modifications to the plan should be considered changes. It is very common to make changes during a project. As a project progresses, the business environment often changes, which brings new requirements; errors in planning are discovered; and new ideas are suggested. Through the process of resolving issues (see previous section), requests for changes may also occur. It can sometimes seem that the project is in a constant state of change.

However, these changes may be beneficial to the project. The new information received, whether from new requirements, corrected plans, or new ideas, may result in an improvement to the results of the project.

On the other hand, changes can be disruptive to the project's execution. Each time a change is made, plans need to be updated and work may need to be redone. Changes, particularly those made quickly or at the last minute, can introduce defects to the project. Changes may also dampen the mood of the project team, who may become increasingly uncertain about whether further changes will be coming.

As discussed in chapter 11: "Executing, Monitoring, and Controlling the Plan," scope creep may also occur, causing small, incremental changes to occur in the project scope. If scope creep is not controlled, the small changes may significantly increase the project scope over time and ultimately negatively affect the project.

The challenge is to determine which changes should be implemented because they are beneficial to the project and which should not be implemented because they are disruptive to the project. To help make this determination, a **change control process** should be developed.

As part of developing a change control process, a person or group who will approve changes should be identified. Normally, this would include the Project Sponsor. However, in large projects, this role could be performed by a committee of individuals from across the organization.

For changes that are proposed during a project, the steps shown in figure 12.2 are performed.

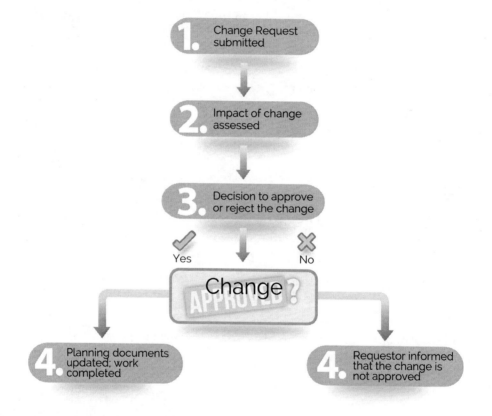

Figure 12.2: Change Control Process

The following is additional information about each step in the change control process:

1. A **Change Request** is submitted by the person requesting the change. This request should include the following information:
    *   A description of the requested change
    *   A description of the potential benefit to the project resulting from the change

2. The Project Manager, in consultation with project team members, assesses any impacts to the project including the following:
   - An increase in the cost of the project
   - A delay to the end date of the project or other milestones
   - A change to the capabilities of the delivered outcomes of the project
   - A change to the level of risk present for the project
3. The information contained in steps 1 and 2 is presented to the person or committee that approves the changes. This may be done either as the change is requested or on a periodic basis (e.g., weekly). Based on a comparison of the benefits and impact, a decision is made to either approve or reject the change.
4. If the change is approved, the appropriate planning documents (e.g., project schedule, Project Scope Statement) should be updated to reflect the change and the work should be performed as required. If not approved, the person requesting the change should be informed.

The following is the template for a Change Request:

DECO PRODUCTIONS	**CHANGE REQUEST**
Project Name	[This section contains the project name that should appear consistently on all project documents. Organizations often have project naming conventions.]
Requested by	[Name of the person requesting the change]
Request Date	[The date this form was submitted]
1. Description of the Requested Change (Completed by the Requestor)	
[Complete description of the requested change to the project]	
2. Benefit of the Requested Change (Completed by the Requestor)	
[Complete description of the benefit to the project if the requested change is made]	
3. Impacts to the Project (Completed by the Project Manager)	
[Complete description of the impact to the project's scope, quality, schedule, cost, risk, etc.]	
4. Change Request Decision (Completed by the Project Change Committee)	
[An indication of whether the change is approved in full, approved in part, or rejected]	

Case Study Update: Managing Project Change

Just as Sophie arrives in the morning, she sees a message from Chris Sandburg, the Graphic Designer assigned to the project, asking her to contact him about the trade show giveaways deliverable. Seeing that he is currently online in the Morocco office, she starts a video call with him. Once they connect, he begins talking excitedly about a great idea that came to him on the way to work.

"Instead of producing postcards for the trade show giveaways, why don't we change them to look like picture frames? This will support the idea that DecoCam can do more than make a postcard."

Even though the timing is very tight to make this change, Sophie asks Chris to fill out a Change Request so that the idea will be considered as soon as possible.

That afternoon, Sophie checks her email inbox and notices that she has received another request for a possible change. In the email, Zoe Purdie of the DecoCam V4 Development project indicates that a special version of the DecoCam software could be created and used in the multimedia demo, providing a superior experience for the trade show participants. In her reply, Sophie thanks Zoe for sending the idea and asks her to complete a Change Request.

Both requests are received later that day. Due to the tight timing, Sophie meets with her team members immediately in order to develop accurate estimates of the potential impact of making each change.

The next day, the Project Change Committee has its weekly meeting. The members of the committee are Sophie Featherstone, the Project Manager; Arun Singh, the Project Sponsor; and Fatehjit Kumar, the Business Analyst. The committee reviews both Change Requests and discusses the pros and cons of each at length. The postcard/picture frame Change Request is approved, as the committee feels that the benefit is significant for a relatively modest cost. While they are tempted by the benefits of the multimedia request, they feel that the cost and the risk of errors occurring at the trade show are just not worth it. Therefore, this request is not approved.

After the meeting, Sophie checks her notes and makes the appropriate changes to the project plans. The Project Scope Statement is updated to reflect the change in scope, and the Project Budget is updated to reflect the change in the project cost. The project schedule is not affected.

The following are the two Change Requests that were created:

DECO PRODUCTIONS   **CHANGE REQUEST**

Project Name	DCV4Launch—DecoCam V4 Product Launch
Requested by	Chris Sandburg
Request Date	April 7, 2026

**1. Description of the Requested Change
(Completed by the Requestor)**

Change the trade show giveaways to resemble a picture frame rather than a postcard.

**2. Benefit of the Requested Change
(Completed by the Requestor)**

A picture frame would more accurately demonstrate the benefit of the DecoCam software—it would allow the user to take outstanding pictures that would subsequently be framed. A postcard may be confusing, as it suggests a travel theme, which is unrelated to DecoCam.

**3. Impacts to the Project
(Completed by the Project Manager)**

The impacts to the project are as follows:
• There is no change to the work effort or project schedule.
• The supplier could produce a card that would resemble a picture frame. The unit cost would increase from $1.00 to $1.20. For the 2,000 cards that will be ordered, this results in a $400 budget increase to order the cards.
• There is no change in the quality.
• There is no change to the risk.

**4. Change Request Decision
(Completed by the Project Change Committee)**

The Project Change Committee approved this request. The picture frame trade show giveaway will be more effective and memorable than the postcard. This benefit outweighed the $400 cost increase.

DECO PRODUCTIONS   **CHANGE REQUEST**

Project Name	DCV4Launch—DecoCam V4 Product Launch
Requested by	Zoe Purdie
Request Date	April 7, 2026

**1. Description of the Requested Change
(Completed by the Requestor)**

Develop a modified version of the DecoCam V4 software to be used in the trade show multimedia demo.

(continued)

2. Benefit of the Requested Change (Completed by the Requestor)
The modified version would have restricted functionality but would allow the user to fully experience the system rather than using the simulated slideshow application that is currently being planned.
3. Impacts to the Project **(Completed by the Project Manager)**
The impacts to the project are as follows: • The modified version of the software could be completed for $6,000. • There is no change to the project schedule. • There is an increased risk that the new software contains errors that become evident during the trade show.
4. Change Request Decision **(Completed by the Project Change Committee)**
The Project Change Committee rejected this request. While the potential for this modified software is appealing, the increased cost would cause the project to exceed its $60,000 budget. As well, the increased potential for problems at the trade show is not acceptable.

Resolve project Change Requests by using a change control process.

KEY TERMINOLOGY

Change Control Process: A formal process to approve or reject proposed changes to the project

Change Request: A document containing information related to a proposed project change that is used during the change control process

Issue: A condition or situation that, if left unresolved, will reduce the performance or effectiveness of the project

Issue Log: A document containing information about the project issues that have occurred

KEY CONCEPTS

1. Document project issues in an Issue Log.
2. Resolve issues in priority order using a systematic problem-solving approach.
3. Resolve project Change Requests by using a change control process.

DISCUSSION QUESTIONS

1. The problem-solving process described in this chapter could be viewed as being slow and ponderous by some who might want to just "do something" quickly. How would you respond to this viewpoint?

2. Do all issues result in Change Requests? Explain why issues would and would not require the change control process.

3. When developing a change control process, who should approve the proposed changes? Describe the factors that should be considered when making this decision.

4. Perform an online search to research project issues. Summarize five common issues that occur during projects.

5. Should all issues in the Issue Log be listed on the Project Status Report? What types of issues should potentially not be included?

13 Managing the Human Resources Aspects of the Project

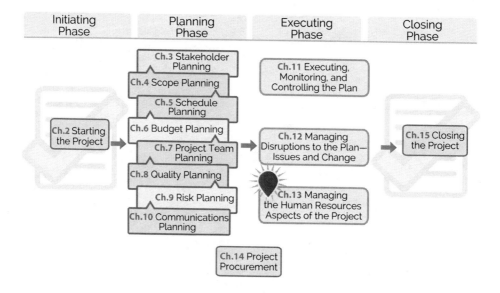

INTRODUCTION TO MANAGING THE HUMAN RESOURCES ASPECTS OF THE PROJECT

Projects are performed by people (the project team) for people (the project stakeholders). The way that each of these groups interacts has a tremendous bearing on the success of the project. It is therefore important to focus on the management of the people aspects of the project.

In order for a project to be successful, Project Managers need to accomplish the objectives of the project through the work of others. This involves actions such as assigning work to be completed, making decisions, achieving consensus, and resolving conflict.

UNDERSTANDING POWER AND INFLUENCE

In many organizations, the Project Manager has the responsibility to complete the project but often lacks the positional power of others in the organization, such as the Directors and Vice-Presidents. Team members are assigned to the project team but do not always report directly to the Project Manager. In order to function effectively in this environment, Project Managers will benefit from an understanding of **power** and **influence** and their effective use (see figure 13.1).

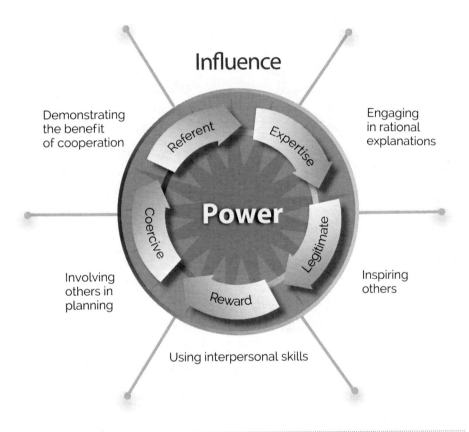

Figure 13.1: Power and Influence

Power

The concept of power was introduced in chapter 3 and was defined as the capacity to influence others to change their attitude and behaviour. People derive power from a number of sources. Research performed by J. R. P. French and B. H. Raven (1959, p. 151) identified the following five sources of power.

Referent Power

Referent power is based on people's desire to be identified with an individual. Someone with referent power inspires trust, respect, and admiration, which may be earned through their ethical and honest behaviour as well as their interpersonal skills, energy, and charisma.[1]

Imagine you are working for an organization and there are two managers you interact with:

- The first manager is someone you admire due to their honesty, their integrity, and their general concern for your welfare. You find yourself feeling positive when working for this manager.
- The second manager is someone you do not trust due to their words and behaviour. You find yourself feeling negative when working for this manager.

If each manager asks you to do something, it is much more likely that you will enthusiastically perform the task for the first manager, perhaps even going above and beyond what was asked. As for the second manager, the likely outcome is that you would only comply with the request because they "are your boss."

Expertise Power

Expertise power is based on the perception of the individual's knowledge and expertise. That is, we are more likely to be influenced by someone we perceive as being knowledgeable, compared to someone we perceive as not being knowledgeable.

As an example of expertise power, say that you have a minor ailment, and you receive advice from two sources: your doctor and a friend who read something about your symptoms online. You are much more likely to be influenced by the advice of your doctor, given your perception of their expertise relative to that of your friend.

---

[1]   Some people speculate that the researchers published a typo and meant this to be "reverent" power. Reverence is really what is described here.
(See https://en.wikipedia.org/wiki/Referent_power#:~:text=Referent%20power%20may%20be%20 defined,appropriate%20label%20being%20reverent%20power.)

Legitimate Power

Legitimate power is based on the individual's formal position within an organization.

Imagine that you are working for an organization and following takes place:

- Your co-worker asks you to help them complete a task that is required by the end of the day.
- The Vice-President of your division asks you to produce a report, also by the end of day.

Because of the Vice-President's legitimate power, it is much more likely that you will comply with their request rather than your co-worker's request.

Reward Power

Reward power is based on the ability to provide resources, pay raises, promotions, and so on to others.

If you are working as a salesperson, there will likely be a sales incentive or bonus structure that forms part of your compensation. This tends to influence you to sell more products or work harder for the organization.

Coercive Power

Coercive power is based on the ability to penalize others or withdraw privileges.

As an example of coercive power, you are working for a manager who provides your annual performance review and future salary increases. Your concern that you could receive a negative review or low salary increase would motivate your performance.

There are many considerations involved in a Project Manager's power. As discussed, Project Managers have limited legitimate power and therefore cannot generally rely heavily on this source. A Project Manager's reward power will be restricted by the project budget and is therefore also limited. Power through coercive methods is generally only used in rare circumstances and is not recommended as an ongoing approach.

This leaves referent and expertise power as the key sources of power for Project Managers. Referent power should be continually developed through a number of approaches, including the effective use of communication, interpersonal skills, honesty, and ethical behaviour. Project Managers should also continually increase their expert power by adopting an attitude of continual learning and by understanding the knowledge they require in order to effectively manage a project.

Influence

The development of power is not an end in itself but instead is required in order to influence others. Influence is defined as the exercise of power to bring about change. There are many tactics that may be used to influence people, such as the following:

Engaging in Rational Explanations

This method of influence involves convincing others through sound reasoning and explanations. In many instances, if the logic of an approach or decision is effectively communicated, others will be more likely to comply.

> During a project, team members could disagree about whether the image files should be in JPG or PNG format. In this case, the Project Manager could list the pros and cons of each format—engaging in rational explanations—in order to determine the optimal format and to increase the support of the decision by the team members.

Inspiring Others

This method involves inspiring others with a higher purpose or vision that goes beyond the details of the scope of the project.

> During a project to create a light rail transit system, team members may become demotivated due to the long duration and difficulty of the project. To help influence the team, the Project Manager may communicate the higher purpose of light rail transit: to provide economical transportation, especially for disadvantaged groups, and to reduce carbon emissions.

Using Interpersonal Skills

This method involves the use of interpersonal skills such as communication, empathy, and a willingness to listen, as well as acts of thoughtfulness or kindness. This is often very effective, as others will respond similarly to how they are treated.

During a project, a team member comes to the Project Manager to say that they need to take off a few days to look after a sick relative. Instead of just reading them the HR policy for personal emergencies, the Project Manager shows genuine concern for the team member, including how they are feeling, and explores additional ways to help the team member. The team member appreciates the concern and works diligently on the project once they return.

Involving Others in the Planning Process

This method involves not just presenting a plan to others but also involving them in the planning process and seeking out their advice. This tends to increase support for the plan, as they will have a sense of ownership for it.

 A Project Manager realizes that their project is running late and that overtime will likely be required. Rather than just announcing this decision to the team, the Project Manager discusses the schedule issue with them and asks for their input. Together, they develop a plan that includes a number of schedule improvements, including some overtime. Being involved in the planning process increases the project team's support for the plan.

Demonstrating the Benefit of Cooperation

This method involves showing how a certain course of action would benefit the other person. This requires empathy in order to see things from their point of view. This can also be described as finding win-win solutions.

 During a project, a team member may not want to perform a certain task, as it is something they haven't done before. Rather than forcing the team member to do so, the Project Manager points out that acquiring this new skill would position them for new and interesting project roles. The team member feels better about taking on the new task.

The effectiveness of each of the above influencing techniques is enhanced to varying degrees by the Project Manager's power. Project Managers should therefore be continually considering and developing their sources of power. The use of power and influence better enables the Project Manager to manage the project team, manage stakeholder relationships, and resolve conflict during the project.

Case Study Update: Understanding Power and Influence

Periodically, Sophie reflects on her work experience prior to becoming a Project Manager. Her background is in business communications, and her first job at Deco Productions was as a Communications Specialist.

Once she became a Project Manager, she assumed that, because of her position, she could just tell people what to do and they would do it. However, she quickly realized that, because her team members didn't report directly to her (they reported to other managers in the organization), she lacked this type of positional power.

She shudders when she thinks of some of her early projects. On one project, she set up a series of deadlines and pointed out team members who didn't meet their deadlines during the weekly team meetings. She quickly found that her team members felt they were being publicly shamed in front of their teammates and were being punished for delays that were often beyond their control. Instead of being motivated, the team was becoming hostile toward her. On another project, she decided to give out small bonuses and gift certificates whenever team members achieved something exceptional. But then she found that team members started to expect a bonus and were demotivated if they didn't receive one. In addition, she exceeded her discretionary budget halfway through the project.

Over time, she came to realize that she shouldn't rely on the use of rewards or disciplinary actions to influence her team. Instead, she found that her team would be much more likely to perform effectively if she gained their confidence and respect. She now focuses on activities such as the following:

- Interacting with each team member on a personal level
- Involving team members in the decision-making process
- Being flexible and open to new ideas, including admitting when she is wrong
- Clearly communicating the reasons for project decisions and actions

The results of her efforts have been positive. Team members see her not only as a competent Project Manager but also as a reasonable and fair person. Sophie learned the hard way how important power and influence can be when managing people. She keeps these strategies in mind as she completes her current project.

Project Managers should develop their sources of power in order to increase their effective use of influence during the project.

MANAGING THE PROJECT TEAM

The stakeholder group that normally requires the Project Manager's greatest attention is the project team. Team management consists of the following two functions:

- Managing the project team's activities
- Building the project team's capabilities

Managing the Project Team's Activities

An important aspect of the Project Manager role is to manage the performance of team members as they complete the work of the project. P. Hersey, K. Blanchard, and D. Johnson (2013, pp. 124–128) theorized that the management style used should match the characteristics of the team member. That is, Project Managers should vary their approach depending on the expertise of each team member (see figure 13.2).

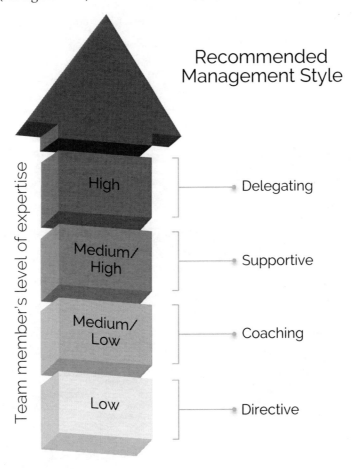

Figure 13.2: Recommended Management Style

Each management style, from the lowest level of team member expertise to the highest, is as follows:

- Directive involves close supervision, including providing direct instructions and frequent reviews of their work.
- Coaching involves less supervision, with the Project Manager providing guidance and coaching to the team member.
- Supportive involves very little supervision and direction, with support and encouragement provided as needed.
- Delegating involves very little involvement by the Project Manager other than periodic updates. Responsibility for completion of the work is delegated to the team member.

During projects, particularly those with long durations, the expertise levels of team members may change during the project.

The use of the Project Manager's power and influence will be important for the effective completion of the work assignments. During the project, there will be many interactions between the Project Manager and team members where additional work may be required, an additional approach may be suggested, or a new issue may need to be solved.

Case Study Update: Managing the Project Team's Activities

Sophie studies the project schedule, reviewing which team members are assigned to each project activity. During a recent team meeting, the schedule was distributed to all team members to ensure that everyone was aware of their own activities.

However, this isn't the end of Sophie's involvement. She considers each of her team members and how she should manage them:

- The Communications Specialist: the company has recently hired Sarah, and while she's eager to learn, she's also inexperienced. Sophie will work very closely with her, helping her draft a daily to-do list and encouraging her to ask questions as they arise.

- The Marketing Specialist: Maddy has been in her current position for over a year and is becoming comfortable in her role. Sophie makes a mental note to drop by to see her every few days to provide support as needed.
- The Graphic Designer: Chris has extensive experience. Unless he asks a question or raises an issue, Sophie does not need to spend additional time with him.

She continues this process with each of the remaining team members. She feels confident about her planned interaction with each team member, as she'll be able to provide the right amount of time and support for their needs.

The Project Manager should vary their management style according to the expertise level of each team member.

Building the Project Team's Capabilities

The goal of the Project Manager should be to help team members achieve a higher state of expertise and productivity. This benefits the project in a number of ways, including increased output, lower costs, and higher-quality deliverables.

The expertise and productivity of team members will generally improve without intervention, as the completion of the work itself will increase a team member's experience. This can be enhanced through the following:

- The team member may undergo training, either formally within a class-room or online course or informally through on-the-job mentoring. Time may be set aside in the project schedule for training.
- Ongoing feedback should be provided, particularly for team members with lower levels of expertise. This may take the form of day-to-day informal feedback or regularly scheduled formal appraisals.

The Project Manager should also create a positive environment in which the project team can effectively perform. Timely recognition of an individual's or team's accomplishments can be a powerful motivator for increased performance. This recognition may be financial (e.g., bonus, paid lunch) or non-financial (e.g., thanking the team for their efforts).

The Project Manager should also consider the use of team-building activities to create an effective team environment. Team-building activities may be informal (e.g., fostering an open-door policy) or organized (e.g., organizing an occasional team lunch or social event). Activities such as these are helpful, as teams usually perform more effectively as familiarity among members increases.

Case Study Update: Building the Project Team's Capabilities

As she organizes her project team, Sophie's thoughts turn to the performance of her team. She knows that the success of the project is tied to how well her team members perform individually and as a group.

Deco Productions supports the team members' ongoing skills training by sending employees to take courses as needed. Sophie also knows that on-the-job training takes place during her projects, and she allots time for this within her project schedule.

While these training opportunities will improve individual performance, Sophie knows that the group also needs to perform effectively as a team. She recalls one of her projects from a couple of years ago when it looked like she had a very strong team. Each person assigned to her project was competent in their respective fields. However, once the project was underway, Sophie realized that something was wrong. The team seemed to act more like a group of strangers, and the reduced communication and cooperation among them began to negatively affect the project. She also found that the team became consumed by the amount of work required and the project issues, creating a dark cloud over the project. The end result was a failed project with many of the team members blaming each other for the failure.

For the DecoCam project, a number of the team members do not know each other well, so there is a chance that history could repeat itself. Sophie plans to gather her team at a local restaurant and pay for the first couple of appetizers. It will serve as an informal project kickoff and help the team members get to know each other outside of the day-to-day work. Chris happens to be travelling to the main office from the Morocco office for some other meetings, so she schedules this gathering to coincide with his trip.

Additionally, Sophie likes to begin her team meetings with humorous stories about the latest thing that her four-year-old daughter said or some unlikely situation that occurred during a family outing. Often, other team members share their own stories as well. This tends to bring the team closer together, lighten the mood, and create a positive environment in which the team can tackle the challenges in front of them.

Sophie hopes these types of team-building activities will help her avoid the pitfalls of the previous project.

The Project Manager should strive to build the capabilities of the project team.

MANAGING THE STAKEHOLDER RELATIONSHIPS

In addition to interacting with the project team, the Project Manager also interacts with a number of other project stakeholders during the project. During project planning, an analysis of the project stakeholders and the development of a Stakeholder Engagement Plan were completed.

As the project is executed, the Project Manager should continue to engage with the various project stakeholders. Based on these interactions, the Stakeholder Engagement Plan should be continually refined as required. As with the management of team members, the Project Manager's power and use of influence are extremely important, especially since many project stakeholders often possess more legitimate power than the Project Manager does.

Case Study Update: Managing the Stakeholder Relationships

It's the end of a long week, and the pace of the project is increasing significantly. At this point, it can be easy to get swept up into the urgent daily activities of the project.

Even though she is busy, Sophie spends a few minutes each week considering her ongoing relationship with the project stakeholders. She pulls up the Stakeholder Engagement Plan on her laptop to review her planned actions with each stakeholder. The plan has been updated numerous times throughout the project as Sophie has gained a greater understanding of the project and its stakeholders.

Looking at the plan, she jots down a couple of new entries on her daily to-do list. She hasn't dropped by to see Casey lately, so she adds this to the list. She also realizes that there have been a few changes to her schedule and that she should send a quick update to the other DecoCam Project Managers. They always appreciate these extra updates that she sends.

After a few additional updates to the Stakeholder Engagement Plan, she saves the file and closes her laptop. Looking at her to-do list, she decides to head to Casey's office first.

The Project Manager should continually engage with the project stakeholders as defined in the Stakeholder Engagement Plan.

MANAGING CONFLICT

The goal of creating something unique in a finite period of time with a limited budget can lead to situations where conflict is likely. Disagreements are common during projects, both within the project team and with project stakeholders.

Some level of conflict is productive for a project. A moderate level of disagreement is a sign that stakeholders are able to provide input to the project, and these discussions can result in superior project designs and solutions. However, a high level of conflict can cause the project to become unproductive.

As discussed in other sections of this chapter, the Project Manager's power and use of influence are important because conflict management relies heavily on communication and interpersonal relationships.

R. R. Blake and J. S. Mouton (1975, p. 31) created the following model to manage conflict. For any given situation where conflict exists, there are two characteristics that need to be determined:

- The importance of the situation (rated from low to high): some situations causing conflict are fairly minor or trivial, while others may be critical.
- The importance of maintaining the relationship between the people involved in the conflict (rated from low to high): in some situations, when the people will continue to work together during the current and future projects, the importance of maintaining the relationship is likely to be high. On the other hand, when future contact is unlikely or likely only in emergency situations, the importance is likely to be low.

Once these two characteristics are determined, a suitable conflict management approach can be chosen, as shown in figure 13.3.

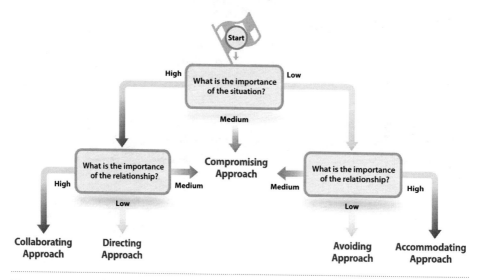

Figure 13.3: Conflict Management

Table 13.1 explains each conflict management approach.

Table 13.1: Description of Conflict Management Approaches

		Low	Medium	High
Importance of Situation	High	**Directing** *(situation—high, relationship—low)* This approach involves resolving the conflict without input from the other party. It is often used in situations such as emergencies or the enforcement of company policies.		**Collaborating** *(situation—high, relationship—high)* This approach involves both parties working together to develop a solution to the conflict. Because of this collaboration, this approach usually takes the greatest amount of time compared to the other conflict management approaches.
	Medium		**Compromising** *(situation—medium, relationship—medium)* This approach involves each side conceding something in order to achieve an agreement. This varies from collaboration in that compromise involves finding a middle ground, while collaboration involves developing alternative solutions and possibilities.	
	Low	**Avoiding** *(situation—low, relationship—low)* This approach involves not participating in, or withdrawing from, the conflict. This is appropriate, as the importance of both the situation and the relationship is deemed unimportant.		**Accommodating** *(situation—low, relationship—high)* This approach involves adapting to the other person's viewpoint. Not only does this eliminate the conflict over an unimportant situation, but it also tends to generate goodwill that may be useful for future interactions.
		Low	Medium	High
			Importance of Relationship	

Managing conflict is important during projects because if it is not addressed, it will likely affect not only the situation causing the conflict but also the ongoing stakeholder relationships. Stakeholder management is important because all of the conflict management approaches are more easily and effectively implemented if there is a strong relationship with the stakeholders involved.

Additionally, for each of the conflict management approaches, the use of appropriate interpersonal skills is beneficial. For example, the directing approach does not imply that the interpersonal style should be harsh. An open and respectful interpersonal style is recommended regardless of which approach is chosen.

Case Study Update: Managing Conflict

One of the things that Sophie didn't realize when she became a Project Manager was the number of disagreements that would occur. At times, by the end of the week, she feels like a referee! But over time, by analyzing the characteristics of each new conflict, she has more success with conflict management.

Just this week, there were two potential conflicts with her Project Sponsor. Arun is a key stakeholder of the project, and maintaining a positive relationship with him is very important. The first conflict arose because Arun felt strongly that the project should be completed one week earlier so that the Marketing team would be able to create a better marketing plan for the DecoCam V4 project. Sophie saw this as a significant change that could affect the budget of the project and add significant risk. To address this conflict, she booked a meeting with Arun during which they explored each of their concerns and searched for possible solutions. In the end, they settled on a new approach: the original project due date will be maintained, but Sophie will meet with the Marketing team one week before this due date to present all of the product launch deliverables. By using a collaborative approach, both Sophie and Arun were satisfied with the resolution.

The second conflict had to do with the weekly status report. As part of the Communication Management Plan, Arun receives a weekly status report, sent as an electronic file attached to an email. Arun recently requested that Sophie also send him a printed copy of the report. Sophie sighed when she received the request, as this is just one more thing she would need to do each week. In addition, the company policy has been to reduce paper use wherever possible. However, when she thinks about it, this issue really isn't important to her, and apparently it's important to Arun. Therefore, she accommodates the request by adding this extra step to her weekly processes.

Also during the week, Sophie ran into a situation with her project team. During a team meeting, Sarah and Eli said that rather than recording the number of hours that they worked on the project on a daily basis, they would prefer to estimate their hours at the end of the project. Sophie explained why having current information on a regular basis is useful to her effective management of the project. This satisfies Sarah, but Eli digs in and states that he still doesn't want to record his hours during the project. Given the high importance of timely project information and that this is a company policy that cannot be changed, Sophie takes a directing approach and lets Eli know that while she understands his concerns, it must be done.

A day later, one of the employees from the Finance department drops by her office. It seems that her team was "very loud" as they celebrated the completion of a key milestone earlier in the week. She asks Sophie to speak to her team to make sure they are quiet next time. Sophie recalls that she was probably laughing the loudest at the meeting. Overall, she feels that this issue is somewhat trivial since it was a very brief period of celebrating and they didn't exceed the normal noise levels in the office. She also doesn't know the employee and probably won't have any further interactions with her. She thanks the employee for the feedback but politely indicates that she won't be pursuing this further. By avoiding any further discussion, she limits the time spent on this issue. She doesn't expect to hear any more about it.

And finally, while meeting with the Project Managers of the other DecoCam V4 projects, two of the Project Managers ask if the Project Status Report could be sent to them by 8:00 a.m. on Thursdays, rather than by noon. They would like more time to prepare for the Friday meeting. This concerns Sophie, as she usually arrives at the office at 8:30 a.m., after dropping her daughter off at daycare. She feels that it's not an overly important issue, though she knows that maintaining a good relationship with the other Project Managers is important. They reach a compromise that the Project Status Report will be sent by 10:00 a.m.

By the end of the week, Sophie feels she has effectively managed each of the conflicts that came up. She is sure, though, that there will be more problems to address next week.

The Project Manager should assess and manage conflict between project stakeholders to ensure the effective execution of the project.

KEY TERMINOLOGY

Influence: The exercise of power to bring about change

Power: The capacity to influence others to change their attitude and behaviour

KEY CONCEPTS

1. Project Managers should develop their sources of power in order to increase their effective use of influence during the project.

2. The Project Manager should vary their management style according to the expertise level of each team member.

3.   The Project Manager should strive to build the capabilities of the project team.

4.   The Project Manager should continually engage with the project stakeholders as defined in the Stakeholder Engagement Plan.

5.   The Project Manager should assess and manage conflict between project stakeholders to ensure the effective execution of the project.

DISCUSSION QUESTIONS

1.   Review the five sources of power. Which one do you think is your greatest source of power? Which is your weakest?

2.   For each source of power, an example was provided. What is another example of each source of power?

3.   Consider the different approaches to influence others mentioned in this chapter. Which approach do you use most often? Is there another approach that would be more effective?

4.   For each of the different approaches to influence, an example was provided. For each example, what would be the primary source of power that would enable the use of influence?

5.   Think of a recent conflict that you were involved in. What approach did you use to manage the conflict? According to the conflict management model, what approach should have been used?

6.   Perform an online search to research project team development. List any additional team development ideas that you find beyond those described in this chapter.

14 Project Procurement

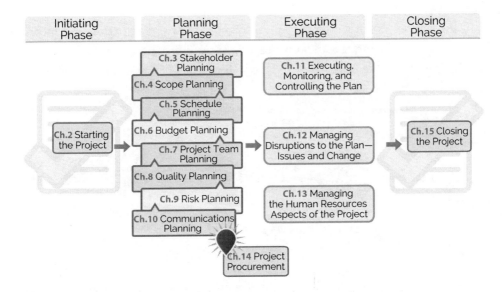

Initiating Phase	Planning Phase	Executing Phase	Closing Phase

- Ch.2 Starting the Project
- Ch.3 Stakeholder Planning
- Ch.4 Scope Planning
- Ch.5 Schedule Planning
- Ch.6 Budget Planning
- Ch.7 Project Team Planning
- Ch.8 Quality Planning
- Ch.9 Risk Planning
- Ch.10 Communications Planning
- Ch.11 Executing, Monitoring, and Controlling the Plan
- Ch.12 Managing Disruptions to the Plan— Issues and Change
- Ch.13 Managing the Human Resources Aspects of the Project
- Ch.14 Project Procurement
- Ch.15 Closing the Project

INTRODUCTION TO PROJECT PROCUREMENT

Up to this point in the text, the project management processes and tools have been presented with the assumption that all work will be completed within the same organization that receives the output of the project. While this is true for many projects, there is another classification of processes for projects in which one organization performs project work for another. This is known as project procurement. Internal projects and projects involving procurement share many processes and tools. Therefore, most of the concepts covered up to this point in the text apply to projects involving procurement. However, there are some additional processes and tools to be explored.

During the case study project, employees of Deco Productions completed all of the work. However, there are many reasons for work to be completed externally, including the following:

- The potential for lower cost or earlier delivery
- Gaining access to skills or knowledge not present internally
- Internal resources being unavailable

The amount of work performed externally may be either a small or a significant percentage of the total project. Terms used to describe this work include *outsourcing, purchasing,* and *procurement.*

Throughout the procurement process, there are two main parties: the **buyer** and the **seller**. The buyer is the organization that purchases the product, service, or result from another organization. The seller is the organization that produces the product, service, or result for sale to another organization.

Figure 14.1 shows the stages of project procurement.

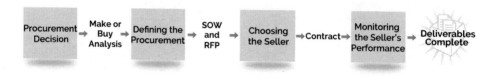

Figure 14.1: Stages of Project Procurement

When planning the work of a project, an important decision is to determine which deliverables will be created internally and which deliverables will be created externally. A **Make or Buy Analysis** can help determine whether to "make" the project deliverables or "buy" the project deliverables.

If there are deliverables that will be created externally based on the results of the Make or Buy Analysis, the procurement process begins. During this stage, the procurement is defined in detail in the **Statement of Work** (SOW) and the **Request for Proposal** (RFP), which are described later in the chapter.

Once the Statement of Work and Request for Proposal are produced, the process of choosing the seller begins. When the seller is chosen, a **contract** is created and signed by both the buyer and the seller.

The final stage occurs when the seller produces the deliverables. The buyer's role is to monitor the seller's performance to ensure the work is performed according to the terms of the contract.

MAKE OR BUY ANALYSIS

When deciding whether to make or buy the deliverables for projects, it is useful to divide the deliverables into three categories:

- Deliverables that will definitely be made internally
- Deliverables that will definitely be bought externally
- Deliverables that could be made internally or could be bought externally

For projects that fall into the first two categories, the decision of whether the work should be performed internally or externally is obvious and no further analysis is required. For the first category, this may be work that has been traditionally performed within the organization. For the second, the organization may lack the expertise or the resources to perform this work.

However, for the third category, the decision of whether to perform the project work internally or externally is not obvious, and therefore further analysis is required. This process, known as a Make or Buy Analysis, consists of comparing the "make" option and the "buy" option according to the expected cost, quality, time required, and risk of each option.

Other factors may also affect this analysis. The buyer may currently lack the necessary resources to perform the work due to other projects or priorities. Or the strategy of the buyer's organization could be changing to increase the amount of project work performed externally.

Case Study Update: Performing the Make or Buy Analysis

Early in the Planning Phase, Sophie reviews the Work Breakdown Structure of the project. As usual, time is limited and resources are scarce, so if there are any opportunities to outsource any of the work, now is the time to consider the options.

Most of the deliverables are typical of the work performed by Deco Productions and therefore will be produced internally. However, two deliverables catch Sophie's eye: the multimedia demo and social media content. Both could potentially be completed externally, so further analysis is required.

Sophie first considers the multimedia demo. Enlisting help from her project team, the following analysis is completed:

Criterion	Make Option	Buy Option
Cost	Current estimate is $4,400.	The expected cost is $5,000.
Scope	Includes all scope.	Includes all scope.
Risk	There is a risk that Chris may be required to work on other projects and will not be able to complete this work as scheduled.	An external organization will not be as familiar with the DecoCam product. The quality may not be as high.

(continued)

After further consideration and discussion with the Project Sponsor, the decision is made to outsource the production of the multimedia demo despite the higher cost. The risk that Chris may be pulled onto another project was too high to ignore.

Next, Sophie considers the Social Media deliverable:

Criterion	Make Option	Buy Option
Cost	Current estimate is $2,400.	Expected cost is $2,400.
Scope	Includes all scope.	Includes all scope.
Risk	Moderate to low risk due to the Marketing team's familiarity with the organization and product.	Lack of familiarity with the organization and product may increase the risk of lower-quality social media posts being produced.

After consulting with the Project Sponsor, Sophie decides that the social media work will not be outsourced and will remain with the project team. The risk of an external company producing lower-quality social media posts was unacceptable to Sophie.

A Make or Buy Analysis is used to determine whether the work of a project should be produced internally by the project team (Make) or by an external organization (Buy).

DEFINING THE PROCUREMENT

Once the buyer decides to procure work from outside the organization, the next challenge is to define the characteristics of the procurement so that prospective sellers understand the needs of the buyer.

This definition consists of two documents: the Statement of Work (SOW) and Request for Proposal (RFP).

The Statement of Work

The purpose of the SOW is to completely describe the work to be completed during the procurement. Its content may vary depending on the type, size, and complexity of the project. However, the following type of information is typically contained in a SOW:

- The specifications of the work to be completed
- The required quantity
- The required quality or level of performance
- The period of performance for the work

- The location where the work will be performed
- Any other special requirements

The SOW may include other documents, such as design documents, schematics, and blueprints. It may also include information contained in the Project Scope Statement.

The following is the Statement of Work template:

STATEMENT OF WORK	
Organization	[Name of buyer organization]
Project Name	[This section contains the project name that should appear consistently on all project documents. Organizations often have project naming conventions.]
Date Produced	[Date that the Statement of Work is produced]
Technical Specifications	
[Description of the work to be completed by the seller organization]	
Time Period/Key Milestones	
[Description of the time period for the work to be completed, including a list of key milestones]	
Location of Work	
[Description of where the work will be performed]	
Special Requirements	
[Description of any special requirements not covered above]	

The Request for Proposal

The purpose of the RFP is to describe the process that prospective sellers will use to submit proposals to the buyer.

RFPs are used in situations where the proposals provided by the prospective sellers may contain unique solutions. In situations where the solutions of each seller are identical or very similar, a Request for Quote (RFQ) will be used. RFQs are commonly used for purchasing materials or other off-the-shelf items. In situations where the buyer is seeking information, a Request for Information (RFI) will be used. The remainder of this chapter will describe the use of an RFP.

As with the SOW, the content of an RFP will vary significantly depending on the type, size, and complexity of the project. The following is the type of information typically found in an RFP:

- Process details regarding how the prospective seller should submit their proposal, including the required information, format, number of copies, and the date and time that the proposal must be submitted
- The Statement of Work

- Any required contract provisions
- An indication of how the proposal will be evaluated (e.g., cost, quality)

The RFP and SOW should be considered a package that fully describes the project procurement to prospective sellers and therefore enables the seller to develop and submit a proposal.

The following is the Request for Proposal template:

REQUEST FOR PROPOSAL	
Organization	[Name of buyer organization]
Project Name	[This section contains the project name that should appear consistently on all project documents. Organizations often have project naming conventions.]
Date Produced	[Date that the Request for Proposal is produced]
Background	[Background information about the buyer organization and the project that led to this RFP]
Proposal Requirements	
[Description of the required content of the proposal to be submitted]	
Evaluation Criteria	
[Description of the criteria that will be used to evaluate the proposals received]	
Contract Requirements	
[Description of the required contract type and payment schedule]	
Submission Requirements	
[Description of the timing and format of the proposal submission]	

Case Study Update: Defining the Procurement

With the decision to procure the multimedia demo from outside the organization, Sophie begins to develop two new documents: the Statement of Work and the Request for Proposal.

Sophie knows that the procurement process, especially for large procurements, can be a complex process. She finds that it is often advisable to seek out assistance from those with procurement expertise. At Deco Productions, they are usually found in the purchasing, supply chain, or logistics areas of the organization. She knows it is also important to obtain legal assistance, particularly at the point when the contract is created.

So, in order to have a successful procurement process, Sophie negotiates the assistance of representatives from the Supply Chain and Logistics Department and the Legal Department. She asks each of the representatives to review her documentation and provide advice throughout the procurement process.

Given the amount of planning work that has been performed, creating the SOW is fairly straightforward. Using the WBS and Project Scope Statement as a guide, she describes the key features of the multimedia demo in detail. To ensure the demo is ready by the product launch date (May 8), she is very specific about the due date for the work. Sophie also includes a number of technical requirements in the Special Requirements section of the SOW.

At the same time that she begins to work on the SOW, she starts to work on the RFP. Looking at the project schedule, she selects April 10 as the date that proposals must be submitted. The proposal itself should provide a description of the proposed multimedia demo, a cost estimate, and a list of the key milestones, including the final delivery date. She indicates that the contract for this procurement will require a fixed price, meaning that the seller guarantees the price, which will not change.

Sophie also develops the criteria that will be used to select the winning proposal. Deco Productions is known for the reliability of its products, so she sets quality as the highest requirement. Though not as important as quality, her project has a fairly tight budget, so the cost of the demo is set as the second criterion. Sophie has always found that a seller's reputation is important, so she makes this the third factor. This results in the following criteria:

- Professional quality   50%
- Cost (fixed price)   30%
- Seller reputation   20%

Deco Productions has a standard legal contract template for work of this type. Sophie includes this template as an appendix. Finally, she adds the SOW as a second appendix.

Reading through the RFP and SOW documentation, she feels confident that prospective sellers will have the information they need to submit a proposal. Now, on to the next step: creating the list of prospective sellers who will receive these documents.

The following are the Statement of Work and Request for Proposal documents created for the case study project:

DECO PRODUCTIONS	**STATEMENT OF WORK**
Organization	Deco Productions
Project Name	DCV4Launch—DecoCam V4 Product Launch
Date Produced	March 31, 2026

(continued)

Technical Specifications

The scope of work required is to create a multimedia demo to be used at trade shows to demonstrate the functionality of the DecoCam product. The following are the specifications for this work:
• Mural
  ◦ Dimensions: 3 metres wide by 1 metre high
  ◦ Should be laminated and able to be rolled up for transport
  ◦ Contains an urban scene for visual interest—to be provided by Deco Productions
  ◦ High-resolution colour photo quality
  ◦ Quantity required: two (2)
• Mobile phones and tripods
  ◦ Quantity: two (2) of each
• Slideshow
  ◦ A slideshow simulating the user experience of using the DecoCam Photo Assistant feature to be programmed and installed on each phone
  ◦ Slideshow to consist of four slides

Time Period/Key Milestones

The performance period for this work is from April 16, 2026, to May 6, 2026.
The following are the milestones for this work:

Mural design: April 23, 2026
Demo of slideshow: April 28, 2026
Work complete: May 6, 2026

Location of Work

The work is to be completed at the seller's location. Meetings to be conducted through video conferencing.

Special Requirements

The Project Manager for the work should be professionally certified.
Non-disclosure agreements will be required for all personnel working on this project.

DECO PRODUCTIONS

REQUEST FOR PROPOSAL

Organization	Deco Productions
Project Name	DCV4Launch—DecoCam V4 Product Launch
Date Produced	March 31, 2026
Background	Deco Productions is a software company founded in 2012 that develops software related to photography and video production. The company serves both the consumer and business markets.
	A new version of the industry-leading DecoCam software is currently in development. To support the rollout, a product launch project is underway.
	This RFP pertains to a key deliverable of this project: to develop a multimedia demo to be used at trade shows to demonstrate the functionality of the new DecoCam version.

Proposal Requirements
See the attached Statement of Work.   The proposal should include the following: • A description of the seller company, including the number of years in business and its ownership structure   • An overview of past work, including references (3)   • A brief description of the approach to be taken for each element of the Statement of Work   • Quote for the work
Evaluation Criteria
Proposals received will be assessed according to the following criteria: • Professional quality   50%   • Cost   30%   • Seller reputation   20%
Contract Requirements
The contract for this work will be fixed-priced.
Submission Requirements
Proposals must be submitted in PDF format to proposal@decoprd.com by 5:00 p.m. EST, April 10, 2026.

In order to communicate the requirements of a procurement, an SOW and an RFP should be produced and sent to prospective sellers.

CHOOSING THE SELLER

During this stage of the procurement process, potential sellers are identified through activities such as the following:

- The Project Manager's expertise and awareness of potential sellers
- Consultation with colleagues or consultants
- Online or similar searches of potential sellers

In addition, organizations may maintain preferred vendor lists. These are lists of vendors (sellers) who have been previously assessed by the buying organization. Advertising may also be placed online or in industry journals in order to make prospective sellers aware of an upcoming procurement. Public (government) projects normally require that advertising take place, so that all potential sellers have an opportunity to participate. Once prospective sellers are identified, the prepared RFP and SOW documents are sent to each company.

Identify prospective sellers and send the procurements documents (SOW and RFP) to them.

It is now up to the sellers to decide whether they will respond to the procurement. From the seller's perspective, they will assess whether they have the capabilities and resources available to provide the requested work. The prospective sellers who decide to participate will create a proposal based on the requirements of the RFP and SOW.

After a period of time, the buyer should receive a number of proposals from the prospective sellers. The challenge for the buyer is to choose one of the proposals. Various methods may be used to evaluate the proposals, including the following:

- Analysis of the proposal documents
- Discussion with the prospective sellers
- Site visits to the prospective sellers' facilities
- Presentations or demonstrations by the sellers

Evaluate the proposals received in order to choose a seller to complete the procurement.

Once the buyer is selected, the next activity is the creation of a contract between the buyer and the seller. For large, complex procurements, the development of a contract can be a large effort, taking a significant amount of time. The information contained in the contract should include specific details regarding the following:

- The deliverables to be produced
- The due dates for all deliverables
- The price to be paid by the buyer
- The process to report and monitor the status of the work
- The process to accept the deliverables
- The process to manage changes to the required work
- The process to resolve disagreement

The importance of the contract cannot be overstated, as it defines all aspects of the work to be completed by the seller and all obligations each party has to the other. Any disagreements that occur during the course of the procurement will be resolved according to the wording of the contract. Once both parties sign the contract, the work of the procurement may begin.

Create the contract with the seller so the procurement work can begin.

Case Study Update: Choosing the Seller

Sophie puts the finishing touches on the Statement of Work document and saves it on her laptop. Now that she has completed the documentation of the procurement requirements, her mind turns to the challenge of finding an organization to complete the work.

Sophie understands the importance of taking care when selecting a seller, as whatever they accomplish during the project will reflect (either positively or negatively) on the project team and Deco Productions. She knows from experience that customers will hold her accountable for the quality of the final product regardless of who actually performed the work.

From personal experience, Sophie knows of one company that could perform the job. After making phone calls to her colleagues, she adds two more companies to the list. Finally, after an online search, she finds a few more companies that look promising. After locating the addresses of each of the potential sellers, Sophie sends the RFP and SOW to each company. They now have until the due date defined in the RFP to reply with a proposal.

As the April 10 deadline approaches, a number of proposals arrive. Sophie looks through the options and weighs the pros and cons of each. After a period of time, she picks her top three proposals, from CityScape Inc., Designview Video, and TDR Online.

In preparation for the selection of the winning proposal, Sophie organizes an evaluation committee consisting of Arun (the Project Sponsor), Fatehjit (the Business Analyst), and herself. Sophie also calls each of the references provided in the proposals. Sophie knows that "talking a good game" in a proposal is easy, but a satisfied customer who is willing to be used as a reference is a much greater indicator of future success.

Glancing at her watch and realizing it's time for the evaluation meeting, Sophie gathers the proposals and heads to the meeting room. She writes the evaluation criteria previously developed (professional quality, cost, and seller reputation) on a flip chart. She then goes around the table asking each person to provide a ranking from 1 to 10 for each. Once the ranking is complete and the results are compiled in a spreadsheet, Designview Video emerges as the clear winner.

Following the meeting, Sophie contacts Designview Video to inform them that they have been selected for the project. During the discussion, she indicates that she'll send the contract to them shortly. Over the next few days, both parties make a number of adjustments to the contract. After a final review, both parties sign the contract, and the work is ready to begin.

The following is the spreadsheet that was used to evaluate the three sellers. The assessment of each seller was entered under the Score column. The Weighted Score column was then calculated (by multiplying the score times the weight). This generated a total weighted score for each seller.

Criterion	Weight	CityScape Inc.		Designview Video		TDR Online	
		Score	Weighted Score	Score	Weighted Score	Score	Weighted Score
Professional Quality	50%	8	4.0	8	4.0	6	3.0
Cost	30%	6	1.8	9	2.7	5	1.5
Seller Reputation	20%	7	1.4	9	1.8	9	1.8
Total			7.2		8.5		6.3

MONITORING THE SELLER'S PERFORMANCE

Now that the seller has been selected and the contract has been signed, the seller may begin to perform the work of the procurement. It is very important to have a detailed and accurate contract, as it guides the seller and defines what will be performed for the project.

While the buyer is not producing the deliverables, they still have a significant role during this stage of the procurement. There are three main activities to be performed:

1. Monitoring the progress of the procurement work
2. Verifying the deliverables
3. Managing issues and changes

A regular status reporting process should be defined in the contract, indicating how the seller reports their progress to the buyer on a regular basis. This may include regular status meetings, status reports, visits to the seller's facilities, and demonstrations of the work in progress. For most projects, there will also be work performed internally, so the status report created by the seller will be added to or merged with the overall project status information.

As the work is being performed, the buyer will be involved in verifying that the deliverables meet the quality levels defined in the contract. This may be a formal Quality Control process or may involve a simpler inspection of the deliverables.

Issues and changes are almost certain to occur during a project procurement. Similarly to internal project work, processes should be established to manage the resolution of issues and the management of change. Changes that occur during a procurement often require the contract to be updated, which may then impact other contract provisions, such as extending the delivery date or increasing the price.

Throughout the project, disagreements between the buyer and seller often occur and are normally handled through ongoing communication and negotiation. In some instances, disagreements may occur that cannot be resolved through negotiation. In these cases, legal remedies will be required. Depending on the disagreement, the buyer and seller could agree to mediation (where an external mediator facilitates a non-binding agreement) or arbitration (where an external arbitrator creates a binding agreement). The ultimate resolution is litigation, which occurs if the buyer or seller sues the other party.

Once all work is complete as defined by the terms in the contract, final payments are made and the contract is closed.

> Monitor the seller's performance. Once the work is complete and approved, the contract is closed, ending the procurement.

KEY TERMINOLOGY

Buyer: The organization that purchases the product, service, or result from another organization

Contract: A legal agreement between the buyer and seller that documents the content and conditions of the procurement

Make or Buy Analysis: The process of comparing the creation of products, services, or results within the project to their creation by another organization

Request for Proposal: A document that describes the characteristics of a procurement to enable prospective sellers to submit proposals to the buyer

Seller: The organization that produces the product, service, or result for sale to another organization

Statement of Work: A description of the product, services, or results to be provided during a project

KEY CONCEPTS

1.   A Make or Buy Analysis is used to determine whether the work of a project should be produced internally by the project team (Make) or by an external organization (Buy).

2. In order to communicate the requirements of a procurement, a Statement of Work (SOW) and Request for Proposal (RFP) should be produced and sent to prospective sellers.

3. Identify prospective sellers and send the procurement documents (SOW and RFP) to them.

4. Evaluate the proposals received in order to choose a seller to complete the procurement.

5. Create the contract with the seller so the procurement work can begin.

6. Monitor the seller's performance. Once the work is complete and approved, the contract is closed, ending the procurement.

DISCUSSION QUESTIONS

1. Given recent business trends, do you think that companies will increase or decrease their procurement activities? Explain your reasoning.

2. Does the procurement process increase or decrease the amount of planning and documentation required for a project that may otherwise have been completed internally?

3. Does the presence of a legal contract change the way the project is managed?

4. Perform an online search to research problems that occur during project procurement. Summarize five common problems that may occur.

15 Closing the Project

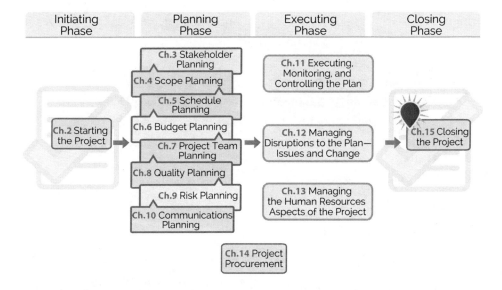

Initiating Phase	Planning Phase	Executing Phase	Closing Phase

Ch.3 Stakeholder Planning

Ch.4 Scope Planning

Ch.5 Schedule Planning

Ch.6 Budget Planning

Ch.7 Project Team Planning

Ch.8 Quality Planning

Ch.9 Risk Planning

Ch.10 Communications Planning

Ch.2 Starting the Project

Ch.11 Executing, Monitoring, and Controlling the Plan

Ch.12 Managing Disruptions to the Plan—Issues and Change

Ch.13 Managing the Human Resources Aspects of the Project

Ch.14 Project Procurement

Ch.15 Closing the Project

INTRODUCTION TO CLOSING THE PROJECT

Once all of the deliverables of the project are created and all activities are executed, the Executing Phase ends. The project now enters the fourth and final phase of the project, the Closing Phase.

While the Closing Phase is important, it often receives insufficient attention. As new projects are initiated, there is a risk that the focus will shift to the new projects at the expense of the closing activities of an existing project. This tendency should be avoided, and the following closing activities should take place:

- Transitioning to the operations of the organization
- Reporting the results of the project
- Storing the project documents and files
- Documenting the lessons learned

TRANSITIONING TO THE OPERATIONS OF THE ORGANIZATION

Most projects create output that will remain in the organization beyond the end of the project. For example, while the project to create a new product will end, the product will be marketed, distributed, and supported by the organization. It is therefore imperative that the output of the project is effectively transitioned to the operations of the organization.

Depending on the complexity of the project's deliverables, a plan should be developed in order to ensure effective transition. A great deal of knowledge regarding the project's scope should have been gained during the project, and it is important that this knowledge isn't lost once the project ends. Therefore, this plan should consider the following actions:

- Providing a demonstration of the project's features and capabilities
- Providing training and mentoring to the operations personnel
- Creating or updating user manuals or similar process documents
- Updating the policies and procedures of the organization to reflect the changes that resulted from the project
- Transferring project personnel to the operations area (on either a temporary or permanent basis)

Case Study Update: Transitioning to the Operations of the Organization

The May 8 deadline to complete the project's deliverables has arrived, and Sophie is happy to report to Arun that the product launch is ready. While it was a great deal of work and there were more than a few tense moments, it all came together in the end.

Sophie knows, though, that this is not the end of the project. She remembers a project from a couple of years ago when she didn't pay enough attention to the closing activities and instead shifted her focus to a new initiative. The resulting problems were enormous—the operations personnel at Deco Productions struggled to understand and support the new product without her guidance. Not only did this detract from the success of her project, but it also caused some damage to her relationship with the operations managers. Chalking it up to inexperience, she resolved to never ignore the closing activities again.

Checking the project schedule, she sees that three days of closing activities are planned. Her first priority is to ensure that the Marketing department has all the information they need to effectively support this product launch. Pulling out her notepad, she jots down the following activities:

- Schedule a demonstration of the trade show products (e.g., the banners, holographic cards, multimedia demo)
- Schedule a presentation of the promotional video to the Project Sponsor and key stakeholders
- Update the Marketing department's documentation to reorder banner stands, holographic cards, cameras, and tripods

Given these activities, she's confident that the Marketing department will have everything they need to successfully market the product.

The product, service, or results of the project should be transferred to the operations of the organization.

REPORTING THE RESULTS OF THE PROJECT

At the end of the project, it is useful to remember that the project was initiated based on the anticipated costs and benefits. The Business Case and Project Charter, created during the Initiating Phase, contain this information.

The question of whether the project achieved the costs and benefits that were originally documented must be answered. Accurately answering this question is important, as it may cause changes in processes for future projects. For example, if a project was unsuccessful, this may prompt a review of how the project was managed. The determination of the project results may also cause changes in compensation (e.g., project bonuses, salary raises) or promotions, depending on the success of the project.

The results of the project are documented in a **Final Project Report**. This report should measure whether the project achieved its objectives and should give a detailed report regarding the project's scope, budget, and schedule performance. The Final Project Report will be distributed to the Project Sponsor and other key stakeholders.

Depending on the objectives of the project, research may be required in order to gather the project stakeholders' feedback or measure the project's performance. One of the challenges of this measurement is that the objectives of projects often include performance measures that may only become known in the future (e.g., within the next quarter or next year).

In addition to the creation of the Final Project Report, a final review meeting is often scheduled with the Project Sponsor and other key stakeholders. The agenda for the meeting would normally follow the outline of the Final Project Report and would demonstrate the results and performance of the project.

The Final Project Report template is as follows:

FINAL PROJECT REPORT	
Project Name	[This section contains the project name that should appear consistently on all project documents. Organizations often have project naming conventions.]
Date Produced	[Date the Final Project Report is produced]
Project Sponsor	[Name of Project Sponsor]
Project Manager	[Name of Project Manager]
Project Goals	
Project Charter	[The project goals from the Project Charter]
Actual Results	[The actual results achieved for each of the project goals from the Project Charter]
Project Objectives	
Project Charter	[The project objectives from the Project Charter]
Actual Results	[The actual results achieved for each of the project objectives from the Project Charter]
Completion Date	
Project Charter	[The target date(s) from the Project Charter]
Actual Results	[The actual date(s) achieved for each of the target date(s) from the Project Charter]
Budget	
Project Charter	[The budget from the Project Charter plus approved budget changes made during the project]
Actual Results	[The actual costs incurred for the project]

Case Study Update: Reporting the Results of the Project

Checking the Communication Management Plan, Sophie sees that the Final Project Meeting is scheduled for May 13. The Final Project Report will be reviewed at this meeting, so it's time to get started on this document. The CEO, Casey Serrador, who is known for asking very detailed questions, will attend this meeting. It will be important to thoroughly prepare beforehand.

Overall, the project performed extremely well. All of the project goals and objectives were met. While the project's final cost of $61,250 did exceed the original budget of $60,000, there were two approved project changes that added $2,000 to the project budget, and the decision to outsource the multimedia demo added $600 to the budget. Therefore, Sophie was actually $1,350 under budget for the project. This reminds her of the importance of an effective change management process. Without the documentation of the approved changes, she might have found herself explaining why she was over budget.

As she completes the Final Project Report, she's feeling great about the results of the project. After sending a copy of the report to Casey and Arun, she also sends a copy to the project team with a note of thanks for another terrific effort on their part.

The Final Project Report produced for the case study project is as follows:

DECO PRODUCTIONS	**FINAL PROJECT REPORT**
Project Name	DCV4Launch—DecoCam V4 Product Launch
Date Produced	May 13, 2026
Project Sponsor	Arun Singh
Project Manager	Sophie Featherstone
Project Goals	
Project Charter	The goal of the project is to successfully launch DecoCam V4 in order to support the company's goal of a 5% increase in DecoCam's market share.
Actual Results	As all objectives were completed, this project supported the company's goals of a 5% increase in market share. The assessment of the market share achieved will become known in the next six months.

(continued)

Project Objectives	
Project Charter	The objectives of the project are, by May 8, 2026: • Update the product information on the company website and printed materials. • Promote DecoCam V4 through existing communication channels. • Create a promotional video that achieves 10,000 views within three months. • Create the trade show materials. • Complete the project within the $60,000 budget.
Actual Results	All of the project objectives were achieved.
Completion Date	
Project Charter	May 8, 2026 (product launch) May 13, 2026 (project complete)
Actual Results	The project is ready to launch by May 7, 2026 (one day early). The project will be closed on May 13, 2026.
Budget	
Project Charter	$60,000
Actual Results	The final costs for the project were $61,250. The original Project Charter budget was increased to $62,600 during the project due to the following approved changes: • Change the trade show giveaways to resemble a picture frame rather than a postcard ($400). • Upgrade the software required to create the multimedia demo ($1,600). • Outsource the development of the multimedia demo ($600). Based on the modified budget, the project was under budget by $1,350.

The results of the project should be summarized and reported.

STORING THE PROJECT DOCUMENTS AND FILES

During the project, a number of project documents are created. This includes project management documents, such as the Project Charter, Project Scope Statement, and Project Status Reports. Retention of these documents is useful for future teams, as reviewing the plans and progress of past projects can be helpful.

The Project Documentation Guidelines that were creating during the communications planning outline the storage location for the project documents. During the Closing Phase, the Project Manager should ensure that all project documents are stored as required.

Additionally, a number of files, such as spreadsheets, graphics files, and software files, are created during projects. These files may be needed for future projects and for the operations area of the company in order to provide ongoing support. The Project Manager should also ensure that all of the project files are stored as required.

Case Study Update: Storing the Project Documents and Files

Without a doubt, one of Sophie's least favourite closing activities is locating and storing all of the project documents and files. Inevitably, despite her careful creation of the Project Documentation Guidelines, many of the documents and files are scattered in various locations.

However, she knows that it is an important activity to complete. During the DecoCam project, she reviewed the project documents from a previous product launch project on a number of occasions. This information was only available to her because a Project Manager from a previous project stored the documents and files at the end of the project. With this in mind, she starts moving documents and files into the appropriate folders.

All project-related documentation should be archived for possible future reference.

DOCUMENTING THE LESSONS LEARNED

While each project is unique, many project processes are repeated. Taking the opportunity to review these processes, identify improvements, and document what was learned is key to the improvement of project performance. This also promotes sharing project-based learning within the organization.

Collecting and documenting the lessons learned should involve as many project team members and other stakeholders as possible. Often the discussion of a problem encountered will generate ideas for potential improvements on future projects.

Care should be taken that this process does not become a discussion of performance problems or an opportunity to assign blame. Issues related to individual performance should not be raised during this meeting. When holding a Lessons Learned Meeting, the ground rules for the meeting should be discussed beforehand.

The following is the **Lessons Learned Report** template:

LESSONS LEARNED REPORT	
Project Name	[This section contains the project name that should appear consistently on all project documents. Organizations often have project naming conventions.]
Project Sponsor	[Name of Project Sponsor]
Project Manager	[Name of Project Manager]

(continued)

What went well during the project?	
[List something that went well or was successful during the project.]	
What did not go well during the project?	
[List something that did not go well or was unsuccessful during the project.]	
What should we do differently next time?	**How will this be done?**
[List ideas for process improvements for future projects.]	[Provide detail about how the process improvement could be performed or achieved.]

Case Study Update: Documenting the Lessons Learned

At the end of each project, Sophie schedules a meeting in order to gather feedback from those involved in the project. She invites the project team, the Project Sponsor (Arun), and the Resource Manager (Anand Bhandari) to an online Lessons Learned Meeting.

First, she asks each person to brainstorm on the following questions:

- What went well during the project?
- What did not go well during the project?
- What could be improved upon for the next project?

Using the video conferencing software's virtual whiteboard, Sophie asks each person to post virtual sticky notes on the whiteboard under one of three headings: "Went well," "Did not go well," or "Do differently next time."

As Sophie facilitates the discussion, she groups similar notes together, as multiple people will often come up with the same or similar ideas. She discusses each idea with the group in order to ensure that she understands it fully and that she gathers all of the important information. Once the discussion is complete, she records the results of the meeting in a Lessons Learned Report.

Sophie finds that this process helps her effectively manage the meeting so that each person is able to provide input and it is less likely that anyone will be able to dominate the discussion.

The following is the Lessons Learned Report created for the project.

DECO PRODUCTIONS	**LESSONS LEARNED REPORT**
Project Name	DCV4Launch—DecoCam V4 Product Launch
Project Sponsor	Arun Singh
Project Manager	Sophie Featherstone

What went well during the project?
The Project Kickoff Meeting was very effective. The stakeholders found that it was informative, and they were able to understand the objectives of the project.
The Project Scope Statement contained a useful level of detail, and team members found that it was helpful as they completed their tasks during the project.
The duration estimates for the project's activities were accurate. Most activities were completed within the planned duration.
The on-the-job training provided by Maddy to Eli seemed to work well.
The level of risk management seemed to be effective. There were no significant surprises during the project.

What did not go well during the project?
Team members were not quite sure when their tasks were to be completed. While this information was contained in the project management software, they did not have access to it and were often unsure about the schedule.
The cost estimates for materials seemed to be optimistic—when they were purchased, the prices tended to be higher than estimated. The sales tax also didn't seem to be included in the original estimates.
The team members were not always available when originally planned in the Project HR Requirements spreadsheet. This necessitated that the project schedule be updated numerous times.
There were times during the project when there wasn't enough communication among project team members. This caused problems regarding the project's quality that needed to be addressed later in the project.
A number of problems regarding the project's quality came up at the end of the project. A great deal of work took place to correct the issues.

What should we do differently next time?	**How will this be done?**
Ensure team members know what their tasks are for each week.	Investigate ways to produce individual weekly task reports for each team member. This will ensure each team member is aware of their tasks.
Improve cost estimating.	Spend additional time validating the material resources estimates through online checks of the supplier websites. Be sure to include the sales tax in the estimate and assume an additional 10% cost to account for possible price increases.

(continued)

What should we do differently next time?	How will this be done?
Improve resource estimating and management.	Plan a biweekly meeting between the Project Manager and the Resource Manager to ensure the Project HR Requirements spreadsheet remains accurate.
Improve the communication within the project team.	In future projects, ensure that all team members understand that the daily huddle is a mandatory meeting.
Put more focus on project quality.	Once the Quality Assurance Plan is created, hold a team meeting to review the document and provide feedback.

The project's performance should be reviewed in order to document the lessons learned for future projects.

Case Study Update: Epilogue

Arun Singh settles into his seat at the Consumer Electronics Show in Las Vegas, Nevada. Casey Serrador, the CEO of Deco Productions, is the keynote speaker. While he awaits Casey's introduction, he thinks about the recently completed DecoCam V4 project. As the Project Sponsor, he is pleased that the product launch was successful. The articles and blog reviews have been extremely positive. Activity on the company's social media channels has increased significantly, and the promotional video has been viewed more than 100,000 times.

After Casey's presentation, Arun walks over to the trade show area. On his way, he waves to Sophie, Chris, and Maddy, who are on their way to another presentation. As he walks up to the Deco Productions booth, he notices a number of things. The DecoCam signs are very noticeable and are attracting many of the conference attendees, who seem to like the holographic picture frames—a few are even asking if they can have one or two more. There are also small lineups forming to view the multimedia demo. Arun makes a mental note to order at least two more cameras and tripods for the next conference. At that moment, Casey walks up to him.

"Hello, Arun! Your launch of DecoCam was just great. Thank you for getting this done."

"Thanks, Casey. But I couldn't have done it without Sophie and her fantastic team. They really did some great work."

Smiling, Casey replies, "Well, that's good. Version 5 of DecoCam is already on the drawing board, so your team will have a new product to launch soon!"

KEY TERMINOLOGY

Final Project Report: A closing document that contains a summary of the results of the project

Lessons Learned Report: A closing document that summarizes the experiences of a project, including what went well, what did not go well, and what should be done differently for the next project

KEY CONCEPTS

1. The product, service, or results of the project should be transferred to the operations of the organization.
2. The results of the project should be summarized and reported.
3. All project-related documentation should be archived for possible future reference.
4. The project's performance should be reviewed in order to document the lessons learned for future projects.

DISCUSSION QUESTIONS

1. Why is it important to transfer the output of the project to the operations area of the company? What could happen if this step isn't performed effectively?
2. Often the results of a project will not be known until a future date, sometimes long after a project has been completed. For example, if one of the product's goals was to increase the market share of a product, this objective cannot be determined until at least six months or more following the completion of the project. What effect does this have on the Final Project Report?
3. Conducting a Lessons Learned Meeting can be challenging, as team members may feel they are being criticized for mistakes they may have made. How can you run the meeting so that it does not focus on individual performance?
4. Perform an online search to research project closing checklists. Describe any other activities that may take place during closing that were not mentioned in this chapter.

PART III

AGILE AND HYBRID PROJECT MANAGEMENT

During part II of the text, the focus was on the tools and techniques of waterfall project management, which is based on the predictive life cycle. However, there are other life cycles, including iterative, incremental, and agile, to consider.

In chapter 16: "An Overview of Agile," the origins of agile, including the Agile Manifesto, will be examined, as well as the agile mindset and an overview of different agile approaches. Chapter 17: "The Scrum Framework" will provide an introduction to a popular agile approach, Scrum, along with a DecoCam case study highlighting the use of Scrum to complete a software development project.

Finally, in chapter 18: "Hybrid Project Management," a number of approaches that combine features of both waterfall and agile will be examined.

16 An Overview of Agile

INTRODUCTION

The development of agile has occurred over a number of decades, so before specific agile approaches and processes are reviewed, it will be useful to trace its origins in order to more fully understand its characteristics and advantages. The agile process consists of a repetitive cycle of planning, building, testing, reviewing, and deployment (see figure 16.1).

The term *agile* itself may be used in many contexts. It can refer to a specific approach, such as **Scrum** or **Kanban**, both of which will be introduced later in this chapter. It can refer to the Agile Manifesto, a document created in order to summarize and promote agile approaches. It can also refer to a mindset that organizations are looking to adopt in order to become more flexible and responsive to their customers.

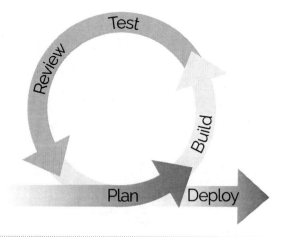

Figure 16.1: Agile Process

Each of these contexts, along with an overview of agile's origins, will be discussed here.

SETTING THE STAGE FOR AGILE

In the past, software development projects often used waterfall and typically comprised phases such as those demonstrated in figure 16.2.

Figure 16.2: Software Development Using Waterfall

Over time, and as software development became more complex and interconnected, issues with using a waterfall approach became increasingly apparent. Business personnel who were expected to provide detailed requirements early in the project, often found accurately articulating these requirements difficult. This would often lead to problems later in the project.

In 1994, the Standish Group published a report that studied a number of software development projects. They concluded that only 16% of projects studied were considered successful (completed on time, on budget, and with all scope delivered), with the remainder often leading to significant cost overruns and schedule delays.

The study participants were asked to describe the factors leading to project failure, which resulted in these top three responses:

- Lack of user input
- Incomplete requirements and specifications
- Changing requirements and specifications

While there are many potential causes for this underperformance, the research was pointing toward the processes involved in the definition of requirements and specifications, as well as the management of ongoing changes and involvement of the customer.

There were also many efforts already underway to develop alternative approaches to improve the systems development process. A few highlights are as follows:

- Following World War II, the foundations of Lean Manufacturing were developed by Taiichi Ohno and a number of others at the Toyota Motor Corporation.
- In 1986, Barry Boehm published a paper describing the Spiral Model, which incorporated iterations into the software development process.
- In 1986, Hirotaka Takeuchi and Ikujiro Nonaka published "The New New Product Development Game," which described the concept of Scrum.
- In 1991, James Martin published the book *Rapid Application Development*, which focuses on rapid iterations and prototyping.
- In 1995, Jeff Sutherland and Ken Schwaber presented the Scrum Development Framework at the OOPSLA 1995 conference.
- Throughout the 1990s, a number of software development frameworks were being created, such as the following:
  - Extreme Programming (XP), which emphasized customer collaboration, incremental development, and continuous testing (developed by Kent Beck).
  - Crystal, which emphasized frequent communication, collaboration, and iterative development (developed by Alistair Cockburn).
- In 2001, the Agile Manifesto was published.

Issues encountered while using waterfall for software projects prompted the development of alternative approaches using iterative and incremental development techniques, leading to the publication of the Agile Manifesto.

THE AGILE MANIFESTO

In early 2001, a series of meetings took place at Snowbird, Utah, which brought together 17 prominent figures in the software industry, including Kent Beck, Ken Schwaber, and Jeff Sutherland. These individuals were advocates of alternative software development approaches, including Scrum, XP, and others. Their goal was to find a common set of principles that would capture the essence of their approaches.

Their discussions produced the Manifesto for Agile Software Development, or Agile Manifesto (Agile Alliance, 2001). The idea was that this would be a lightweight alternative to the heavyweight software development processes common in many organizations at the time.

The Agile Manifesto Values

The Agile Manifesto defines four values for software development. They are shown in pairs, with the item on the left side of each pair given more importance than the item on the right. The importance given to the values on the left indicates a change in thinking from plan-based concepts to an approach that is more adaptable and customer-oriented. The values are as follows:

- Individuals and interactions over process and tools
- Working software over comprehensive documentation
- Customer collaboration over contract negotiation
- Responding to change over following a plan

The Agile Manifesto also states the following:

> While there is value in the items on the right, we value the items on the left more.

The above statement of values is often misinterpreted as meaning that the values on the right (i.e., those involving process and tools, comprehensive documentation, contract negotiation, and following a plan) have *no or very limited value* and therefore that agile is somehow free from documentation and planning.

To the contrary, the Agile Manifesto is stating that the values on the right remain important and relevant within agile approaches. The point being made is that the values on the left (individuals and interactions, working software, customer collaboration, and responding to change) should receive *a greater emphasis* within agile approaches.

The Agile Manifesto Principles

The Agile Manifesto also lists 12 principles that provide more detailed guidance on how to apply the four core principles in agile software development. The 12 principles are as follows:

1. Our highest priority is to satisfy the customer through early and continuous delivery of valuable software.
2. Welcome changing requirements, even late in development. Agile processes harness change for the customer's competitive advantage.
3. Deliver working software frequently, from a couple of weeks to a couple of months, with a preference to the shorter timescale.

4. Business people and developers must work together daily throughout the project.

5. Build projects around motivated individuals. Give them the environment and support they need, and trust them to get the job done.

6. The most efficient and effective way of conveying information to and within a development team is face-to-face conversation.

7. Working software is the primary measure of progress.

8. Agile processes promote sustainable development. The sponsors, developers, and users should be able to maintain a constant pace indefinitely.

9. Continuous attention to technical excellence and good design enhances agility.

10. Simplicity—the art of maximizing the amount of work not done—is essential.

11. The best architectures, requirements, and designs emerge from self-organizing teams.

12. At regular intervals, the team reflects on how to become more effective, then tunes and adjusts its behaviour accordingly.

These principles provide guidance for teams adopting agile approaches by promoting flexibility and collaboration, and providing value to customers.

Overall, the Agile Manifesto's impact on the software development industry has been significant, with the increasing adoption of agile approaches such as Scrum, XP, and Kanban. The Agile Alliance was founded in 2001 and the Scrum Alliance in 2002. The Agile Manifesto has also influenced other domains beyond software development, such as project management, product management, and more.

THE AGILE MINDSET

Agile has come to mean not only an approach to software development and project management but also a mindset to be fostered within organizations. The agile mindset is the embodiment of the Agile Manifesto and places the interactions of people at the forefront. An agile mindset recognizes that some level of process is necessary but that ultimately it is the people involved who make the difference.

Those with an agile mindset prefer to deliver value early and often. The focus is on the continual development and delivery of product increments in order to meet customer needs. It is also based on a belief that delivering in smaller increments allows for quicker response to changing requirements and customer feedback.

This mindset places a high priority on collaboration and favours an environment of empowered teams rather than decisions being made by top-down hierarchies. As well, the agile mindset encourages an openness to change and uncertainty. It recognizes that change is common and often represents an opportunity for improvement rather than an exception to be controlled. This creates an environment of continual improvement where teams learn from their work and strive to improve through each iteration.

The Agile Manifesto prioritizes individuals, collaboration, and adaptability during software development over extensive planning and documentation. An agile mindset is the embodiment of the Agile Manifesto.

AGILE TRANSFORMATION

As the benefit of agile has become apparent, many organizations have embarked on a strategy of agile transformation or "going agile." Agile transformation is the process of shifting to agile ways of working by applying values and principles such as those documented in the Agile Manifesto.

Agile transformation involves more than just adopting an agile approach (such as documented in this chapter) and then following new processes. It also requires a shift in the organizational culture in order to accept a new way of working. A number of considerations will be documented in the following sections.

Product Focus

Instead of a project having a team built around it, an agile approach involves building a team with an agile mindset and then the team becoming the constant. The team is provided work to be performed in a constant, sustainable manner. This shifts the focus away from the project-based lens of start and end date, project budget, and defined project scope to a continuous flow of product development. The term *product* often replaces the term *project*.

The Agile Manifesto value "Working software over comprehensive documentation" may also be realized with this focus. Unlike a waterfall project team that disappears when the project ends, the agile team continues indefinitely.

This team's continuing support and update of the product may then reduce the need for the type of comprehensive documentation that often needs to be created at the end of a project.

Management Structure and Support

An effective agile transformation is often dependent on management's understanding and commitment to agile principles. Within a waterfall approach, a high degree of decision-making is concentrated centrally within senior management, the Project Sponsor, and the Project Manager. Within agile, there is an increased level of decision-making distributed to the agile teams.

The Agile Manifesto value "Individuals and interactions over processes and tools" is central to the realignment of management's role. A greater focus needs to be placed on the individuals and interactions within agile teams and the interactions with customers.

Increased Collaboration

Central to an agile organization is the belief in the value and benefits of collaboration within the organization. Embracing cross-functional roles and teams while resisting the segmentation of work into specialized roles and teams with minimal communication is essential.

The Agile Manifesto value "Customer collaboration over contract negotiation" supports this need. The goal is to break down barriers to communication and collaboration within the organization by creating opportunities for collaboration between the agile teams and customers.

Acceptance of Uncertainty

A great deal of the process of waterfall project management is the reduction of uncertainty through detailed planning. The planning process attempts to define the complete scope of the project and therefore reduce or eliminate uncertainty.

An agile transformation takes a different approach. Uncertainties are managed by effectively responding to change through the agile process. Many uncertainties are difficult to identify up front, and effectively responding to change allows for decisions to be made once the uncertainty becomes apparent. The Agile Manifesto value "Responding to change over following a plan" requires this acceptance of uncertainty.

An agile transformation requires a shift in the organizational culture in order to embrace agile characteristics such as a product focus rather than a project focus, increased decision-making within the agile teams, increased collaboration, and an acceptance of uncertainty.

AGILE APPROACHES

While the Agile Manifesto defined agile as a series of values and principles, a number of approaches have been developed to provide direction for the implementation of agile:

- Scrum
- Kanban
- XP
- Lean Development
- Crystal
- And others

The approaches listed above tend to share a number of common characteristics that are fundamental to the agile mindset. These include the following:

- Iterative: the product is developed over a number of successive time periods in order to continually refine the product. These iterations facilitate frequent review and feedback opportunities.
- Incremental: the delivery of project outcomes occurs in smaller batches, allowing the outcomes to reach the customer sooner.
- Collaborative: agile approaches tend to be very collaborative, with team members working closely with each other and with customers on a regular basis.
- Flexible and adaptive: change is embraced in order to adapt to evolving requirements, often late in the development timeline.
- Visible: visible tools such as Kanban boards are often used, allowing for the work to be easily accessible.
- Small, cross-functional, empowered teams: agile approaches tend to favour teams that are small, self-organizing, and empowered to make

decisions about the delivery of the product. Team members also tend to be cross-functional rather than highly specialized.

Two popular approaches, Scrum and Kanban, are described here.

Scrum

The term *Scrum* comes from rugby, a sport where players come together in a scrum to restart a game after a rule infringement. The rugby scrum involves bringing team members closely together and coordinating their efforts in order move the ball forward. This aligns with the collaborative and adaptive nature of agile development. In agile development, the team works closely together, reassessing priorities and adapting to change in order to move the product forward.

In Scrum, work is organized into time-boxed iterations called **Sprints**, which typically last one to four weeks. The goal is to be able to deliver a usable product to the customer by the end of each Sprint. During each Sprint, the following takes place:

- The work to be completed during the Sprint is planned.
- The work is completed (this accounts for the majority of the Sprint's duration).
- The work of the Sprint (the usable product that could be delivered to the customer) is reviewed and feedback is gathered.
- The processes used during the Sprint, as well as any other related processes, are reviewed in order to identify possible improvements.

The completion of the Sprint is then followed by the start of the next Sprint, and the cycle continues (see figure 16.3). Underlying Scrum are the principles of transparency, inspection, and adaptation, known as the three pillars of Scrum. Each will be discussed here.

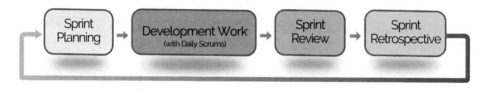

Figure 16.3: Sprint Overview

Transparency

During Scrum, transparency is achieved through open communication and visibility of relevant information. Scrum promotes transparency by making all aspects of the project visible. The visibility of the work selected for the Sprint and the usable product produced during the Sprint provides a clear understanding of the work in progress, priorities, and the current state of the product.

Regular meetings throughout the Sprint promote open dialogue among team members, allowing for the identification of issues and the sharing of progress. By emphasizing openness and accessibility to information, Scrum enables stakeholders to share a common understanding of the content and progress of the work being completed.

Inspection

Scrum emphasizes frequent inspection of both the product being developed and the processes being used to complete the work. For example, each day the team discusses their progress and any obstacles to the successful completion of the Sprint. Near the end of the Sprint, the completed work is inspected by various stakeholders in order to provide feedback to the team, and the processes of the Sprint are inspected for possible areas of improvement.

By regularly inspecting the product and process, continual improvement is built into Scrum, as the frequent inspections facilitate the incorporation of feedback into the next Sprint.

Adaptation

The third principle, adaptation, is achieved through regular adjustments made based on the insights gained from inspection. Daily meetings provide an opportunity for the team to synchronize their work. The inspections performed near the end of the Sprint allow the team to make adjustments to both the product and the development process during future Sprints.

Through these opportunities for adjustments, Scrum provides an environment of adaptability, allowing teams to effectively respond to changing requirements and priorities.

Use of Scrum

Scrum's time-boxed Sprints and incremental delivery enable frequent customer feedback and adaptation to changing requirements. The Scrum process helps ensure the product aligns with evolving customer needs, making it well-suited for the dynamic nature of product development.

Scrum is a popular agile approach involving the completion of iterations known as Sprints and emphasizes transparency, inspection, and adaptation.

Kanban

Kanban is a visual system for managing and tracking workflow. Unlike many other agile approaches, Kanban doesn't rely on time-boxed iterations but instead employs a continuous flow of work. The **Kanban board** is a visual representation of the workflow, with columns representing different stages of the process (see figure 16.4). Work items are represented as cards that contain essential information about the work, such as its status, priority, and relevant details.

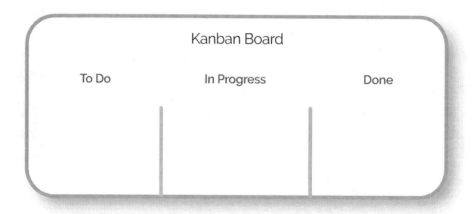

Figure 16.4: Kanban Board

A key aspect of Kanban is to limit the work in progress. This is accomplished by setting limits on the amount of work allowed into each column of the Kanban board. This helps prevent overloading any particular stage of the process and ensures a more balanced workflow.

Kanban is based on a **pull system** in which the team pulls new work into the To Do column when there is capacity to do so (see figure 16.5). This is based on an understanding of the maximum work-in-progress items; therefore, new work may be pulled into the Kanban board only when there is capacity for it. Cards are moved from one column to the next as work progresses.

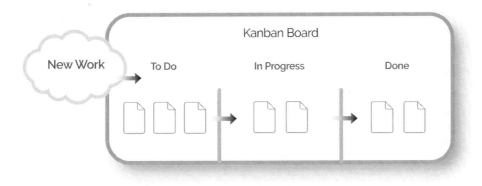

Figure 16.5: Kanban Pull System

Kanban enables predictable delivery times by visualizing and optimizing workflow, which allows teams to limit work in progress, identify bottlenecks, and continually improve efficiency (see figure 16.6). By observing how long work takes, teams are able to more accurately predict delivery times.

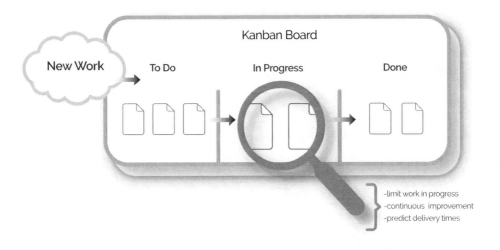

Figure 16.6: Visualization and Optimization of Workflow

Use of Kanban
While Kanban may be used for many types of projects, it is particularly well-suited for work environments such as software maintenance and support areas. For example, an IT help desk could employ a Kanban approach to manage the flow and processing of IT support requests (tickets). The Kanban approach

enables the visualization of support tickets, the limiting of work in progress to ensure that the number of tickets does not overwhelm the support team, and the measurement and optimization of the workflow in order to increase the overall effectiveness of the IT support provided.

Kanban is a visual system for managing and tracking workflow that emphasizes continual delivery and efficiency through real-time monitoring of tasks on a Kanban board.

KEY TERMINOLOGY

Kanban: A visual system for managing and tracking workflow

Kanban board: A visual display of work progress in columns such as To Do, In Progress, and Done

Pull system: A method in which new work is started only when there is capacity for it

Scrum: An agile approach that involves the repetition of fixed time periods (Sprints) to develop the product

Sprint: A set period of time during which work is completed and demonstrated

KEY CONCEPTS

1. Issues encountered while using waterfall for software projects prompted the development of alternative approaches using iterative and incremental development techniques, leading to the publication of the Agile Manifesto.

2. The Agile Manifesto prioritizes individuals, collaboration, and adaptability during software development over extensive planning and documentation. An agile mindset is the embodiment of the Agile Manifesto.

3. An agile transformation requires a shift in the organizational culture in order to embrace agile characteristics such as a product focus rather than project focus, increased decision-making within the agile teams, increased collaboration, and an acceptance of uncertainty.

4. Scrum is a popular agile approach involving the completion of iterations known as Sprints and emphasizes transparency, inspection, and adaptation.

5. Kanban is a visual system for managing and tracking workflow that emphasizes continual delivery and efficiency through real-time monitoring of tasks on a Kanban board.

DISCUSSION QUESTIONS

1. Why did Agile initially evolve within the context of software development projects?

2. Besides software development, what other types of projects may benefit from the use of agile approaches?

3. Review the four values listed in the Agile Manifesto. What potential challenges can you identify for organizations implementing these values within their project work?

4. How would you describe the key elements of an agile mindset, and in what way would cultivating such a mindset benefit project teams?

5. Perform an online search for the agile approaches discussed in this chapter (Scrum and Kanban). Indicate the strengths and weaknesses of each approach.

17 The Scrum Framework

INTRODUCTION TO THE SCRUM FRAMEWORK

While many agile approaches have been developed, the most widely used is Scrum. This chapter will describe Scrum in detail and will demonstrate the approach in a Scrum case study.

Introduction to the Scrum Case Study

While Deco Productions uses waterfall project management for many of its projects, a few years ago, the company moved to using an agile approach for its software development. After some consideration, Scrum was selected.

A number of Scrum Teams have been formed to support Deco Productions' various software products. While there have been some additional challenges of coordinating the activities of waterfall projects and agile projects, overall the results have been very positive. The ability of Deco Productions' software projects to adapt to change effectively and ship new features to customers on an almost continuous basis has contributed to the company's overall performance.

One of the company's Scrum Teams supports the DecoCam product. With the announcement of the Photo Assistant capability, the DecoCam team expects that they will be focused on updating the DecoCam application to include many new features.

SCRUM DEFINITIONS

Before the Scrum process is examined, a number of Scrum foundational concepts need to be defined.

Sprints

During Scrum, a number of iterations, known as Sprints, are performed. Each Sprint is relatively brief, usually lasting one to four weeks (see figure 17.1). Each Sprint is the same length. For example, a two-week Sprint should not be followed by a four-week Sprint. A consistent Sprint duration creates a rhythm that can be productive for the team.

Sprint (1 to 4 weeks)

Figure 17.1: Sprints

During Scrum, work is completed through the repetition of fixed time periods called Sprints.

Scrum Artifacts

During Scrum, three artifacts are created to help manage the work:

- **Product Backlog**: a prioritized and continually updated list of desired product requirements
- **Sprint Backlog**: a subset of the Product Backlog to be developed during a Sprint
- **Product Increment**: a potentially releasable product developed during a Sprint

The Product Backlog is available at the outset of the Sprint, during which the Sprint Backlog and the Product Increment are created (see figure 17.2).

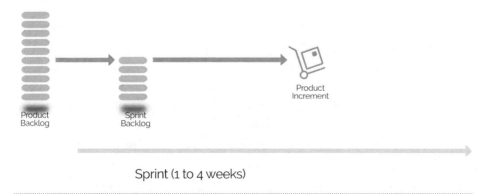

Sprint (1 to 4 weeks)

Figure 17.2: Scrum Artifacts

During Scrum, three artifacts are created: the Product Backlog, the Sprint Backlog, and the Product Increment.

User Stories and Epics

Product Backlog items are often written as **user stories** and use the following format:

> As a [*who wants to accomplish something*], I want [*what they want to accomplish*] so that [*why they want to accomplish it*].

A user story for an online banking system could be written as follows:

- As a customer, I want to be able to view a graphic of my monthly spending so that I can budget more effectively.

Epics are user stories that are too large to be delivered in a single Sprint and therefore need to be broken down into smaller user stories. Epics are normally not completed within a single Sprint but instead span a number of Sprints.

Product Backlog items are often written as user stories. Epics are user stories that are too large to be delivered in a single Sprint and are subsequently broken down into smaller user stories.

The Scrum Team

The three roles that make up the **Scrum Team** are the **Product Owner**, **Developers**, and **Scrum Master** (see figure 17.3).

Product Owner

The Product Owner has the responsibility of managing the Product Backlog, which is a highly visible document that is central to Scrum. The Product Owner also works with the Developers to ensure they understand the items contained in the Product Backlog, their business context, and their priority level. The Product Owner defines the acceptance criteria required to accept the deliverables produced by the Developers.

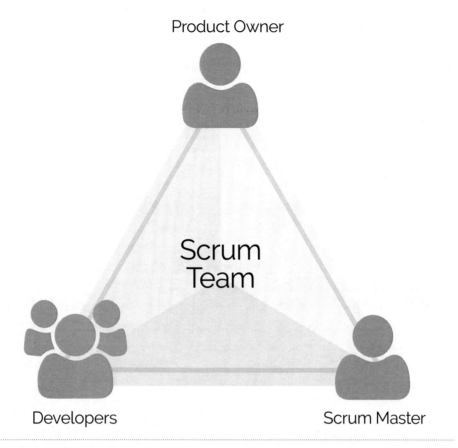

Figure 17.3: The Scrum Team

Although the Product Owner is a single person on the team, they may represent the views of a number of individual stakeholders or a committee. Only the Product Owner may change the Product Backlog.

Developers

The Developers are responsible for completing the work of each sprint and are part of a self-directed, cross-functional team that completes all aspects of the Development Work.

While individuals may have specific skill sets, Developers are not organized into sub-teams based on specialized skills (e.g., a programming team or a testing team). Each Developer is expected to perform various functions as required during the Sprint, with accountability for the work residing with the Developers as a whole.

In addition to completing the work, the Developers have other responsibilities:

- Attend a daily meeting to review the development progress.
- Work with the Product Owner to maintain the Product Backlog.
- Participate in the planning of the work to be completed.
- Inspect and adapt both the product and the development process.

Scrum Master

The Scrum Master is responsible for ensuring that Scrum values, principles, and practices are understood and followed. They do not directly manage the work performed by the Development team. Instead, the Scrum Master provides advice and coaching as required and works to remove obstacles to the Developers' progress. Rather than directly managing the Developers, the Scrum Master focuses on their growth and ensuring their needs are met.

The Scrum Master shields the Developers from outside interference and interacts with project stakeholders as needed. This allows the Developers to remain focused on delivering the Sprint Backlog items.

The three roles that make up the Scrum Team are the Product Owner, Developers, and the Scrum Master.

Scrum Case Study Update: The Scrum Team

Within the Deco Productions Software Development area, a dedicated Scrum Team is responsible for the development and delivery of product support related to the DecoCam application.

Jordan Kovac is the Product Owner and Zoe Purdie is the Scrum Master. The Developers are Lauren Wetlauffer, Dima Gibaldi, Miguel Hani, and Teacen Freitas. While each of the Developers possesses specific skills, they are expected to perform the work as required, including work inside and outside of their own specialties. This requires communication, cross-training, and mentoring.

With the upcoming release of DecoCam V4, a significant number of updates to the DecoCam application are likely required. This will be the focus of the next few Sprints.

THE SCRUM PROCESS

Product Backlog Refinement

The Product Backlog is a highly visible document that is central to the Scrum framework. Most items contained in the Product Backlog are features (functionality that provides value to the customer), though they may be other requirements, such as defects to be corrected or technical improvements (see figure 17.4).

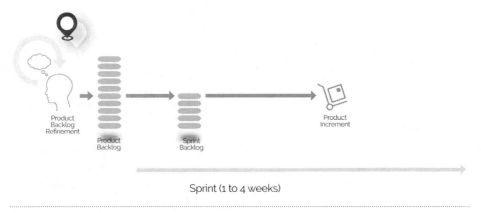

Sprint (1 to 4 weeks)

Figure 17.4: Product Backlog Refinement

The Product Backlog is continually updated so that it always reflects the current needs and desired functionality of the organization. The Product Owner is responsible for maintaining the Product Backlog with input and consultation with the Developers and other stakeholders. Updates may include the addition of new items, changes to the priority order, and development of estimates.

Estimates for Product Backlog items are usually developed on a regular basis, particularly for those that are high priority and likely to be developed in the near future. The items may be estimated using either **story points** or person-days. Story points represent a relative measure to describe the magnitude of a Product Backlog item. For example, a small item may be assigned two points, while a larger item (perhaps four times the size) would be assigned eight points. Person-days represent an estimate of the effort that would be required to complete the item. For the remainder of this chapter, story points will be used.

A common technique for sizing Product Backlog items is known as **planning poker**. This is a consensus-based approach that involves the members of the Scrum Team. To begin, each Developer receives a number of playing cards; each card contains a number from a sequence. While there are different number sequences that may be used, one method is to use the Fibonacci sequence (1, 2, 3, 5, 8, 13, 21, 34, 55, etc.) as there are more numbers at the lower end and fewer at the larger end.

When using planning poker, the full Scrum Team participates. The Product Owner presents and clarifies the Product Backlog items. The Scrum Master coaches the team to effectively use the planning poker process. The Developers collaboratively create the estimates. For each Product Backlog item, the following process is followed:

- The Product Owner describes the Product Backlog item.
- The Developers discuss the item, asking questions of the Product Owner as required.
- Each Developer privately selects a card that they feel best represents the effort required.
- All Developers reveal their card at the same time.
- If the estimates are not the same, there may be discussion about any assumptions that were made, and the Developers with the highest and lowest story points can provide an explanation of their reasoning.

This process repeats until there is consensus, that is, until all Developers agree on a story point amount for the Product Backlog item.

The value of planning poker is not only the development of Product Backlog item estimates but also the discussion and shared understanding that results.

The template for the Product Backlog is as follows:

DECO PRODUCTIONS	**PRODUCT BACKLOG: DECOCAM**	
#	**Description**	**Estimate (story points)**
[Product Backlog item number]	[Description of the Product Backlog item]	[Story points for this Product Backlog item]

Scrum Case Study Update: Product Backlog Refinement

With the recent announcement of DecoCam V4, the Product Owner, Jordan, has been busy adding new items for the DecoCam Product Backlog. So far, he has added 17 new user stories.

The next step is to develop estimates for the newly added user stories. For this, Jordan will need the input of the Developers. He sets up a meeting with the DecoCam Scrum Team.

During the meeting, Jordan selects the first user story: "As a user, I want to be able to adjust the settings of my camera before taking a picture, based on the advice provided by the Photo Assistant, so that I can improve the quality of my photos."

Jordan reads the user story out loud to the team, and the Developers start discussing the details of the required work. They talk about the different settings that users might want to adjust, such as brightness, contrast, and focus. They also discuss the potential complexity involved in developing the Photo Assistant feature that would provide advice to users about which settings to adjust.

Once the team has a clear understanding of the user story and the possible complexities, they use planning poker cards to estimate the effort required. In the first round of planning poker, the estimates range from 5 to 21, with an average of 10. Miguel and Lauren provide the rationale for their estimates, as they provided the lowest and highest estimates. In the second round, the estimates range from 3 to 13, with an average of 7. The team feels that they are getting closer to consensus, but they still have some differences to be resolved. Miguel and Teacen provide the rationale for their estimates. In the third round, all four Developers choose 8 as their estimate. They all agree that the work is moderately complex and will require some effort to implement the Photo Assistant feature and user interface for adjusting settings.

This process continues for the remaining user stories in the Product Backlog.

The following are the new items added to the Product Backlog, including the estimates developed:

DECO PRODUCTIONS   **PRODUCT BACKLOG: DECOCAM**

#	Description	Estimate (story points)
00367	As a user, I want to be able to adjust the settings of my camera before taking a picture, based on the advice provided by the Photo Assistant, so that I can improve the quality of my photos.	8

(continued)

#	Description	Estimate (story points)
00368	As a user, I want the Photo Assistant to be able to identify the subject of the photo, so that I can take aesthetically pleasing photos.	5
00369	As a user, I want the Photo Assistant to be able to detect and advise on lighting conditions, so that I can make necessary adjustments to my camera settings to improve my photos.	3
00370	As a user, I want the Photo Assistant to be able to provide specific advice for different types of photography, such as portrait, landscape, and action, so that I can take better photos in various photography styles.	8
00371	As a user, I want to be able to turn off the Photo Assistant feature if I prefer to take pictures without its advice, so that I have the option to choose how I want to take my photos.	1
00372	As a user, I want the Photo Assistant to be able to recognize and give specific advice for different types of scenes, such as beach, sunset, and city, so that I can take better photos in different environments.	5
00373	As a user, I want the Photo Assistant to be able to provide advice on my camera's ISO, shutter speed, and aperture, so that I can take better photos with the optimal settings.	5
00374	As a user, I want the Photo Assistant to be able to provide advice on post-processing techniques, such as cropping, colour correction, and filters, so that I can improve the final product of my photos.	13
00375	As a user, I want the Photo Assistant to be able to provide advice on how to photograph specific objects, such as animals, architecture, and food, so that I can take better photos of certain subjects.	8
00376	As a user, I want the Photo Assistant to be able to provide advice on how to photograph in different weather conditions, such as rain, snow, and fog, so that I can take better photos in adverse conditions.	8
00377	As a user, I want the Photo Assistant to be able to provide advice on how to photograph in different types of environments, such as low light, backlight, and high contrast, so that I can take better photos in different environments.	3
00378	As a user, I want the Photo Assistant to be able to provide advice on how to use different types of camera equipment, such as tripods, lenses, and flash, so that I can improve my photos with the proper camera equipment.	2
00379	As a user, I want the Photo Assistant to be able to provide advice on how to photograph in different styles, such as black and white, street photography, and fine art, so that I can vary the types of photos taken.	3
00380	As a user, I want the Photo Assistant to be able to provide advice on how to photograph different types of events, such as weddings, concerts, and sports, so that I can take better photos at various events.	5
00381	As a user, I want the Photo Assistant to be able to provide advice on how to photograph in different types of situations, such as macro, night, and underwater, so that I can take better photos in different conditions.	13
00382	As a user, I want the ability to view the original photo alongside the Photo Assistant's analysis and advice, so that I can compare and better understand the changes made to the photo.	8
00383	As a user, I want to be able to save the settings recommended by the Photo Assistant for future use, so that I can take future photos faster.	1
	Total Estimate	99

During Product Backlog refinement, estimates are created for the Product Backlog items.

Sprint Planning

The **Sprint Planning** meeting is attended by the Scrum Team. The length of this meeting will vary depending on the duration of the Sprint. As a guideline, a four-hour Sprint Planning meeting would be appropriate for a two-week Sprint (see figure 17.5).

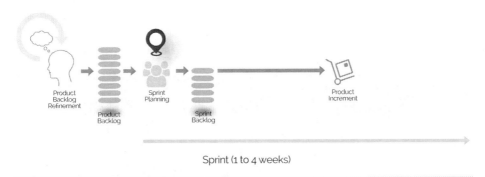

Product Backlog Refinement   Product Backlog   Sprint Planning   Sprint Backlog   Product Increment

Sprint (1 to 4 weeks)

Figure 17.5: Sprint Planning

During the meeting, the **Sprint Goal** is developed, and this becomes the objective for the Sprint. The items contained in the Product Backlog are reviewed and considered for possible inclusion in the Sprint, based on the priorities provided by the Product Owner as well as technical dependencies identified by the Developers.

In order to determine the Product Backlog items to be included in the Sprint, the capacity of the Developers is determined. To do this, the team's **velocity** during recent Sprints is reviewed. The team's velocity may be stated as either the average number of story points accomplished during recent Sprints or the number of story points accomplished during the last Sprint. The predicted velocity for the upcoming Sprint may also be adjusted for other factors, such as non-Sprint commitments (e.g., maintenance or personal time off).

The Product Backlog items that will be accomplished during the Sprint are listed in the Sprint Backlog.

During Sprint Planning, the content of the Sprint is defined and the Developers self-organize to determine how the work will get done.

The following is the Sprint Backlog template:

DECO PRODUCTIONS	**SPRINT BACKLOG: DECOCAM**	
Sprint Starting	[Starting date of the Sprint]	
#	**Description**	**Estimate (story points)**
[Product Backlog item number]	[Description of the Product Backlog item]	[Story points for this Product Backlog item]

Scrum Case Study Update: Sprint Planning

It's 8:30 on Monday morning, and the first Sprint Planning meeting is ready to begin. Since the Sprint is defined to be two weeks, the meeting is scheduled for the next four hours. The Scrum Master (Zoe), the Product Owner (Jordan), and the Developers (Lauren, Dima, Miguel, and Teacen) are in attendance.

"Good morning team," says Jordan. "Our Sprint Goal is to develop the foundational Photo Assistant features that enable more advanced features to be implemented. Based on our recent velocity, our target is to complete a total of 20 story points of work by the end of this Sprint."

The Developers nod in agreement and go to work. They begin by reviewing the Product Backlog and selecting user stories according to the Sprint Goal. They discuss each user story in detail, ensuring they understand the requirements and dependencies before committing to them. They also identify potential risks and obstacles that they may encounter during the Sprint.

After a period of time, the Developers finalize the user stories to be completed during this Sprint and place the items in the Sprint Backlog. They also self-organize in order to determine how the work will be performed during the Sprint.

Throughout this process, the Scrum Master, Zoe, keeps everything moving forward so that the Sprint Planning process is successfully completed in the time allotted. She's careful not to direct the Developers to include certain user stories or to plan their work in a certain way. Her role is to facilitate, not to direct.

The following is the Sprint Backlog for the first Sprint:

DECO PRODUCTIONS	SPRINT BACKLOG: DECOCAM	
Sprint Starting	March 23, 2026	
#	**Description**	**Estimate (story points)**
00367	As a user, I want to be able to adjust the settings of my camera before taking a picture, based on the advice provided by the Photo Assistant, so that I can improve the quality of my photos.	8
00368	As a user, I want the Photo Assistant to be able to identify the subject of the photo, so that I can take aesthetically pleasing photos.	5
00371	As a user, I want to be able to turn off the Photo Assistant feature if I prefer to take pictures without its advice, so that I have the option to choose how I want to take my photos.	1
00373	As a user, I want the Photo Assistant to be able to provide advice on my camera's ISO, shutter speed, and aperture, so that I can take better photos with the correct settings.	5
00383	As a user, I want to be able to save the settings recommended by the Photo Assistant for future use, so that I can take future photos faster.	1
	Total Estimate	20

Development Work

The majority of the Sprint consists of **Development Work** (see figure 17.6). Each of the items contained in the Sprint Backlog will be developed, and

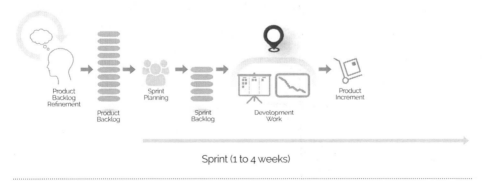

Sprint (1 to 4 weeks)

Figure 17.6: Development Work

the work is self-directed by the Developers. The Product Owner and Scrum Master do not assign work to the Developers or direct them on how to complete the work. The Developers, as a whole, are responsible for the completion of the work.

The progress of the Sprint is displayed on a **Scrum Board**. While there are various ways to organize a Scrum Board, one approach is to include three columns: To Do, In Progress, and Done. Each item from the Sprint Backlog is represented by a sticky note and is placed in the appropriate column. At the start of the Sprint, all of the notes are placed in the To Do column. As work gets underway, the Developers will move the appropriate note to the In Progress column. When an item is completed, it is moved to the Done column.

The progress of the Sprint is also reflected in the **Burndown Chart**. A Burndown Chart displays the total number of story points to be completed during the Sprint. As the work of the Sprint is completed, the number of story points left to be completed will be reduced, which signifies the reduction or "burndown" of the total story points.

Ideally, each Sprint will complete the entire Sprint Backlog and therefore achieve all of the story points estimated for the Sprint. Sometimes this does not happen, and a smaller number of story points is achieved. For example, for a Sprint estimated for 50 story points, imagine that only 42 story points are achieved. The number of story points achieved represents the velocity of the Sprint. A key focus for the Scrum Team would be to manage and increase their velocity in subsequent Sprints. Typically, the velocity of the team will increase over time as the team gains more experience. However, this could vary from Sprint to Sprint for other reasons. For example, if a Developer is on vacation, the velocity achieved during the Sprint will likely be lower.

In the event that any items in the Sprint Backlog were not completed, the Sprint is not extended. Instead, these items are returned to the Product Backlog for consideration in a future Sprint.

The implementation of the items in the Sprint Backlog creates the Product Increment. A Product Increment is not a "work-in-progress" deliverable. Instead, it is a tested, working version of the product that could be released to the customer.

Scrum Case Study Update: Development Work

It's 12:30 p.m., and the Sprint Planning meeting has just ended. The Developers continue to self-organize in order to complete the items contained in the Sprint Backlog. Often, user stories are decomposed to the task level to facilitate the work of the team. Consider the first user story:

> As a user, I want to be able to adjust the settings of my camera before taking a picture, based on the advice provided by the Photo Assistant, so that I can improve the quality of my photos.

The user story is broken down into the following tasks:

- Analyze settings module
- Design settings module changes
- Add new fields to settings table
- Code changes to settings module
- Test changes to settings module

This decomposition to the task level allows the Developers to manage the dependencies between tasks and to better plan and track the work.

Lauren heads over to the Scrum Board and writes the name of each activity to be completed on a separate sticky note. She places each sticky note in the To Do column. Now the Developers begin their work. Frequent discussions take place during the day as different approaches are contemplated, and the work tends to pass back and forth frequently between the Developers. As the days pass, sticky notes are moved from the To Do column to the In Progress column.

A small celebration usually takes place when a sticky note moves to the Done column. The visible reminder of progress provided by the Scrum Board tends to focus and motivate the Developers. The progress is also reflected in the Burndown Chart, another physical reminder of the team's progress.

Jordan drops by periodically during the day to answer questions and provide clarification to the Developers. By answering questions as they come up, the momentum of the project is maintained.

Scrum Board

Partway through the Sprint, the user story and associated tasks mentioned in the case study are positioned on the Scrum Board as shown in figure 17.7 (along with the rest of the Sprint's user stories and associated tasks). Note that in some instances, the progression of user stories rather than tasks from To Do to Done may be tracked on the Scrum Board.

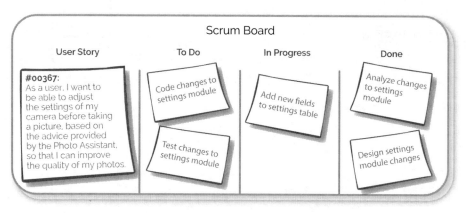

Figure 17.7: Scrum Board

Burndown Chart

Based on the story points completed as of the sixth day, the Burndown Chart appears as shown in figure 17.8. This Burndown Chart demonstrates that for the first five days of the Sprint, the number of story points remaining was higher than planned (assuming an even distribution of story points throughout the 10 days of the Sprint). On the sixth day, the number of story points remaining was lower than planned.

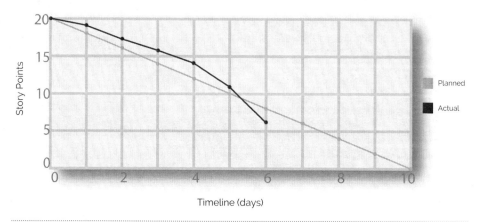

Figure 17.8: Burndown Chart

Daily Scrum

A key element of the Development Work is the **Daily Scrum** (see figure 17.9). This 15-minute meeting is held at the same time on a daily basis and is attended by the Scrum Team. Each person reports the following:

1. What they accomplished during the last workday
2. What they plan to accomplish today
3. Any obstacles that may be blocking their progress

The purpose of this meeting is to help coordinate the work of the Scrum Team through the exchange of progress, plans, and obstacles. However, a discussion of the project's issues and solutions does not take place during this meeting, as the 15-minute time limit does not allow for this level of detailed discussion. Further discussion of this type takes place following the meeting. The Scrum Master ensures that this process is followed.

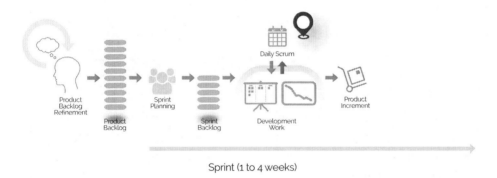

Product
Backlog
Refinement

Product
Backlog

Sprint
Planning

Sprint
Backlog

Daily Scrum

Development
Work

Product
Increment

Sprint (1 to 4 weeks)

Figure 17.9: Daily Scrum

The work of the Sprint is completed during the Development Work. The Daily Scrum takes place at the same time each day for no more than 15 minutes.

Scrum Case Study Update: Daily Scrum

Every morning at 8:30, Zoe meets with the Developers for a 15-minute stand-up meeting called the Daily Scrum.

One by one, each Developer indicates what they accomplished in the last workday, what they plan to accomplish today, and any obstacles in their way. For example, Dima

(continued)

provided the following update today: "Yesterday, I designed the changes to the settings module and added the new fields to the settings table. Today, I expect to complete the code changes to the settings module. However, I am still waiting for feedback from the Customer Experience department before I can start the design work on turning off the Photo Assistant. I'd ideally like to start this tomorrow."

The point is to exchange information and synchronize the activities of the Developers. Zoe makes special note of the obstacles, as these are issues that she will help resolve following the meeting. She is seeing the Director of Customer Experience later today and will check on the issue that Dima raised. This issue, and others raised during the Daily Scrum, are high priority for Zoe in order to help the Developers maintain their progress and complete all of the story points during the Sprint.

The meetings take place every day, at the same time, with everyone attending, no matter what is happening during the Sprint. The Daily Scrum is a vital aspect of the Sprint.

Sprint Review

During the **Sprint Review**, the Product Increment is demonstrated. This meeting is attended by the Scrum Team but may also be attended by other stakeholders within the organization.

The Product Increment should be in a state where the product could be provided to customers if desired. A key benefit of the Sprint Review is that, even if the Product Increment is not provided to customers, the stakeholders are provided with a current view of the product's capabilities. Stakeholders' subsequent feedback may then cause further refinements to the Product Backlog for possible inclusion in future Sprints (see figure 17.10).

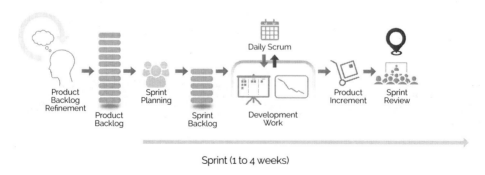

Figure 17.10: Sprint Review

The Product Increment is demonstrated at the Sprint Review.

Scrum Case Study Update: Sprint Review

It's Friday afternoon, and the Sprint Review is about to begin. In addition to the Scrum Team, Arun Singh is attending, as well as Emma Mansfield (Director of Marketing). The company's CEO, Casey Serrador, also attends from time to time and walks through the meeting door just as the meeting is about to start.

The team worked diligently to complete all the items in the Sprint Backlog and are eager to receive feedback from stakeholders. The meeting is taking place in the conference room, where the DecoCam application will be displayed on a large monitor.

The Scrum Master, Zoe, begins the meeting by introducing the team and giving an overview of what they accomplished during the Sprint. She then invites Lauren and Miguel, two of the Developers, to demonstrate the key features of the Photo Assistant developed during this Sprint.

Lauren starts the demonstration by providing an overview of the Photo Assistant. She explains that it uses artificial intelligence to analyze the environment and provide recommendations for optimal camera settings, and she demonstrates how the user can adjust their settings based on these recommendations.

Miguel then demonstrates how the user is able to save their favourite camera settings. He shows how these favourites are accessed and used for future photos. He also demonstrates how these favourites may be edited and deleted as needed.

As each demonstration takes place, a number of comments and possible improvements are suggested. Jordan, the Product Owner, takes notes, as these may be possible additions to the Product Backlog. Overall, the stakeholders are impressed with the team's progress and look forward to seeing what the team will accomplish in the next Sprint.

Sprint Retrospective

After the Sprint Review, the final step is to complete a **Sprint Retrospective** (see figure 17.11). This meeting is an opportunity for the Scrum Team to determine what went well and what did not go well during the Sprint and what could be improved in the next Sprint.

The purpose of this meeting is not to assign blame or assess individual performance, but rather to examine processes in order to make improvements for the next Sprint. A key metric that the Scrum Team will review is the velocity

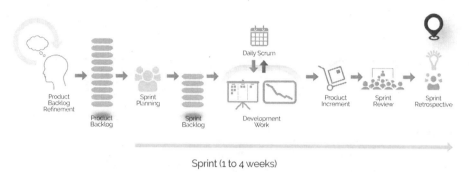

Sprint (1 to 4 weeks)

Figure 17.11: Sprint Retrospective

achieved during the Sprint. The Scrum Team should be constantly refining their processes in order to increase their velocity for future Sprints. The Scrum Master facilitates the Sprint Retrospective process, but the input should come from the entire Scrum Team.

Following the completion of the Sprint Retrospective, the Sprint is complete. The next Sprint, starting with Sprint Planning, is ready to begin.

Processes related to the Sprint and the Scrum Team are refined during the Sprint Retrospective.

Scrum Case Study Update: Sprint Retrospective

Following the Sprint Review, the Scrum Team meets to perform the Sprint Retrospective. At the start of the meeting, Zoe reminds everyone that the purpose of the meeting is to improve how the team will work together during future Sprints. The meeting is not the place to discuss Product Backlog items or specific plans for the next Sprint.

As the discussion gets underway, the team reflects on what went well during the Sprint. Several team members share their thoughts, including how the team collaborated well and successfully completed all the items in the Sprint Backlog. They also discuss the fact that communication within the team was effective and they were able to address issues quickly.

However, many team members agree that the Daily Scrum was a little too early. Deco Productions has a flextime policy that provides employees some flexibility to choose the start and end times of their workday. While most of the team members are in the office by 8:00 a.m., Dima and Teacen both like to arrive between 8:30 a.m. and 9:00 a.m.

Additionally, there were a couple of quality problems where a significant error was missed by the team.

Based on the discussion, the team resolves to do the following:

- Move the Daily Scrum one hour later, to 9:30 a.m., to allow each Developer to resolve issues from the previous day before attending the meeting
- Update their Quality Control processes so that each Developer will ensure that their work is checked and verified by another Developer before it is considered to be done

Since the team completed the Sprint Backlog, the velocity for this Sprint was 20 story points. After some discussion, the team agrees that, based on the results of this Sprint and the process improvements identified in this meeting, they will increase the next Sprint to 22 story points.

The team ends the retrospective by discussing action items that will be performed by team members. This includes assigning tasks to team members and setting deadlines for completion during the next Sprint.

Sprint Planning for the next Sprint is scheduled for first thing Monday morning. It's time for the team to enjoy a well-deserved weekend so they will be ready for next week.

KEY TERMINOLOGY

Burndown Chart: A measurement tool that displays the work completed for the Sprint compared to the total work planned

Daily Scrum: A daily 15-minute meeting to help the team coordinate their work and discuss progress and challenges

Developers: The team members who are responsible for completing the work of each Sprint

Development Work: The period of time during the Sprint when the items contained in the Sprint Backlog are developed

Epic: A collection of user stories that share a common purpose or requirement

Planning Poker: A collaborative technique involving the use of playing cards to develop work estimates

Product Backlog: A prioritized list of all the work items, which is managed by the Product Owner

Product Increment: The updated version of whatever is being produced during the Sprint; it is a tested, working version of the product that could be released to the customer

Product Owner: The team member who is responsible for managing the Product Backlog and is considered the voice of the customer for the project

Scrum Board: A physical display of the current progress of the Sprint showing the work that is awaiting development, in progress, and completed

Scrum Master: The team member who is responsible for ensuring that Scrum processes are understood and followed

Scrum Team: The Product Owner, Developers, and the Scrum Master

Sprint Backlog: The Product Backlog items selected for the current Sprint

Sprint Goal: The objective for the Sprint, which provides guidance for the Developers regarding why the Product Increment is being developed

Sprint Planning: A meeting at the start of the Sprint during which the items from the Product Backlog are selected and a plan for development is completed

Sprint Retrospective: A meeting at the end of the Sprint during which the processes of the Sprint are reviewed in order to determine possible improvements

Sprint Review: A meeting held at the end of the Sprint during which the Product Increment is demonstrated to the project stakeholders

Story Point: A unit of measurement used when estimating an item in a Product Backlog

User Story: A description of a feature of the product, written from the user's point of view

Velocity: The amount of work achieved during a Sprint, expressed in units such as story points or workdays

KEY CONCEPTS

1. During Scrum, work is completed through the repetition of fixed time periods called Sprints.

2. During Scrum, three artifacts are created: the Product Backlog, the Sprint Backlog, and the Product Increment.

3. Product Backlog items are often written as user stories. Epics are user stories that are too large to be delivered in a single Sprint and are subsequently broken down into smaller user stories.

4. The three roles that make up the Scrum Team are the Product Owner, Developers, and the Scrum Master.

5. During Product Backlog refinement, estimates are created for the Product Backlog items.

6. During Sprint Planning, the content of the Sprint is defined and the Developers self-organize to determine how the work will get done.

7. The work of the Sprint is completed during the Development Work. The Daily Scrum takes place at the same time each day for no more than 15 minutes.

8.   The Product Increment is demonstrated at the Sprint Review.

9.   Processes related to the Sprint and the Scrum Team are refined during the Sprint Retrospective.

DISCUSSION QUESTIONS

1.   How does the Scrum Master role differ from the Project Manager role?

2.   The first Sprint is underway, and a key stakeholder asks for a detailed timeline of all the major deliverables. How would you respond to this request?

3.   Why is the Daily Scrum an important part of the Sprint process, and why is it only 15 minutes long?

4.   Why is a Sprint Retrospective completed for each Sprint? Why not just perform one at the end of a few Sprints instead?

5.   Why are Sprints not extended in cases where all items in the Sprint Backlog are not completed?

6.   How does the use of planning poker improve the estimates for the Product Backlog items?

7.   Perform an online search to compare and contrast the use of story points or person-days when estimating Product Backlog items.

18 Hybrid Project Management

INTRODUCTION TO HYBRID PROJECT MANAGEMENT

Thus far, this textbook has examined two main project management approaches: waterfall and agile. Waterfall project management offers stability through detailed planning and is appropriate for many projects, including instances in which specific due dates and comprehensive documentation are required. Agile, on the other hand, excels when requirements are difficult to determine up front and when the need for adaptability and change is high.

For many organizations, strictly choosing one of the above options is not ideal, as both approaches offer benefits. For example, certainty of milestones and due dates is useful, while the ability to readily adapt to changing conditions is also beneficial. For this reason, many organizations resist an "either-or" decision

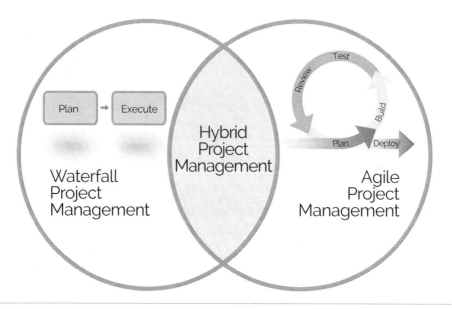

Figure 18.1: Hybrid Project Management

and instead opt to create a project approach that is the "best of both worlds." That is, they develop a hybrid project management approach that employs elements of both waterfall and agile project management (see figure 18.1).

DETERMINING A HYBRID PROJECT MANAGEMENT APPROACH

While there are many frameworks for and approaches to managing projects, each organization's environment is unique in terms of its capabilities, products, business environment, and so on. A key decision for an organization is the development of *how* its projects will be managed.

Table 18.1 contains a number of project characteristics. The relative importance of each characteristic will tend to influence the organization to choose either a waterfall approach or an agile approach.

Table 18.1: Preferred Approach Based on Project Characteristics

Characteristic	Preferred Approach
Certainty of milestones and project due date	Waterfall
Frequent project deliveries to customers	Agile
Ability to define requirements prior to development	Waterfall
Ease of adaptability and change	Agile
Acceptance of uncertainty	Agile
Extensive documentation of the project output	Waterfall

For some projects, the characteristics listed in the table will clearly demonstrate a preference for either waterfall or agile. The following example demonstrates a type of project that clearly aligns with a waterfall approach.

Project #1: The New Light Rail Train (LRT)

A city is planning to create a light rail train (LRT) system to ease traffic congestion and further the city's sustainability strategy. The characteristics of the project and organization are as follows:

- The city needs to include the expected costs in its capital budget, coordinate the construction of the LRT (e.g., the delivery of the trains) with suppliers, and communicate the project's timeline to the various project stakeholders. Therefore, a certainty of milestones and due dates is required. (Result: waterfall is preferred.)

(continued)

- While some interim milestones are planned, they are primarily internal to the project and are not delivered to the customer (i.e., the city and transit users). The output of the project (i.e., a functioning LRT train system) will be primarily delivered all at once. Therefore, frequent project deliveries to customers are not required.

- The requirements of the project's scope (e.g., train route, number of stations, type of train) will need to be completely defined prior to creation of the project deliverables. Therefore, the ability to define requirements prior to development is required. (Result: waterfall is preferred.)

- Given the need for extensive requirement definition and planning, it is not expected that the work will need to be significantly modified during the project. Any changes that may arise will be managed through a change control process. Therefore, ease of adaptability and change is not required.

- Unexpected problems could significantly impact the project. For example, changes to the train route, stations, or contracts with suppliers would likely result in significant cost increases and potential liability. Extensive risk management planning is necessary in order to identify and mitigate possible risks. Therefore, the acceptance of uncertainty is not required.

- As this is a publicly funded project, significant documentation is required, particularly regarding the procurement process with potential suppliers. The features and characteristics would also need to be documented for the users of the LRT system. Therefore, extensive documentation of project output is required. (Result: waterfall is preferred.)

Based on the above, three characteristics indicate that a waterfall approach is preferred and none of the characteristics indicate that an agile approach is preferred. Therefore, a waterfall approach is the most appropriate for this type of project.

The following example demonstrates a type of project that clearly aligns with an agile approach.

Project #2: Self-Serve Banking Application

A financial services company is planning for a revamp of its customer banking application that is used by its customers for day-to-day banking. The interface for the website and mobile app will be updated, and many new functions are planned over the next two to three years.

The characteristics of the project and organization are as follows:

- While the company has defined an overall timeframe for development of the new website and mobile app, specific deadlines for the new functionality have not been defined. Instead, regular updates are desired. Therefore, a certainty of milestones and due dates is not required.
- Rather than waiting until all types of banking functions are defined before implementing the new system, the strategy will be to implement each new function as it is developed. Therefore, frequent project deliveries to customers are required. (Result: agile is preferred.)
- While a list of potential banking functions has been discussed, there may be others that become apparent as the website is being developed and used. Therefore, the ability to define requirements prior to development is not required.
- It is expected that significant insights about the new system will be gained as the development proceeds and from the eventual users of the website and mobile app. The team needs to be prepared to readily adapt to these expected changes. Therefore, the ease of adaptability and change is required. (Result: agile is preferred.)
- Despite some overall planning, issues and challenges will likely be encountered. These will be addressed as the development proceeds. Therefore, the acceptance of uncertainty is required. (Result: agile is preferred.)
- It is expected that the new system will be fairly intuitive, and an extensive user manual is not required. In terms of internal systems documentation, the Agile Manifesto value "Working software over comprehensive documentation" will be followed. Therefore, extensive documentation of project output is not required.

Based on the above, three of the characteristics indicate that an agile approach is preferred and none of the characteristics indicate that a waterfall approach is preferred. Therefore, an agile approach is the most appropriate for this type of project.

However, there are many situations where the project work does not fit neatly into one category or the other. That is, some of the project characteristics may suggest waterfall and others may suggest agile. For example, management within an organization could desire that their projects be delivered on predictable milestones or due dates *and* allow for adaptability and change.

This leads to the development of hybrid project management approaches consisting of elements of both the predictive features of waterfall and the adaptive and incremental elements of agile. Hybrid project management is not a single approach that may be distilled into a single set of processes. Instead, it is a tailored approach designed to draw upon the strengths of both waterfall and agile.

> While projects may favour either a waterfall or agile project management approach, some projects benefit from the use of a hybrid project management approach that combines elements of both agile and waterfall.

The following sections demonstrate a number of possible hybrid approaches. Note that this is not an exhaustive list, and the approaches do not appear in order of importance. Instead, these sections document a number of ways to combine elements of waterfall and agile approaches. The following approaches will be discussed:

- Concurrent waterfall and agile
- Combination of waterfall and agile within a project
- Iterative life cycle
- Incremental life cycle
- **Rolling wave**

CONCURRENT WATERFALL AND AGILE

Using this hybrid approach, some projects are delivered using a waterfall approach, while others are delivered using agile. As projects are initiated, the use of either a waterfall or an agile approach is determined. This allows each project to work within a project management methodology best suited to the requirements of the project.

This hybrid approach is useful when an organization executes categories of projects that are very different from each other and choosing one project management approach for all projects would therefore be inefficient.

The two case studies contained in this textbook provide an example of this type of hybrid project management. The DecoCam Product Launch project employed the use of waterfall project management in order to plan and then execute the work of the project. The software updates made to the DecoCam application demonstrated the use of agile.

The following describes an example of concurrent waterfall and agile projects within an insurance company.

An insurance company's IT department has two upcoming projects to consider. The first is an Actuarial Model Development project, which involves the development of a new set of actuarial models to assess and price the risk for a new insurance product. The second is a Mobile App Development project, which involves the creation of a new mobile app to allow customers to manage their policies, file claims, and access their personal information.

- Waterfall approach for Actuarial Model Development: the work will involve complex calculations, strict regulatory requirements, and precise calculations. A waterfall approach enables the model to be planned in its entirety and verified by actuaries prior to the creation of the system during the Executing Phase. Once the system is developed, extensive testing will be performed prior to the use of the system to price the new insurance product.
- Agile approach for Mobile App Development: insurance is a dynamic and competitive market, and customers expect that mobile apps will change rapidly. The company anticipates the need for continual feature updates and the ability to respond quickly to customer feedback.

The insurance company uses waterfall for a project that requires a high degree of precision and is subject to regulatory compliance, while using agile for customer-facing applications in order to quickly respond to market demand and ongoing feedback.

During a concurrent waterfall and agile hybrid approach, some projects are delivered using waterfall, while others are delivered using agile.

COMBINATION OF WATERFALL AND AGILE WITHIN A PROJECT

When using this hybrid approach, parts of the project are completed using a waterfall approach, while other parts of the project use agile. During the initial planning for the project, the determination of how best to complete each part (using a waterfall or agile approach) is performed. Each part of the project is optimized according to its requirements.

This hybrid approach is useful when projects contain certain elements that benefit from the structure and efficiency of waterfall and other elements that benefit from the flexibility and adaptability of agile.

The following describes an example of a manufacturing company that employs the use of waterfall followed by agile within a project.

A manufacturing company is implementing an Enterprise Resource Planning (ERP) system to enhance its overall business operations. The project involves the deployment of a standardized ERP software package and the development of custom modules according to the needs of departments within the company.

- Waterfall approach for ERP system deployment: the deployment of the standard ERP follows a standard implementation process recommended by the ERP vendor. This process involves detailed planning, installation of the standard ERP modules, and then a conversion of company data to the new system.
- Agile approach for custom module development: this work involves the development of custom modules to address specific requirements unique to the manufacturing environment. The company requires flexibility and responsiveness to the business needs that will likely evolve during the implementation.

The initial implementation of the ERP system is expected to follow a known phased approach and will provide the foundation for the overall system. The subsequent agile development will allow the company to tailor the custom modules according to the unique and changing needs of the organization.

As an alternative, agile can precede the waterfall part of the project. In this configuration, the early part of the project, often the development of requirements and design features, is performed using an agile approach. This is followed by a waterfall approach to complete the project.

The following describes an example of a construction company that employs the use of agile followed by waterfall.

A construction company undertakes a project to build a new office complex. The project involves the development of architectural and interior design plans followed by the construction of the building.

- Agile approach for design: while the project begins with an initial set of design requirements, the customer recognizes that their preferences may change and evolve as various design options are presented. The Design team collaborates closely with the customer, presenting different design options in short iterations. This series of iterations allows the Design team to incorporate the customer feedback and make adjustments to the design.
- Waterfall approach for construction: once the design is approved, the project transitions into a structured construction effort. The team will follow a comprehensive plan including a detailed schedule, assigned tasks, and an approved budget. Any changes that are encountered once construction begins will be handled through formal change management procedures.

Through the use of an agile approach for the design phase followed by the use of waterfall for the construction phase, the project is able to optimize creativity and flexibility early in the project while ensuring a structured and efficient execution of the construction.

 During a combination of waterfall and agile within a hybrid project approach, parts of the project are completed using a waterfall approach, while other parts of the project use agile.

ITERATIVE LIFE CYCLE

An iterative life cycle is a variation of the traditional sequential project life cycle that occurs during waterfall. Instead of completing all planning prior to the Executing Phase, when using an iterative life cycle, the output of the project is developed and refined through multiple iterations of planning followed by creation of deliverables. Following each iteration, insights are gained that influence the planning for the next iteration (see figure 18.2).

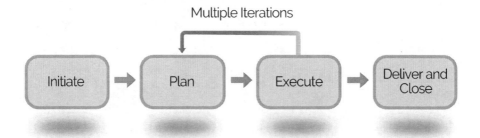

Figure 18.2: Iterative Life Cycle

This hybrid approach is useful for situations in which a traditional phased approach is desired but the project scope contains a high degree of complexity or when frequent stakeholder changes are expected.

The following describes an example of a technology company that uses an iterative life cycle for a product development project.

A technology company is setting out to develop a new electronic product. The concept is to develop a new type of smart wearable device. Using an iterative life cycle, the following iterations will take place:

- Iteration 1—initial design: during this initial iteration, the Product Development team defines the design concept, main features, and initial requirements for the smart wearable device. This initial design is reviewed by potential users in order to gather feedback.
- Iteration 2—prototyping: a working prototype of the smart wearable device is created based on the initial design created in the previous iteration. The prototype is tested by potential users to gain feedback regarding the features and user experience.
- Iteration 3—refinement and technology integration: based on the feedback received in the previous iteration, the design is refined and integrated with the necessary technology.
- Iteration 4—production: during this iteration, the final version of the device is created and the steps required to move the device into ongoing production are performed.

Through an iterative life cycle, the team adapts to current consumer preferences and the available technology to help ensure an effective development of the product.

During an iterative life cycle hybrid approach, the output of the project is developed and refined through multiple iterations of planning followed by the creation of deliverables.

INCREMENTAL LIFE CYCLE

When using an incremental life cycle, the scope of the project is created in portions and then provided to the customer in a series of deliveries (see figure 18.3). Following the definition of the overall requirements, the project may be divided into a series of increments, with each being planned, created, and delivered separately. An advantage of an incremental life cycle is the reduction of execution

Figure 18.3: Incremental Life Cycle

complexity because rather than the entire scope of the project needing to be man-aged at once, each increment may be managed as a smaller sub-project. Other advantages of an incremental life cycle include an increased ability to adapt to changing requirements, early delivery of value to the customer, and an increased level of customer involvement throughout the project.

This approach is appropriate when the speed of delivery is highly important and the customer does not need to wait until all deliverables are complete.

The following describes an example of a house construction project that uses an incremental life cycle.

A building contractor meets with customers to define the overall requirements of a house to be built. The overall design is agreed upon and architectural drawings are created during an Overall Requirements Phase.

The project is then divided into a series of increments to be delivered sequentially to the customer. During each increment, more detailed requirements will be confirmed with the customer and then the construction work will be completed. As each increment is delivered, the customer will be invoiced for work completed. The following are the planned increments:

- Increment 1—foundation and framing: this first increment involves laying the concrete foundation and building the structural frame of the house.
- Increment 2—exterior walls and roof: once the foundation and frame are com-plete, the exterior walls and roof are completed.
- Increment 3—interior walls and utilities: once the house is closed in, this incre-ment focuses on the completion of the interior walls and the installation of utilities such as plumbing and electrical systems.
- Increment 4—interior finishes: the next increment involves the installation of interior finishes such as flooring, kitchens, and bathrooms.
- Increment 5—exterior landscape: the final increment includes the completion of landscaping and a backyard deck.

The process of completing the house in increments allows for flexibility, adaptability, and the increased involvement of the customer.

During an incremental life cycle hybrid approach, the scope of the project is created in portions and then provided to the customer in a series of deliveries.

ROLLING WAVE

Rolling wave is an approach that may be used for large and complex projects where the complete set of requirements is difficult to define all at once and, therefore, the development of a plan for the entire project is challenging. When using this approach, planning is performed iteratively throughout the project, and these planning stages are referred to as rolling waves (see figure 18.4).

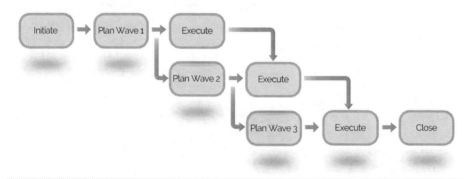

Figure 18.4: Rolling Wave

This approach proceeds as follows:

1. In the first wave, some overall project planning is performed as well as detailed planning for a defined time period (e.g., two months).
2. Once Wave 1 planning is complete, the Wave 1 deliverables are produced.
3. As the Wave 1 deliverables are being produced, Wave 2 planning (for the next time period) takes place.
4. This process repeats until the project's total scope is produced.

Each wave produces detailed plans for only the next time period rather than for the entire project. The advantage of the approach is that each successive wave benefits from the knowledge gained during previous waves and allows the development of the project's output to commence prior to the completion of all project planning. In some cases, the output of a wave may be delivered to customers. In other cases, the output of a wave is not delivered but is instead built upon during the next wave.

This approach is appropriate for projects where a high degree of uncertainty is present and it is not possible to plan every detail of the project up front. Rolling wave may be appropriate for very complex projects, long-term projects, and projects that are heavily affected by external influences such as regulations, technology advancements, or economic conditions. Rolling wave may also be used in emergency response situations, as this approach allows teams to take immediate actions while additional planning takes place as new information becomes available.

Note that rolling wave shares some similarities with the incremental life cycle, discussed earlier. A key difference is that rolling wave is used in situations where it is infeasible to plan the entire scope of the project and, therefore, only the next wave is planned. The incremental life cycle is used when the entire scope is possible to plan to some degree and the detailed planning and execution are contained within each increment.

The following describes the use of rolling wave during an emergency response situation.

A region is hit by a major hurricane and must quickly develop an emergency response plan. While risk response plans have previously been developed, additional planning is required to deal with the unique details of the actual disaster.

Given the uncertainty of the details of the crisis, rolling wave planning is employed as it allows the authorities to take immediate action while additional planning takes place. The following are the details of each wave:

- Wave 1—immediate response: during the first wave, the priority is to perform an assessment of the situation and provide immediate relief (including shelter, food, and first aid) to affected people.
- Wave 2—restoring essential services: during this wave, a more detailed assessment of the damage is performed. Essential services such as electricity and water are restored, and major debris is cleared.
- Wave 3—rebuilding infrastructure: during this wave, the complete damage is assessed, and work is planned to repair damaged infrastructure and public facilities.

The use of rolling wave enables immediate action to take place and then allows for subsequent waves to adapt and improve the response as additional information became available.

During a rolling wave hybrid approach, planning is performed iteratively throughout the project, and these iterations are referred to as rolling waves.

THE CHALLENGES OF HYBRID PROJECT MANAGEMENT

After reviewing the different hybrid approaches in this chapter, one might assume that the coexistence of waterfall and agile in an organization, with the subsequent development of a hybrid approach, is a straightforward, logical process based on the pros and cons of both waterfall and agile.

Unfortunately, this is often not the case. In many organizations, project management approaches and philosophies have been developed over many years. Employees may have experience in one approach and even feel threatened by the advancement of a new approach. For example, long-term employees experienced in waterfall project management could view agile as a new, unproven tool. Newer employees may view agile as the natural replacement for an older project management approach. This can lead to organizational conflict as each side works to maintain its approach to project management.

As discussed during the introduction to this chapter, the pursuit of hybrid project management approaches is motivated by an attempt to create a "best of both worlds" solution. However, there is also a risk of creating complexity when attempting to blend two approaches that possess different philosophies, processes, and terminology. Consider the following, for example:

- Does a project manager direct the team, or is the team self-directed?
- Does the team create requirements or user stories?
- Is the team implementing a project that starts and ends or supporting a product on an ongoing basis?
- Does the team conduct a single Lessons Learned Meeting for frequent retrospectives?

While each of these questions may seem straightforward, the number of differences encountered between the "waterfall world" and the "agile world" tends to add a level of friction when creating a hybrid approach.

The challenge for an organization undertaking a hybrid approach will be to mitigate this risk, primarily through effective leadership and communication. Regardless of the hybrid approach to be pursued, processes and terminology should be clear to team members and stakeholders.

The development of a hybrid project management approach may lead to conflict within the organization. Effective leadership and communication should be used to mitigate this risk.

KEY TERMINOLOGY

Rolling Wave: A project management approach in which planning is performed iteratively throughout the project and each of these iterations is referred to as a rolling wave

KEY CONCEPTS

1. While projects may favour either a waterfall or agile project management approach, some projects benefit from the use of a hybrid project management approach that combines elements of both agile and waterfall.
2. During a concurrent waterfall and agile hybrid approach, some projects are delivered using waterfall, while others are delivered using agile.
3. During a combination of waterfall and agile within a project hybrid approach, parts of the project are completed using a waterfall approach, while other parts of the project use agile.
4. During an iterative life cycle hybrid approach, the output of the project is developed and refined through multiple iterations of planning followed by the creation of deliverables.
5. During an incremental life cycle hybrid approach, the scope of the project is created in portions and then provided to the customer in a series of deliveries.
6. During a rolling wave hybrid approach, planning is performed iteratively throughout the project, and these iterations are referred to as rolling waves.
7. The development of a hybrid project management approach may lead to conflict within the organization. Effective leadership and communication should be used to mitigate this risk.

DISCUSSION QUESTIONS

1. Describe a project that would benefit from the use of agile and a project that would benefit from the use of waterfall. What characteristics of each project led to this assessment?
2. When using agile, the Developers possess more control over the content and planning than they would using waterfall approaches. What are the potential advantages and disadvantages of having the Developers be responsible for the completion of the work?

3. When using waterfall, team members usually perform tasks related to their specialized skills. With agile, team members are cross-functional, often performing tasks outside of their skill set. Compare the benefits and drawbacks of each approach.

4. Would it be possible to use agile for projects that involve procurement? If yes, how would the contract be written to accommodate this approach?

5. You are recommending the development of a hybrid project management approach for your organization. However, the Project Managers who manage waterfall projects and the Scrum Masters from the agile projects object. What approach would you take to convince each of these groups to support a hybrid approach?

6. Perform an online search to find an example of each of the hybrid project management approaches discussed this in chapter. For each example, describe the benefit of employing a hybrid project management approach rather than a waterfall or agile approach.

Appendix 1

Critical Path Analysis—The Calculations

This section demonstrates the calculations that are required to determine the critical path and the amount of total float for a schedule. They are included here to provide a deeper understanding of the critical path and total scope, and not to suggest that they have to be manually calculated during a project.

Calculating the critical path involves looking at the schedule in two distinct ways:

1. Determining the earliest date that each activity may occur by performing a **forward pass** of the schedule—this will determine the **early start** and **early finish** times for each activity.
2. Determining the latest date that each activity may occur by performing a **backward pass** of the schedule—this will determine the **late start** and **late finish** times for each activity.

CRITICAL PATH CALCULATIONS—A SIMPLE EXAMPLE

To demonstrate the forward pass, the vacation project introduced in chapter 5 will be used.

The Forward Pass

In this example, each activity will be assigned a Task ID as follows:

Task ID	Activity
A	Select vacation destination
B	Apply for passport
C	Book vacation
D	Pack for vacation
E	Depart for vacation

On the network diagram, each activity will display the Task ID and duration, as shown in figure A1.1.

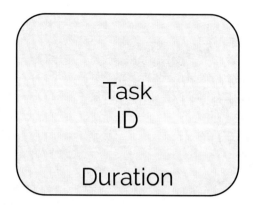

Figure A1.1: Activity with Duration

The resulting network diagram can be seen in figure A1.2.

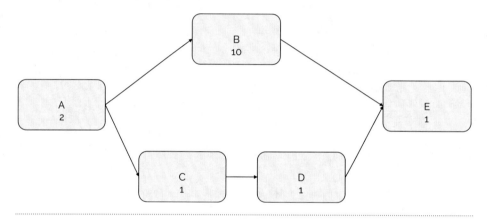

Figure A1.2: Vacation Network Diagram with Durations

The method to calculate the early start (ES) and early finish (EF) of each activity is as follows.

For activities that have no predecessors (i.e., the first activities in the schedule), do the following:

1. Set ES = 1
2. Set EF = ES + activity duration − 1

Moving forward through the network diagram, for each subsequent activity:

3. Set ES = EF + 1 of the preceding activity (if there is more than one preceding activity, use the largest EF + 1)
4. Set EF = ES + activity duration − 1

Using this method, the following calculations are performed:

- For Task ID A:
    - ES $= 1$ (starts on the first day)
    - EF $=$ ES $+$ activity duration $- 1$
        $= 1 + 2 - 1$
        $= 2$
- For Task ID B:
    - ES $=$ EF $+ 1$ of the largest preceding activity
        $= 2 + 1$
        $= 3$
    - EF $=$ ES $+$ activity duration $- 1$
        $= 3 + 10 - 1$
        $= 12$
- For Task ID C:
    - ES $=$ EF $+ 1$ of the largest preceding activity
        $= 2 + 1$
        $= 3$
    - EF $=$ ES $+$ activity duration $- 1$
        $= 3 + 1 - 1$
        $= 3$
- For Task ID D:
    - ES $=$ EF $+ 1$ of the largest preceding activity
        $= 3 + 1$
        $= 4$
    - EF $=$ ES $+$ activity duration $- 1$
        $= 4 + 1 - 1$
        $= 4$
- For Task ID E:
    - ES $=$ EF $+ 1$ of the largest preceding activity
        $= 12 + 1$
        $= 13$
    - EF $=$ ES $+$ activity duration $- 1$
        $= 13 + 1 - 1$
        $= 13$

On the network diagram, each activity will contain the ES and EF (see figure A1.3).

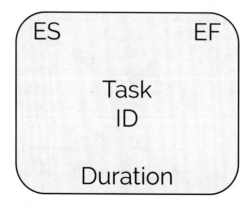

Figure A1.3: Activity with Early Start and Early Finish

The resulting network diagram is shown in figure A1.4.

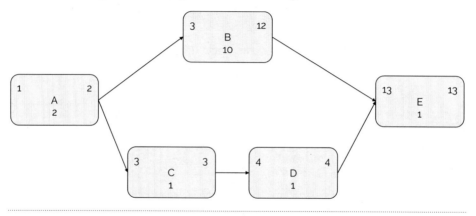

Figure A1.4: Vacation Network Diagram with Early Start and Early Finish

The Backward Pass

The method to calculate the late start (LS) and late finish (LF) of each activity is as follows.

For activities that have no successors (i.e., the final activities in the schedule), do the following:

1. Set LF = EF (which was previously calculated in the forward pass)
2. Set LS = LF – activity duration + 1

Moving backward through the network diagram, for each preceding activity:

3. Set LF = LS – 1 of the succeeding activity (if there are more than one succeeding activities, use the smallest LS – 1)
4. Set LS = LF – activity duration + 1

Using this method, the following calculations are performed:

- For Task ID E:
    - LF = EF (which was previously calculated in the forward pass)
        = 13
    - LS = LF – activity duration + 1
        = 13 – 1 + 1
        = 13
- For Task ID D:
    - LF = LS – 1 of the smallest succeeding activity
        = 13 – 1
        = 12
    - LS = LF – activity duration + 1
        = 12 – 1 + 1
        = 12
- For Task ID C:
    - LF = LS – 1 of the smallest succeeding activity
        = 12 – 1
        = 11
    - LS = LF – activity duration + 1
        = 11 – 1 + 1
        = 11
- For Task ID B:
    - LF = LS – 1 of the smallest succeeding activity
        = 13 – 1
        = 12
    - LS = LF – activity duration + 1
        = 12 – 10 + 1
        = 3
- For Task ID A:
    - LF = LS – 1 of the smallest succeeding activity
        = 3 – 1
        = 2
    - LS = LF – activity duration + 1
        = 2 – 2 + 1
        = 1

On the network diagram, each activity will contain the LS and LF (see figure A1.5).

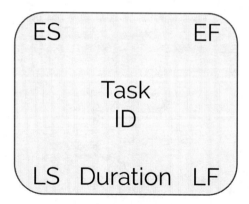

Figure A1.5: Activity with Late Start and Late Finish

The resulting network diagram is shown in figure A1.6.

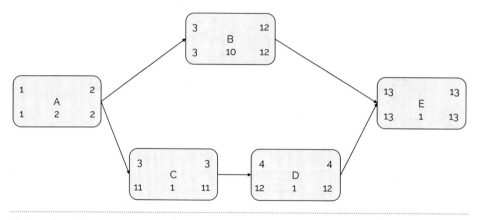

Figure A1.6: Vacation Network Diagram with Late Start and Late Finish

The Total Float

For each activity, the total float is calculated as the difference between the earliest an activity may start/end and the latest an activity may start/end.

- Total Float = LS – ES OR Total Float = LF – EF

On the network diagram, each activity will contain the total float (see figure A1.7).

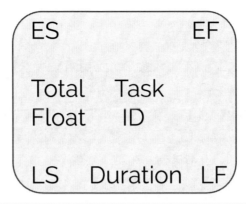

Figure A1.7: Activity with Total Float

The resulting calculations are shown in figure A1.8.

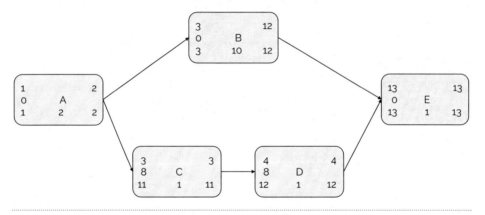

Figure A1.8: Vacation Network Diagram with Total Float

CRITICAL PATH ANALYSIS—THE CASE STUDY PROJECT

Using the same calculation method, the critical path and total float will be manually calculated for the case study project. In this example, each activity will be assigned a Task ID as follows:

Task ID	Activity
A	Initiate the project
B	Plan the project
C	Create sign graphics/text
D	Order banner stands

(continued)

E	Create holographic cards
F	Order cards
G	Create mural for booth
H	Develop demo slideshow
I	Order cameras and tripods
J	Create SM strategy
K	Develop SM post content
L	Update product page
M	Develop online slideshow
N	Create outreach list
O	Perform outreach
P	Create press release
Q	Send press release
R	Develop video concept
S	Develop storyboard and script
T	Film video
U	Edit video
V	Close the project

The Forward Pass

Using the calculation method demonstrated above, the ES and EF may be calculated as shown in figure A1.9.

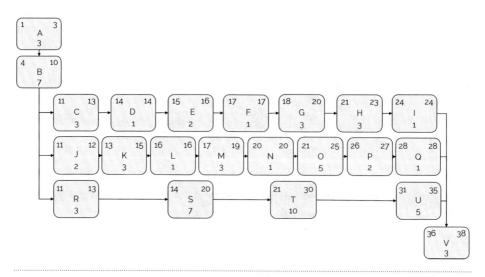

Figure A1.9: DecoCam Network Diagram with Early Start and Early Finish

The Backward Pass

Using the calculation method demonstrated above, the LS and LF may be calculated as shown in figure A1.10.

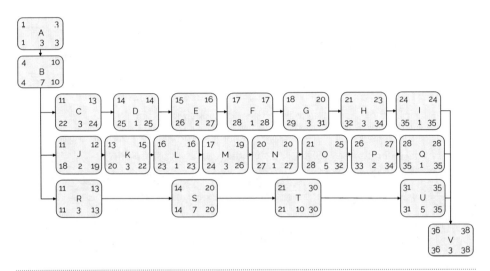

Figure A1.10: DecoCam Network Diagram with Late Start and Late Finish

Total Float

Using the calculation method demonstrated above, the total float may be calculated as shown in figure A1.11.

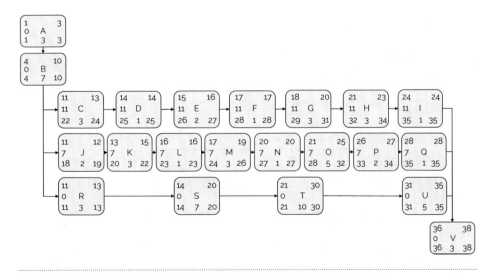

Figure A1.11: DecoCam Network Diagram with Total Float

KEY TERMINOLOGY

Backward Pass: A process that involves moving backward through the project schedule in order to determine the latest date that each task can start and finish

Early Finish: The earliest time that an activity may finish in a project schedule, taking into account the defined dependencies and any other scheduling constraints

Early Start: The earliest time that an activity may start in a project schedule, taking into account the defined dependencies and any other scheduling constraints

Forward Pass: A process that involves moving forward through the project schedule in order to determine the earliest date that each task can start and finish

Late Finish: The latest time that an activity may finish in a project schedule, taking into account the defined dependencies and any other scheduling constraints

Late Start: The latest time that an activity may start in a project schedule, taking into account the defined dependencies and any other scheduling constraints

CRITICAL PATH QUESTIONS

1. For the following network diagram, calculate the
    i.   Critical path
    ii. Planned project duration
    iii. ES, EF, LS, LF, and total float of each activity

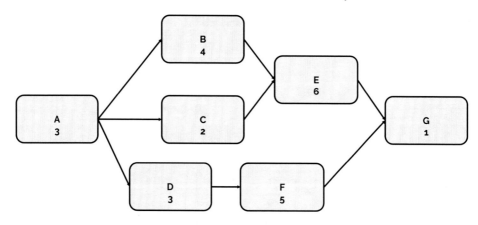

2. For the following network diagram, calculate the
    i.   Critical path
    ii. Planned project duration
    iii. ES, EF, LS, LF, and total float of each activity

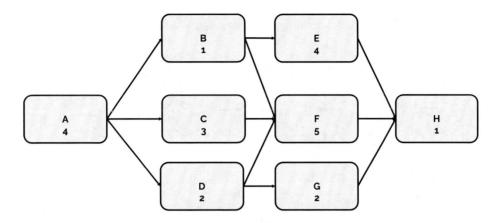

3. For the following network diagram, calculate the
   i. Critical path
   ii. Planned project duration
   iii. ES, EF, LS, LF, and total float of each activity

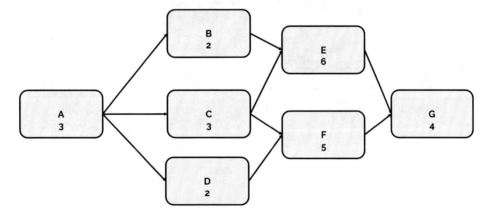

Answers

1. The critical path is A-B-E-G, and the planned duration is 14 days.

Activity	ES	EF	LS	LF	Total Float
A	1	3	1	3	0
B	4	7	4	7	0
C	4	5	6	7	2
D	4	6	6	8	2
E	8	13	8	13	0
F	7	11	9	13	2
G	14	14	14	14	0

2. The critical path is A-C-F-H, and the planned duration is 13 days.

Activity	ES	EF	LS	LF	Total Float
A	1	4	1	4	0
B	5	5	7	7	2
C	5	7	5	7	0
D	5	6	6	7	1
E	6	9	9	12	3
F	8	12	8	12	0
G	7	8	11	12	4
H	13	13	13	13	0

3. The critical path is A-C-E-G, and the planned duration is 16 days.

Activity	ES	EF	LS	LF	Total Float
A	1	3	1	3	0
B	4	5	5	6	1
C	4	6	4	6	0
D	4	5	6	7	2
E	7	12	7	12	0
F	7	11	8	12	1
G	13	16	13	16	0

Appendix 2

An Overview of Earned Value Management

INTRODUCTION

Earned Value Management (EVM) is a project management methodology that integrates schedule, costs, and scope information in order to measure project performance. By comparing the project's planning information with actual progress data, EVM may also be used to forecast future performance and to enable project managers to adjust project plans as required.

EVM is often used in organizations managing large, complex projects that have many stakeholders and a high requirement for budget and schedule control. These types of organizations typically include engineering and construction firms, government agencies, and defence contractors. A large project is one with a multimillion- or even billion-dollar budget, where any small variation can be significant.

EVM will be applied to the textbook case study project. However, it is unlikely that EVM would be used for a project of this duration and budget. The processes and calculations are applied for demonstration purposes.

Note that the term *value* is used extensively within EVM terminology. This should not be confused with the concept of maximizing customer value through the completion of projects. Instead, in the context of EVM, value refers to the cost and the rate of progress of the scope being delivered.

EARNED VALUE MANAGEMENT CORE CONCEPTS

There are a number of core concepts that first need to be understood. The explanation of each concept should be read carefully, as the EVM calculations that are performed later rely on an understanding of these concepts.

Budget at Completion and Original Time Estimate

Budget at Completion (BAC) is the total authorized value of the work to be completed. The **Original Time Estimate** (OTE) is the planned duration of the project.

You are managing a project estimated to be completed in 12 months. The budget is $100,000. The BAC is $100,000. The OTE is 12 months.

Planned Value

Planned Value (PV) is the cumulative value of the scheduled work distributed across the timeline of the project. The PV, which is calculated before the work is actually done, also serves as a baseline. Note that the cumulative value builds progressively to reflect the planned progress of the project work, and at the end of the project, the PV equals the BAC. The formula to calculate PV at any given status reporting date is as follows:

$$PV = (\text{Planned percentage complete}) \times (\text{BAC})$$

You are managing a project estimated to be completed in 12 months (OTE). The budget (BAC) is $100,000. Six months have passed.

> According to the schedule, the planned work should be 50% complete.
> PV = (Planned percentage complete) × (BAC)
>   = 50% × $100,000
>   = $50,000

Earned Value

Earned Value (EV) is the value of the actual work completed to date. The formula to calculate EV is as follows:

$$EV = (\text{Actual percentage complete}) \times (\text{BAC})$$

You are managing a project estimated to be completed in 12 months (OTE). The budget (BAC) is $100,000. Six months have passed.

> Upon reviewing the work performed, 40% is actually complete.
> EV = (Actual percentage complete) × (BAC)
>   = 40% × $100,000
>   = $40,000

Actual Cost

Actual Cost (AC) is the amount of money spent to date.

> You are managing a project estimated to be completed in 12 months (OTE). The budget (BAC) is $100,000. Six months have passed.
>
> Upon reviewing the amount of money spent to date, you find that $35,000 has been spent.
>
> AC = $35,000

Case Study Update: Calculating the Planned Value, Earned Value, and Actual Cost

The DecoCam V4 Product Launch project is nearing the halfway point, with four of the scheduled eight weeks completed.

Sophie looks at the most recent Project Status Report, which was produced as of April 17, 2026. She sees that while one activity, "develop demo slideshow," is ahead of schedule, four other activities are slipping behind schedule. This could be a problem if the trend continues. She is also aware that the actual costs seem to be higher than she originally planned in the Detailed Budget. Her team members have been needing to log additional time to complete their assigned tasks, and the costs of materials purchased have been higher than expected. She wonders if this trend will continue and what this means for the final project costs and completion date.

At that very moment, a chat message pops up on her laptop screen. It is from Arun, the Project Sponsor:

> Hi Sophie. How confident are you that we will make our deadline for the product launch? Marketing is worried that we might be late. Also, how are you feeling about the budget?

At Deco Productions, Earned Value Management is performed on a monthly basis, and this will help her answer these questions. She will need to consult the project schedule, Detailed Budget, and cost reports from Deco Productions' Finance department.

Her first step is to calculate the PV, EV, and AC as of April 17, 2026. She opens a spreadsheet and copies the names of the activities that represent the HR Costs and the Other Costs from the Detailed Budget, placing them in the first column. For each of these

(continued)

costs, she lists the cost estimate for each cost category (from the Detailed Budget) in the Budget at Completion (BAC) column.

Sophie then checks the project schedule to see the planned percentage complete of each activity under HR Costs that was planned to be started by April 17. She also consults the schedule to see the cost percentage planned to be accrued by April 17 for each cost category under Other Costs. She enters this percentage under the Planned Percentage Complete column. She is then able to calculate the Planned Value (PV) column by multiplying the Budget at Completion (BAC) amount by the Planned Percentage Complete.

Next, she checks the most recent Project Status Report to determine the actual percentage complete of each activity by April 17. She enters this percentage under the Actual Percentage Complete column. She is then able to calculate the Earned Value (EV) by multiplying the Budget at Completion (BAC) amount by the Actual Percentage Complete.

Finally, she consults the cost reports from the Finance department in order to determine the actual accrued costs for the project and enters them into the Actual Cost (AC) column.

The following are the resulting EVM calculations:

EVM Metrics (as of April 17, 2026)						
	Budget at Completion (BAC)	Planned Percentage Complete	Planned Value (PV)	Actual Percentage Complete	Earned Value (EV)	Actual Cost (AC)
HR Costs						
Initiate the project	$1,200	100	$1,200	100	$1,200	$1,640
Plan the project	$7,280	100	$7,280	100	$7,280	$9,300
Create sign/ graphics text	$1,200	100	$1,200	100	$1,200	$1,650
Order banner stands	$400	100	$400	100	$400	$560
Create holo-graphic cards	$800	100	$800	100	$800	$980
Order cards	$400	100	$400	100	$400	$650
Create mural for booth	$1,200	100	$1,200	100	$1,200	$1,506
Develop demo slideshow	$1,200	0	$0	0̶ 50	$̶0̶ $600	$846

Order cameras and tripods	$400	0	$0	0	$0	$0
Create SM strategy	$960	100	$960	100	$960	$1,340
Create SM post content	$1,440	100	$1,440	100	$1,440	$1,841
Update product page	$480	100	$480	~~100~~ 50	~~$480~~ $240	$550
Develop online slideshow	$1,440	100	$1,440	~~100~~ 0	~~$1,440~~ $0	$0
Create outreach list	$480	100	$480	~~100~~ 0	~~$480~~ $0	$0
Perform outreach	$2,400	0	$0	0	$0	$0
Create press release	$960	0	$0	0	$0	$0
Send press release	$480	0	$0	0	$0	$0
Develop video content	$1,440	100	$1,440	100	$1,440	$1,970
Develop story-board and script	$3,360	100	$3,360	~~100~~ 50	~~$3,360~~ $1,680	$1,980
Film video	$8,800	0	$0	0	$0	$0
Edit video	$4,400	0	$0	0	$0	$0
Monitor and control	$10,000	40	$4,000	40	$4,000	$4901
Close the project	$1,200	0	$0	0	$0	$0
Other Costs						
Banner stands	$1,000	100	$1,000	100	$1,000	$1,200
Holographic cards	$2,000	100	$2,000	100	$2,000	$2,936
Murals	$200	100	$200	100	$200	$250
Cameras and tripods	$1,400	0	$0	0	$0	$0
Total	**$56,520**		**$29,280**		**$26,040**	**$34,100**

Note that five costs listed in the table are deviating from the timing indicated in the project schedule. They are highlighted with shaded cells.

	Dur	Week Ending 27-Mar	Week Ending 03-Apr	Week Ending 10-Apr	Week Ending 17-Apr	Week Ending 24-Apr	Week Ending 01-May	Week Ending 08-May	Week Ending May 15
DecoCam V4 Prod Launch		M T W T F	M T W T F	M T W T F	M T W T F	M T W T F	M T W T F	M T W T F	M T W T F
Develop demo slideshow	3d								

Figure A2.1: Activity Starting Ahead of Schedule

One activity, "develop demo slideshow," has started ahead of schedule (see figure A2.1). This leads to the following results for this activity:

- The PV is $0 (the activity was not scheduled to start by April 17).
- The EV is $600 (the activity was estimated to be 50% complete by April 17).

	Dur	Week Ending 27-Mar	Week Ending 03-Apr	Week Ending 10-Apr	Week Ending 17-Apr	Week Ending 24-Apr	Week Ending 01-May	Week Ending 08-May	Week Ending May 15
DecoCam V4 Prod Launch		M T W T F	M T W T F	M T W T F	M T W T F	M T W T F	M T W T F	M T W T F	M T W T F
Create outreach list	1d								

Figure A2.2: Activity That Is Behind Schedule

Four activities are behind schedule. For example, see "create outreach list" in figure A2.2. This leads to the following results for this activity:

- The PV is $480 (the activity was scheduled to start by April 17).
- The EV is $0 (the activity has been estimated to be 0% complete by April 17).

Note that the Actual Cost regularly diverges from the Planned Value and Earned Value. For HR Costs, the actual effort required to complete an activity often varies from the planned work effort. For Other Costs, the actual purchase price may differ from the planned cost for a number of reasons (e.g., inflation, low estimates).

Once all the information has been entered, the following EVM metrics for the project are determined:

- BAC: $56,520
- PV: $29,280
- EV: $26,040
- AC: $34,100

Note that the PV, EV, and AC amounts are cumulative as of a point in time during the project. For example, the AC of $34,100 means that this is the total actual accrued costs of the project to date.

VARIANCE ANALYSIS

When managing a project, it is imperative to understand how the project is performing in terms of cost and schedule. That is, based on the progress of the project so far, is the project on budget, over budget, or under budget? Similarly, is the project on schedule, behind schedule, or ahead of schedule? The use of **Cost Variance** and **Schedule Variance** will help the project manager analyze the project's progress (i.e., how the project is performing in terms of schedule and cost).

Cost Variance

Cost Variance (CV) is the difference between the budgeted value of the work completed to date (EV) and the actual amount of money spent to date (AC). That is, it compares the value of what you *have done* by now to what you *have spent* by now.

The formula to calculate CV is as follows:

$$CV = EV - AC$$

This formula can be used to determine whether a project is progressing on budget.

Cost Variance	Value of Work	Project Progress
CV is greater than zero (positive)	Work completed (EV) is more than money spent (AC)	Under budget
CV is equal to zero	Work completed (EV) is equal to the money spent (AC)	On budget
CV is less than zero (negative)	Work completed (EV) is less than the money spent (AC)	Over budget

You are managing a project estimated to be completed in 12 months (OTE). The budget (BAC) is $100,000. Six months have passed.

You have calculated the EV to be $40,000 and the AC to be $35,000.

$$CV = EV - AC$$
$$= \$40,000 - \$35,000$$
$$= \$5,000$$

Therefore, the project is under budget at this point.

Schedule Variance

Schedule Variance (SV) is the difference between the budgeted value of the actual work completed to date (EV) and the budgeted value of the planned work to be completed to date (PV). That is, it compares what you *have* done by now to what you *should* have done by now.

The formula to calculate SV is as follows:

$$SV = EV - PV$$

This formula can be used to determine whether a project is progressing on schedule.

Schedule Variance	Value of Work	Project Progress
SV is greater than zero (positive)	Work actually completed (EV) is more than the work planned to be completed (PV)	Ahead of schedule
SV is equal to zero	Work actually completed (EV) is equal to the work planned to be completed (PV)	On schedule
SV is less than zero (negative)	Work actually completed (EV) is less than the work planned to be completed (PV)	Behind schedule

You are managing a project estimated to be completed in 12 months (OTE). The budget (BAC) is $100,000. Six months have passed.

You have calculated the EV to be $40,000 and the PV to be $50,000.

$$
\begin{aligned}
SV &= EV - PV \\
&= \$40,000 - \$50,000 \\
&= -\$10,000
\end{aligned}
$$

Therefore, the project is behind schedule at this point.

Case Study Update: Variance Analysis

Sophie looks at the EVM metrics that she previously calculated:

- BAC: $56,520
- PV: $29,280
- EV: $26,040
- AC: $34,100

At first glance, the numbers do not look good. It appears that progress is less than she would like because the Earned Value is less than what was planned to be complete by this point. In addition, the actual costs are a lot higher than they should be to this point based on the progress made.

Sophie realizes, though, that she needs to dig deeper into these metrics and apply variance analysis. While her intuition tells her that the project is behind schedule and over budget, she needs to determine the magnitude. When she responds to Arun, she wants to make sure she has the hard evidence to support her answer.

The following are the resulting variance calculations:

Cost Variance:

$$CV = EV - AC$$
$$= \$26{,}040 - \$34{,}100$$
$$= -\$8{,}060 \text{ (over budget)}$$

Schedule Variance:

$$SV = EV - PV$$
$$= \$26{,}040 - \$29{,}280$$
$$= -\$3{,}240 \text{ (behind schedule)}$$

Figure A2.3 demonstrates the PV throughout the project duration and the EV and AC to the current date in the project.

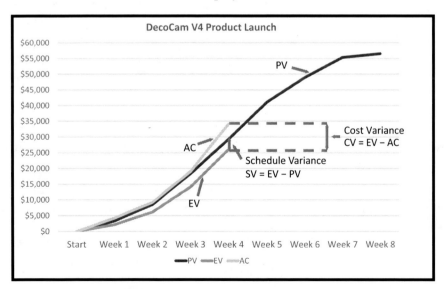

Figure A2.3: DecoCam V4 Product Launch: Earned Value Management Graph

Negative Schedule Variance is demonstrated, as the EV line is lower than the PV line as of the current date. Likewise, negative Cost Variance is demonstrated, as the EV line is lower than the AC line as of the current date.

PERFORMANCE INDEXES

In addition to variance analysis, two performance indexes may be calculated: the **Cost Performance Index** and the **Schedule Performance Index**. As with the variance calculations, they will determine whether the project is on, under, or over budget and on, ahead of, or behind schedule. However, they also facilitate the forecasting of future performance based on the project performance to date.

Cost Performance Index

The Cost Performance Index (CPI) is a measurement of the project's cost efficiency by comparing the budgeted value of the actual work completed to date (EV) to the amount of actual money spent to date (AC). That is, it compares what you *have done* by now to what you *have spent* by now.

The formula to calculate CPI is as follows:

$$CPI = EV / AC$$

This formula can be used to determine whether a project is progressing on budget.

CPI	Value of Work	Project Progress
CPI is greater than 1	Work completed (EV) is more than the money spent (AC)	Under budget
CPI is equal to 1	Work completed (EV) is equal to the money spent (AC)	On budget
CPI is less than 1	Work completed (EV) is less than the money spent (AC)	Over budget

Once CPI is calculated, it is also possible to forecast the final cost of the project, assuming that no corrective action is taken and the current CPI trend continues until project completion. This is based on the assumption that cost performance will be consistent throughout the project. The **Estimate at Completion** (EAC) is the predicted final cost of the project based on the cost performance to date.

The formula to calculate EAC is as follows:

$$EAC = BAC / CPI$$

You are managing a project estimated to be completed in 12 months (OTE). The budget (BAC) is $100,000. Six months have passed.

 You have calculated the EV to be $40,000 and the AC to be $35,000.

$$
\begin{aligned}
CPI &= EV / AC \\
&= \$40,000 / \$35,000 \\
&= 1.14
\end{aligned}
$$

Therefore, the project is under budget at this point. In addition, the EAC may be calculated as follows:

$$
\begin{aligned}
EAC &= BAC / CPI \\
&= \$100,000 / 1.14 \\
&= \$87,719.30
\end{aligned}
$$

The EAC is forecasting that the final costs of the project will be less than the original budgeted amount.

 Note that the precision in this forecast would not be communicated to project stakeholders. Instead, a forecast of a rounded amount, such as $88,000, would be more appropriate.

Schedule Performance Index

The Schedule Performance Index (SPI) measures the project's schedule efficiency by comparing the value of the actual work completed to date (EV) to the value of the planned work to be completed to date (PV). That is, it compares what you *have* done by now to what you *should* have done by now.

 The formula to calculate SPI is as follows:

$$SPI = EV / PV$$

This formula can be used to determine whether a project is progressing on schedule.

SPI	Value of Work	Project Progress
SPI is greater than 1	Work actually completed (EV) is more than the work planned to be completed (PV)	Ahead of schedule
SPI is equal to 1	Work actually completed (EV) is equal to the work planned to be completed (PV)	On schedule
SPI is less than 1	Work actually completed (EV) is less than the work planned to be completed (PV)	Behind schedule

It is also possible to forecast the final duration of the project by applying the SPI to the OTE. This is based on the assumption that schedule performance will be consistent throughout the project. The **New Time Estimate** (NTE) is the predicted final duration of the project based on the schedule performance to date.

The formula to calculate NTE is as follows:

$$NTE = OTE / SPI$$

You are managing a project estimated to be completed in 12 months (OTE). The budget (BAC) is $100,000. Six months have passed.

You have calculated the EV to be $40,000 and the PV to be $50,000.

SPI = EV / PV
= $40,000 / $50,000
= 0.8

Therefore, the project is behind schedule at this point. In addition, the NTE may be calculated as follows:

NTE = OTE / SPI
= 12 months / 0.8
= 15 months

This indicates the project's predicted duration is 15 months (three months behind schedule).

Limitations of the Schedule Performance Index

The SPI has a number of limitations that should be considered when assessing the status of a project's schedule. The calculation of the SPI does not take the specific status of activities on the critical path into account. In other words, the SPI calculations do not differentiate the critical path activities from the non-critical activities. This creates the potential for the SPI forecasting a project that is ahead of (or behind) schedule that is contrary to the status of the critical path.

The use of project management software can help validate the true schedule performance by tracking the progress of activities on the critical path, comparing their actual duration to the baseline duration. This additional focus on the critical path performance can help overcome the limitations of the SPI.

Also, because SPI is a ratio of EV to PV, the SPI will eventually converge to 1 by the end of the schedule. That is, the work will eventually be completed (EV) and, as this occurs, will become equal to the PV. This then means that the SPI and resulting project duration forecast has reduced relevance in the latter stages of the project since there may be insufficient time available to implement corrective actions.

Case Study Update: Performance Indexes

Sophie looks at the variance analysis that she just completed:

- CV: –$8,060 (over budget)
- SV: –$3,240 (behind schedule)

While this isn't the news Sophie would prefer, knowing this information now allows her time to address these cost and schedule issues. The CV indicates that the project is currently over budget. The SV also indicates bad news: that the project is currently behind schedule.

She understands that if nothing is done, this trend will likely continue and that her project is on course to be both over budget and late. These are not the result that she wants.

The next question is "How far over budget and how late is the project going to be if nothing is done to fix this situation?" To answer this question, her next step in the EVM process is to use performance indexes to forecast the estimated budget and project duration. To do so, she reviews the EVM metrics previously calculated:

- BAC: $56,520
- PV: $29,280
- EV: $26,040
- AC: $34,100

In addition, she needs the planned project duration, which she knows is 40 days.

The CPI and SPI are calculated as follows:

$$CPI = EV / AC$$
$$= \$26,040 / \$34,100$$
$$= 0.76 \text{ (less than one means over budget)}$$
$$SPI = EV / PV$$
$$= \$26,040 / \$29,280$$
$$= 0.89 \text{ (less than one means behind schedule)}$$

The EAC may then be calculated as follows:

$$EAC = BAC / CPI$$
$$= \$56,520 / 0.76$$
$$= \$74,368.42$$

The NTE may then be calculated as follows:

$$NTE = OTE / SPI$$
$$= 40 \text{ days} / 0.89$$
$$= 44.9 \text{ days}$$

Case Study Update: Earned Value Management Analysis

Sophie looks at the EVM calculations on her spreadsheet. Her calculations definitely indicate significant trouble for the project. However, she appreciates having this information now rather than at the end of the project, when it is too late to do anything about it.

First, she looks at the EAC. Her EVM calculations show that the budget is forecasted to grow to over $74,000, which is significantly higher than both her original project estimate of $56,320 and the total budget of $60,000 available to the project. She makes a mental note to determine the reason for the increased costs and hopefully reverse this trend for the remainder of the project. She certainly doesn't want to exceed $60,000.

She then turns her attention to the NTE. The EVM calculations indicate that the project's duration will increase from 40 days to 45 days (44.9, rounded to 45). This raises alarm bells in her mind, as being five days late would be a significant problem.

However, she remembers that the SPI does not consider the project's critical path, so she quickly turns to her critical path calculations. To her relief, three of the late activities ("update product page," "develop online slideshow," and "create outreach list") are not on the critical path, so this might not be as big a problem as she first thought. As it turns out, the three activities share a total of seven days of total float and therefore may be delayed somewhat without impacting the project's completion date. However, she makes a mental note to investigate further ways to keep a close eye on these activities.

She then turns her attention to the activity that is behind schedule and is on the critical path: "develop storyboard and script." Taking out her phone, she sends a quick text to Maddy to set up a meeting for later that afternoon.

She then decides to call Arun. This might be a difficult conversation, but she knows that Arun appreciates her candid assessment of the project's status. Based on her EVM calculations, she plans to let Arun know that there are signs of a significant cost overrun but that she will investigate it immediately in order to find ways to meet the original budget. Regarding the project schedule, she plans to state that she is cautiously optimistic and will outline the steps she will take to mitigate the risk of the project missing its due date.

EARNED VALUE MANAGEMENT AND AGILE

The use of EVM has traditionally been used during waterfall projects. That is, the scope is defined during project planning, the baseline is set, and then EVM is used to monitor project performance.

EVM may also be applied when using agile. The calculations of the EVM variances and indexes are based on agile metrics such as story points, providing agile projects with the benefits of EVM.

KEY TERMINOLOGY

Actual Cost: The amount of money spent to date

Budget at Completion: The total authorized value of the work to be completed

Cost Performance Index: A measurement of the project's cost efficiency comparing the value of the work completed to date (EV) to the amount of money spent to date (AC)

Cost Variance: The difference between the value of the work completed to date (EV) and the amount of money spent to date (AC)

Earned Value: The budgeted value of the actual work completed to date

Earned Value Management: A project management methodology that integrates schedule, cost, and scope information in order to measure project performance

Estimate at Completion: The forecasted final cost of the project based on the current performance

New Time Estimate: The predicted final duration of the project based on the schedule performance to date

Original Time Estimate: The planned duration of the project

Planned Value: The cumulative authorized value of the scheduled work distributed across the timeline of the project

Schedule Performance Index: A measurement of the project's schedule efficiency comparing the value of the actual work completed to date (EV) to the value of the work planned to be completed to date (PV)

Schedule Variance: The difference between the value of the actual work completed to date (EV) and the value of the planned work to be completed to date (PV)

EARNED VALUE MANAGEMENT QUESTIONS

1. Consider a project with an initial budget of $200,000, a planned duration of six months, and current progress indicators such as EV of $120,000, AC of $150,000, and PV of $140,000. Calculate the EAC and NTE for this project. What would your message be to the Project Sponsor about the performance of the project?

2. Consider a project with an initial budget estimate of $300,000 and a planned duration of eight months. At the current stage, the value of the planned work is $250,000. However, the project has spent $200,000, and 75% of the project has been completed. Is the project currently over or under budget, and is the project currently ahead of or behind schedule? Calculate the EAC and NTE of the project based on the given information.

3. Consider a project with an initial budget estimate of $500,000 and a planned duration of 12 months. At the six-month mark, the value of the planned work is $240,000, the project has spent $320,000, and 60% of the project has been completed. Calculate the CPI, SPI, EAC, and the NTE based on the given information.

Answers

1. BAC = $200,000; OTE = 6 months; EV = $120,000; AC = $150,000; PV = $140,000; CPI = 0.8; SPI = 0.857; EAC = $250,000; NTE = 7 months. The message to the Project Sponsor would be "The project is currently over budget and behind schedule. The forecasted final cost is $250,000, and the new estimated project duration is seven months."

2. BAC = $300,000; OTE = 8 months; EV = $225,000; AC = $200,000; PV = $250,000; CPI = 1.125; SPI = 0.9; EAC = $266,666.67; NTE = 8.9 months. The project is under budget but behind schedule.

3. BAC = $500,000; OTE = 12 months; EV = $300,000; AC = $320,000; PV = $240,000; CPI = 0.9375; SPI = 1.25; EAC = $533,333.33; NTE = 9.6 months. The project is over budget but ahead of schedule.

References and Works Consulted

Agile Alliance. (2001). *Agile manifesto.* agilealliance.org/agile101/the-agile-manifesto/

Arora, M., & Baronikian, H. (2013). *Leadership in project management* (2nd ed.). Leadership Publishing House.

AXELOS. (2017). *Managing successful projects with Prince2.* TSO.

Baca, C. M. (2007). *Project management for mere mortals.* Addison-Wesley.

Barkley, B. T. (2004). *Project risk management.* McGraw-Hill.

Barrett, D. J. (2011). *Leadership communication* (3rd ed.). McGraw-Hill.

Basu, R. (2012). *Managing quality in projects.* Gower.

Berkun, S. (2005). *The art of project management.* O'Reilly Media.

Blake, R. R., & Mouton, J. S. (1964). *The managerial grid.* Gulf.

Blake, R. R., & Mouton, J. S. (1975). An overview of the grid. *Training and Development Journal, 29*(5), 29–37.

Blanchard, K., Zigarmi, P., & Zigarmi, D. (1985). *Leadership and the one minute manager.* William Morrow.

Campbell, M. (2009). *Communication skills for project managers.* AMACOM.

Cleland, D. I., & Ireland, L. R. (2006). *Project management strategic design and implementation* (5th ed.). McGraw-Hill.

Cook, C. R. (2005). *Just enough project management.* McGraw-Hill.

Crosby, B. C., Bryson, J. M., & Anderson, S. R. (2003). *Leadership for the common good fieldbook.* University of Minnesota Extension Service.

Darnall, R. W., & Preston, J. M. (2013). *Project management from simple to complex.* Flat World Knowledge.

Deming, W. E. (2000). *Out of the crisis.* MIT Press.

Dinsmore, P. C., & Cabanis-Brewin, J. (2011). *The AMA handbook of project management* (3rd ed.). AMACOM.

Eden, C., & Ackermann, F. (1998). *Making strategy: The journey of strategic management.* Sage.

Eisenhower, D. D. (1957). *Remarks at the National Defense Executive Research Conference.* www.presidency.ucsb.edu/documents/remarks-the-national-defense-executive-reserve-conference

Fleming, Q. W. (2003). *Project procurement management: Contracting, subcontracting, teaming.* FMC Press.

French, J. R. P., & Raven, B. H. (1959). The bases of social power. In D. Cartwright (Ed.), *Studies of social power* (pp. 150–167). Institute for Social Research.

Garton, E., & Noble, A. (2017, July 19). *How to make agile work for the C-suite.* www.hbr.org/2017/07/how-to-make-agile-work-for-the-c-suite

Gido, J., & Clements, J. P. (2009). *Successful project management* (5th ed.). South-Western Cengage Learning.

Goodman, L. J., & Love, R. N. (1980). *Project planning and management: An integrated approach.* Pergamon Press.

Gross, J. M., & McGinnis, K. R. (2003). *Kanban made simple.* AMACOM.

Handy, C. (1993). *Understanding organizations.* Penguin.

Hansen, B. J. (1964). *Practical pert.* America House.

Heldman, K. (2005). *Project manager's spotlight on risk management.* Jossey-Bass.

Hersey, P., Blanchard, K., & Johnson, D. (2013). *Management of organizational behaviour: Leading human resources.* Pearson.

Hill, G. M. (2010). *The complete project management methodology and toolkit.* CRC Press.

Holpp, L. (1999). *Managing teams.* McGraw-Hill.

Huemann, M. (2015). *Human resource management in the project-oriented organization.* Gower.

Hughes, R. L., Ginnett, R. C., & Curphy, G. J. (2014). *Leadership: Enhancing the lessons of experience* (8th ed.). McGraw-Hill.

Juran, J. M., & De Feo, J. A. (2010). *Juran's quality handbook: The complete guide to performance excellence.* McGraw-Hill.

Kerzner, H. (2013). *Project management: A systems approach to planning, scheduling, and controlling.* John Wiley & Sons.

Klastorin, T. (2004). *Project management tools and trade-offs.* John Wiley & Sons.

Kneafsey, S. *A short history of scrum.* www.thescrummaster.co.uk/scrum/short-history-scrum/

Kwak, Y. H. (2005). Brief history of project management. In E. G. Carayannis, Y. H. Kwak, & F. T. Anbari, *The story of managing projects.* Praeger Publishers.

Lewis, J. P. (2008). *Mastering project management.* McGraw-Hill.

Martin, J. (1991). *Rapid application development.* Macmillan.

Meredith, J. R., & Mantel, S. J. (2003). *Project management: A managerial approach* (5th ed.). John Wiley & Sons.

Munter, M. (1997). *Guide to managerial communication* (4th ed.). Prentice Hill.

Neave, H. R. (1990). *The deming dimension.* SPC Press.

Nutt, P. C., & Backoff, R. W. (1992). *Strategic management of public and third sector organizations: A handbook for leaders.* Jossey-Bass.

Olson, D. (2022). *The myth of the "waterfall" SDLC.* www.bawiki.com/wiki/Waterfall.html

Pelrine, J. (2011). *Is software development complex?* www.thecynefin.co/is-software-development-complex/

Peters, T. J., & Waterman, R. H., Jr. (2004). *In search of excellence: Lessons from America's best-run companies.* HarperCollins.

Pinto, J. K. (2016). *Project management: Achieving competitive advantage.* Pearson Education.

Portny, S. E., Mantel, S. J., Meredith, J. R., Shafer, S. M., & Sutton, M. M. (2008). *Project management: Planning, scheduling, and controlling projects.* John Wiley & Sons.

Project Management Institute. (2006). *PMI Code of Ethics and Professional Conduct.* www.pmi.org/codeofethics

Project Management Institute. (2021). *A guide to the project management body of knowledge (PMBOK Guide)* (7th ed.). Project Management Institute.

Project Management Institute. (2024). Pulse of the profession 2024. www.pmi.org/learning/thought-leadership/pulse/future-of-project-work

Rose, K. H. (2005). *Project quality management: Why, what and how.* J. Ross.

Royce, W. C. (1970). *Managing the development of large software systems.* www.praxisframework.org/files/royce1970.pdf

Royer, P. S. (2002). *Project risk management: A proactive approach.* Management Concepts.

Santo, D. E. (2022). *Top 5 main agile methodologies: Advantages and disadvantages.* www.xpand-it.com/blog/top-5-agile-methodologies/

Schwaber, K. (1997). Scrum development process. In J. Sutherland, D. Patel, C. Casanave, J. Miller, & G. Hollowell (Eds.), *Business object design and implementation: OOPSLA '95 workshop proceedings* (pp. 117–134). Springer.

Schwaber, K. (2004). *Agile project management with scrum.* Microsoft Press.

Shtub, A., Bard, J. F., & Globerson, S. (2005). *Project management: Processes, methodologies, and economics* (2nd ed.). Pearson.

Smith, K. A. (2014). *Teamwork and project management.* McGraw-Hill.

The Standish Group. (1995). *The chaos report (1994).* https://www.standishgroup.com/sample_research_files/chaos_report_1994.pdf

Summers, D. C. S. (2005). *Quality management.* Pearson Prentice Hall.

Sutherland, J. (2014). *Scrum: The art of doing twice the work in half the time.* Crown Business.

Sutherland, J., & Schwaber, K. (2020). *The scrum guide.* www.scrumguides.org/scrum-guide.html

Takeuchi, H., & Nonaka, I. (1986). The new new product development game. *Harvard Business Review.* hbr.org/1986/01/the-new-new-product-development-game

Van Vliet, V. (2012). *Henry Gantt.* www.toolshero.com/toolsheroes/henry-gantt

Yukl, G. A. (2010). *Leadership in organizations.* Pearson Prentice Hall.

Index